MORTAL
REPUBLIC

Also by Edward J. Watts:
Hypatia
The Final Pagan Generation
Riot in Alexandria
City and School in Late Antique Athens and Alexandria

MORTAL REPUBLIC

HOW ROME FELL INTO TYRANNY

EDWARD J. WATTS

BASIC BOOKS

New York

Basic Books
Hachette Book Group
1290 Avenue of the Americas, New York, NY 10104
www.basicbooks.com

Printed in the United States of America

First Edition: November 2018

Published by Basic Books, an imprint of Perseus Books, LLC, a subsidiary of Hachette Book Group, Inc. The Basic Books name and logo is a trademark of the Hachette Book Group.

The Hachette Speakers Bureau provides a wide range of authors for speaking events. To find out more, go to www.hachettespeakersbureau.com or call (866) 376-6591.

The publisher is not responsible for websites (or their content) that are not owned by the publisher.

Print book interior design by Amy Quinn.

Library of Congress Cataloging-in-Publication Data

Names: Watts, Edward Jay, 1975- author.
Title: Mortal republic : how Rome fell into tyranny / Edward J. Watts.
Description: First edition. | New York : Basic Books, 2018. | Includes bibliographical references and index.
Identifiers: LCCN 2018018024 (print) | LCCN 2018036256 (ebook) | ISBN 9780465093823 (ebook) | ISBN 9780465093816 | ISBN (hardcover)
Subjects: LCSH: Rome—Politics and government—265-30 B.C. | Rome—History—Republic, 265-30 B.C.
Classification: LCC DG254.2 (ebook) | LCC DG254.2 .W38 2018 (print) | DDC 937/.05—dc23
LC record available at https://lccn.loc.gov/2018018024

ISBNs: 978-0-465-09381-6 (hardcover), 978-0-465-09382-3 (ebook)

LSC-C

10 9 8 7 6 5 4 3 2

To Nate and Zoe

CONTENTS

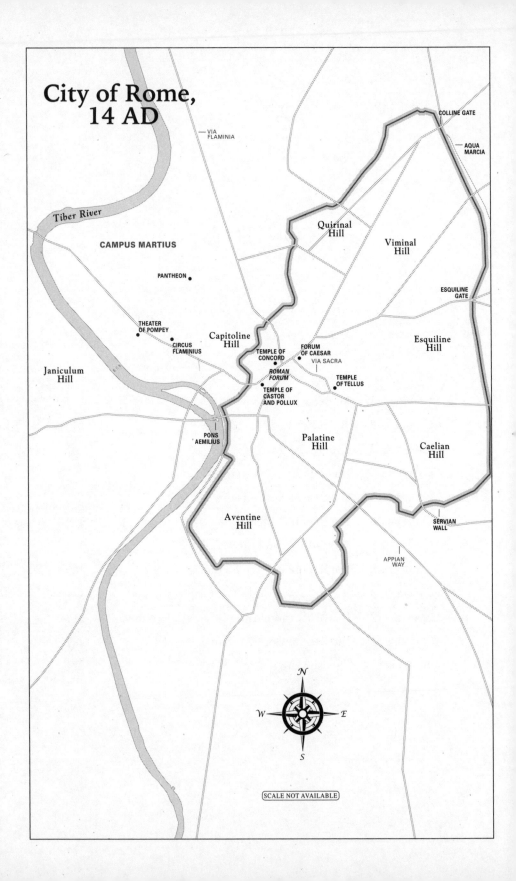

City of Rome,
14 AD

Tiber River

CAMPUS MARTIUS

— VIA FLAMINIA

COLLINE GATE

AQUA MARCIA

Quirinal Hill

Viminal Hill

ESQUILINE GATE

PANTHEON

THEATER OF POMPEY

CIRCUS FLAMINIUS

Capitoline Hill

TEMPLE OF CONCORD

FORUM OF CAESAR

VIA SACRA

Esquiline Hill

Janiculum Hill

ROMAN FORUM

TEMPLE OF CASTOR AND POLLUX

TEMPLE OF TELLUS

PONS AEMILIUS

Palatine Hill

Caelian Hill

Aventine Hill

SERVIAN WALL

APPIAN WAY

N
W E
S

SCALE NOT AVAILABLE

Republican Roman Italy

Alps

Alps

Alps

VENETIA

ILLYRICUM

LIGURIA

Po River

Trebia River

CISALPINE GAUL

Mutina

Bononia

Faesulae

Luca

Rubicon River

Arminium

Auximum

UMBRIA

Perusia

Firmum

ETRURIA

Lake Trasimeno

Asculum

Tiber River

PICENUM

Adriatic Sea

— VIA FLAMINIA

ROME

LATIUM

Ostia

Fregellae

Larinum

SAMNIUM

Cannae

Dyrrachium

VIA APPIA

Capua

CAMPANIA

APULIA

Cumae

Apollonia

Herculaneum

Nola

Brundisium

Stabiae

CALABRIA

LUCANIA

Tarentum

Gulf of Taranto

CORSICA

Tyrrhenian Sea

BRUTTIUM

SARDINIA

Straits of Messana

SICILY

Mediterranean   Sea

N

W   E

S

SCALE NOT AVAILABLE

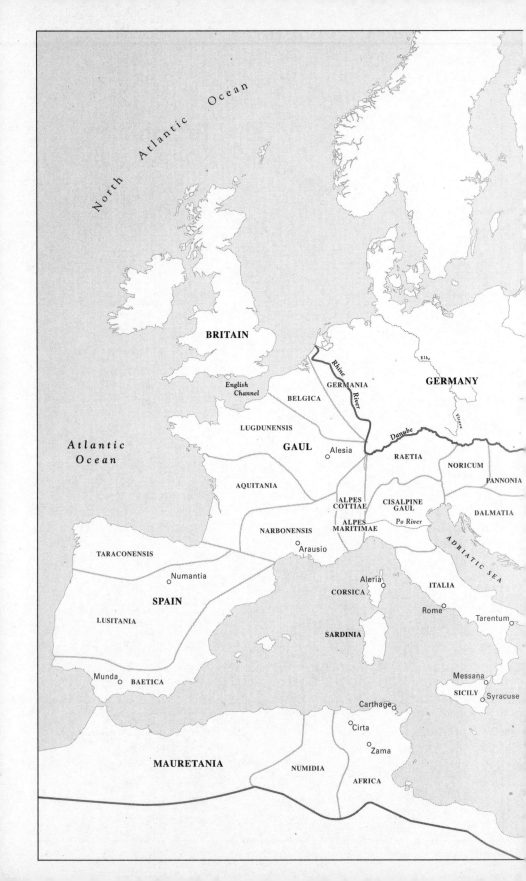

The Roman Empire and the Mediterranean World in 14 AD

DACIA

KINGDOM OF THE BOSPORUS

BLACK SEA

MOESIA

BITHYNIA

PONTUS

ARMENIA

THRACE

GALATIA

CAPPADOCIA

MACEDONIA

Philippi

LYDIA

ASIA

Dyrrachium

Apollonia

AEGEAN SEA

Pergamum

Carrhae

COMMAGENE

EPIRUS

THESSALY

Mytilene

Tarsus

MESOPOTAMIA

Brundisium

Pharsalus

CARIA

CILICIA

PARTHIAN EMPIRE

Delphi

Miletus

Corinth

Athens

LYCIA

Sparta

RHODES

Xanthos

CYPRUS

SYRIA

Crete

Mediterranean Sea

Jericho

JUDAEA

CYRENAICA AND CRETE

Jerusalem

Cyrene

Alexandria

NABATAEA

EGYPT

PREFACE

THIS BOOK GREW OUT OF a series of conversations with my children and my students about the ways in which antiquity can help us understand the challenging and occasionally alarming political realities of our world. Each conversation began with a question about whether history repeats itself, a question that has been asked much more frequently over the past two years as journalists and historians turn to the recent past to try to explain an unpredictable present. The past is no oracle and historians are not prophets, but this does not mean that it is wrong to look to antiquity for help understanding the present. The republics that are now so strained did not, like Athena, spring fully formed from the head of Zeus in the eighteenth century. Their founders modeled them on older, extremely successful republics that preceded them. Rome offered the oldest and most successful republic on which many modern states were patterned. The ancient Roman Republic is, of course, very different from a modern state, but the Roman Republic's distribution of power and its processes for political decision making deeply influenced its modern descendants. The successes and failures of Rome's republic can show how republics built on Rome's model might respond to particular stresses. They also reveal which political behaviors prove particularly corrosive to a republic's long-term health. I hope that this book allows its readers to better appreciate the serious problems that result both from politicians who breach a republic's political norms and from citizens who choose not to punish them for doing so.

A book like this cannot be written without the help, support, and input of many students, friends, and colleagues. I want to first thank the students at Yale, Indiana University, and the University of California, San Diego, I have taught and learned from over the past two decades. Their questions and concerns about the growing political dysfunction descending upon the world around them prompted me to undertake this project. I have benefited greatly from conversations with members of the San Diego Greek community about the relevance of the classical world to contemporary situations. I am particularly thankful to Carol Vassiliadis, whose support for research at UCSD encouraged me to explore more deeply the history of the Roman state that would become Byzantium.

Seth Lerer, Kasey Pfaff, Ben Platt, Denise Demetriou, Karl Gerth, Eric Robinson, Michael Kulikowski, Lieve Van Hoof, Anthony Kaldellis, Gavin Kelly, Scott McGill, David Frankfurter, Peter Van Nuffelen, Johannes Hahn, and Giovanni Alberto Cecconi are among the many friends and colleagues who have shared ideas and suggestions. Josiah Osgood was an amazing resource in the early stages of the project, sharing ideas and a draft manuscript of his wonderful book *Rome and the Making of a World State*. Cristiana Sogno served as an insightful and erudite sounding board as well as a careful editor who offered comments on many chapters. Much of the book manuscript was completed while I was a fellow at the Israel Institute for Advanced Study at the Hebrew University in Jerusalem. I could not have asked for a more intelligent and friendly group of colleagues. I thank Sarit Kattan Gribetz, Alfons Fürst, Maren Niehoff, Gretchen Reydams-Schils, Carlos Levy, Joshua Levinson, Ishay Rosen-Zvi, Al Baumgarten, David Lambert, Laura Nasrallah, Eve-Marie Becker, and Avigail Manekin for creating such a wonderful environment in which to work and think. I am especially grateful to Sarit and Alfons for reading drafts of chapters and offering suggestions for improving the introduction and conclusion. I am also very appreciative of the careful and insightful editing that Brian Distelberg and Christina Palaia have done on this manuscript and the work that Lara Heimert and the rest of the editorial team at Basic Books have done to move the book through production. The book is much better because of the time and energy that all of these people put into it.

My deepest and most profound thanks go to my wife, Manasi Watts, my children, Nate and Zoe, my parents, Dan and Karen Watts, and my in-laws, Brij and Sunanda Bhargava. This book would not have taken form and certainly would not have been completed without their generosity, patience, and forbearance—especially during the time I spent in Jerusalem. The willingness of Brij and Sunanda to visit me in Israel made the time away much easier. These are gifts for which I can never repay any of them. Both Nate and Zoe have the remarkable ability to frame the sorts of insightful and challenging questions that this book cannot answer but that I hope it may equip them to begin to work through on their own. Manasi helped me immensely as I struggled to tell the story of Rome's republic in a way that had relevance for a modern, politically astute audience. Her strength, courage, and personal resilience continually inspire and amaze me. With each sentence I write, I hear her voice telling me to make it more efficient and concrete. Even if my sentences remain too long, I hope, in the end, that this book shows how much I have taken her advice and her example to heart.

Jerusalem
December 12, 2017

CHAPTER 1

AUTOCRATIC FREEDOM

In 22 BC a series of political and economic crises buffeted the regime of Augustus, Rome's first emperor. Augustus had won control of Rome's Mediterranean empire in 30 BC after nearly two decades of civil conflicts, but his hold on power now seemed like it might be slipping. The emperor had only recently recovered from a severe illness that he himself feared would kill him when a series of other misfortunes beset the imperial capital. Plagues and floods hit Rome late in 23, and both returned in early 22. These natural disasters contributed to a food shortage and to such severe rioting that a mob imprisoned the Roman Senate in the senate house and threatened to burn them alive. Augustus could calm the unrest only when he used his own funds to pay for grain to be delivered to the city. It looked like Augustus's empire might quickly come apart.[1]

Things did not improve as the year continued. Augustus felt compelled to appear at the trial of a Roman commander who had attacked a Thracian tribe without legal authority, and, at the hearing, the emperor found himself subjected to an aggressive cross-examination by the advocates of the accused. An assassination plot against him was detected and, although the plotters were executed, the jury embarrassed the emperor by not returning a unanimous verdict against them.[2]

Problems worsened after Augustus left the capital to attend to matters in the empire's eastern provinces. The next year, 21 BC, brought rioting about the selection of Roman magistrates, violence that would recur nearly every year until the emperor returned at the end of 19. Rome, whose population of one million people made it the world's largest city, perpetually sat on the edge of anarchy while its imperial frontiers demanded constant attention. An objective observer might wonder whether one man, even one as skilled as Augustus, could really run so complicated a state. With its seemingly endless problems, Rome's empire under Augustus might by rights look like a failed political experiment in autocracy. Surely, a citizen of a modern republic might assume, Romans would quickly abandon autocracy and return to the representative republic under which Roman elites had shared power with one another for nearly five hundred years. This is how we, who have lived all of our lives under younger representative democracies, have been trained to think about freedom.[3]

But the traumas of those years did not, in fact, push Romans back toward the familiar political structures of the republic. Instead, most Romans seem to have craved the power and authority of Augustus even more. In 22 BC, the Roman mob that threatened to burn the senate house also sought to force Augustus to accept the title of dictator although he already possessed supreme power in the empire. The third-century Roman historian Cassius Dio wrote that the electoral violence of 21 BC showed "clearly that it was impossible for a democratic government to be maintained" among Romans. And, when Augustus returned to the city in 19 BC, the same author wrote: "There was no similarity between the conduct of the people during his absence, when they quarreled, and when he was present." Augustus's presence alone calmed the chaos of Rome and its empire. But Dio added a caveat. Augustus placated Romans only "because they were afraid." Order came to chaos only when freedom was exchanged for fear.

Augustus himself explained the transition from republic to empire very differently. Although Romans had long held that political domination by one individual represented the opposite of liberty, Augustus framed his autocratic control of the Roman state as a sort of democratic act. In Augustus's conception, he had restored liberty (*libertas*) to Rome by first delivering the Roman world from the senators who had seized power by murdering Julius Caesar and by later eliminating the threat of foreign control posed by Cleopatra and her lover Marc Antony.[4] Liberty, as Augustus and his supporters saw it, meant the freedom from domestic unrest and foreign interference that came only with the security and political stability that Augustus provided.[5] Augustus's liberty meant that Roman property rights remained valid. It opened economic opportunities to new segments of the Roman population. And it took control of the city and its empire away from an increasingly corrupt senatorial elite whose mismanagement had led to civil war. In the 20s BC, many Romans agreed with Augustus that liberty could not exist if insecurity persisted. They came to believe that freedom from oppression could only exist in a polity controlled by one man.

This book explains why Rome, still one of the longest-lived republics in world history, traded the liberty of political autonomy for the security of autocracy. It is written at a moment when modern readers need to be particularly aware of both the nature of republics and the consequences of their failure. We live in a time of political crisis, when the structures of republics as diverse as the United States, Venezuela, France, and Turkey are threatened. Many of these republics are the constitutional descendants of Rome and, as such, they have inherited both the tremendous structural strengths that allowed the Roman Republic to thrive for so long and some of the same structural weaknesses that led eventually to its demise. This is particularly true of the United States, a nation whose basic constitutional structure was deliberately patterned on the idealized view of the Roman Republic presented by the second-century BC author Polybius. This conscious borrowing from Rome's model makes it vital for all of us to understand how Rome's republic worked, what it achieved, and why, after nearly five centuries, its citizens ultimately turned away from it and toward the autocracy of Augustus.[6]

No republic is eternal. It lives only as long as its citizens want it. And, in both the twenty-first century AD and the first century BC, when a republic fails to work as intended, its citizens are capable of choosing the stability of autocratic rule over the chaos of a broken republic. When freedom leads to disorder and autocracy promises a functional and responsive government, even citizens of an established republic can become willing to set aside long-standing, principled objections to the rule of one man and embrace its practical benefits. Rome offers a lesson about how citizens and leaders of a republic might avoid forcing their fellow citizens to make such a tortured choice.

Rome shows that the basic, most important function of a republic is to create a political space that is governed by laws, fosters compromise, shares governing responsibility among a group of representatives, and rewards good stewardship. Politics in such a republic should not be a zero-sum game. The politician who wins a political struggle may be honored, but one who loses should not be punished. The Roman Republic did not encourage its leaders to seek complete and total political victory. It was not designed to force one side to accept everything the other wanted. Instead, it offered tools that, like the American filibuster, served to keep the process of political negotiation going until a mutually agreeable compromise was found. This process worked very well in Rome for centuries, but it worked only because most Roman politicians accepted the laws and norms of the Republic. They committed to working out their disputes in the political arena that the republic established rather than through violence in the streets. Republican Rome succeeded in this more than perhaps any other state before or since.

If the early and middle centuries of Rome's republic show how effective this system could be, the last century of the Roman Republic reveals the tremendous dangers that result when political leaders cynically misuse these consensus-building mechanisms to obstruct a republic's functions. Like politicians in modern republics, Romans could use vetoes to block votes on laws, they could claim the presence of unfavorable religious conditions to annul votes they disliked, and they could deploy other parliamentary tools to slow down or shut down the political process if it seemed to be moving too quickly toward an outcome they disliked. When used as intended, these tools helped promote negotiations and political compromises by preventing majorities from imposing solutions on minorities. But, in Rome as in our world, politicians could also employ such devices to prevent the Republic from doing what its citizens needed. The widespread misuse of these tools offered the first signs of sickness in Rome's republic.[7]

Much more serious threats to republics appear when arguments between politicians spill out from the controlled environments of representative assemblies and degenerate into violent confrontations between ordinary people in the streets. Romans had avoided political violence for three centuries before a series of political murders rocked the Republic in the 130s and 120s BC. Once mob violence infected Roman politics, however, the institutions of the Republic quickly lost their ability to control the contexts and content of political disputes. Within a generation of the first political assassination in Rome, politicians had begun to arm their supporters and use the threat of violence to influence the votes of assemblies and the election of magistrates. Within two generations, Rome fell into civil war. And, two generations later, Augustus ruled as Roman emperor. When the Republic lost the ability to regulate the rewards given to political victors and the punishments inflicted on the losers of political conflicts, Roman politics became a zero-sum game in which the winner reaped massive rewards and the losers often paid with their lives.

Above all else, the Roman Republic teaches the citizens of its modern descendants the incredible dangers that come along with condoning political obstruction and courting political violence. Roman history could not more clearly show that, when citizens look away as their leaders engage in these corrosive behaviors, their republic is in mortal danger. Unpunished political dysfunction prevents consensus and encourages violence. In Rome, it eventually led Romans to trade their Republic for the security of an autocracy. This is how a republic dies.

This book begins in the 280s BC, not long after the written record of Roman history becomes more factual than fanciful. The early chapters show how, in moments of crisis throughout the third century BC, Rome's republic proved remarkably resilient. The consensus-building tools of the Republic ensured that it survived after the Carthaginian general Hannibal invaded Italy in 218 and that it remained robust throughout the incredible territorial and economic expansion that followed Hannibal's defeat in 202. The Republic continued to function well as Rome grew into the premier military and political power in the Mediterranean world during the first half of the second century BC. Unlike most other ancient societies, Rome was able to absorb tremendous amounts of territory and generate great economic growth during these years while remaining politically stable.

By the 130s, however, popular anxiety about growing economic inequality began to threaten the Republic's stability. When politicians working within the framework of the Republic failed to reach a consensus about how to respond to their citizens' concerns, some of their rivals opportunistically exploited their inaction by pushing for radical policies in ways that breached the boundaries of acceptable political behavior. The quest for consensus that had made Rome's republic so stable in previous centuries was quickly replaced by a winner-takes-all attitude toward political disputes. Between 137 and 133, senators disavowed a Roman treaty in order to punish particular political opponents, a group of politicians obstructed land reforms aimed to address social and economic inequality, and their opponents resorted to constitutional trickery to get around their obstruction. Then, as 133 drew to a close, Rome saw its first acts of lethal political violence in more than three centuries.

Subsequent chapters show that the political violence that was so shocking in the 130s became increasingly routine as the second century BC drew to a close. The mob violence of those years, however, only set the stage for the violent and destructive civil wars that tore through Roman and Italian societies in the late 90s and most of the 80s BC. The Social War and the Roman civil wars that followed it resulted in tens of thousands of deaths, executions, and confiscations of property. The Republican structures that had once been so robust and resilient failed amid such widespread violence and dysfunction. Although the Republic would be restored before the 70s began, it would never fully recover.[8]

The concluding chapters treat the final decades of the Roman Republic. The Republic remained a source of great pride and enjoyed significant public trust through the 60s, 50s, and even into the 40s BC, but the damage done to it in the first decades of the first century could never be completely repaired. Civil war, widespread political violence, and their enduring economic and political repercussions were now a part of the Roman historical experience. And, as the Republic entered its final civil wars in the 40s, all of these traumas rapidly came back to haunt political life.

This violent political world was the one that Augustus came to control, but this is not how Rome's republic began. In fact, the Republic was expressly designed to prevent the emergence of a figure like Augustus and to limit the political violence that made someone like him possible. It is with this vibrant, capable, and effective Roman Republic that we begin.

CHAPTER 2

THE NEW WORLD ORDER

I N THE SUMMER OF 280 BC, the Mediterranean world's past col-
lided with its future as the armies of the Roman Republic met
those led by the Greek king Pyrrhus of Epirus on a battlefield in
Southern Italy. An ambitious and adventurous commander, Pyrrhus had grown up in a Mediterranean created by the implosion of
Alexander the Great's empire following his death in 323. This was
a world of mercenary armies, patchwork kingdoms, and fluid political boundaries in which Alexander's generals and their descendants
fought among themselves to try to capture as many fragments of
the great Macedonian empire as they could. These kingdoms were
large, but their control of territory was often precarious and the
allegiances of their armies frequently seemed even weaker. This led
ambitious kings and skilled commanders with the right combination of natural talent and good fortune to imagine that they might
build an empire like that of Alexander. And no commander was
more seduced by the idea of conquest than Pyrrhus.

A cousin of Alexander the Great who had briefly held the
Macedonian throne, Pyrrhus had been summoned to Italy by the
former Spartan colony of Tarentum after that city had fallen into
a conflict with Rome. Greeks saw Rome as a rising and dangerous
"barbarian" power that had recently come to control most of Italy,
but they also felt that Rome's recent military successes said little

about its ability to fight against the leading states of the Greek world. The alliance between Pyrrhus and the Tarentines bound two parties who neither knew nor particularly trusted one another. But it served a purpose for both of them. Tarentum was a relatively wealthy city that had a history of calling upon restless commanders from the Greek mainland when it was gravely threatened. The Tarentines hoped that Pyrrhus's arrival could prevent the Romans from threatening the independence of their city and that, after Pyrrhus had fought for them, both he and Rome would leave Tarentum alone.[1]

Pyrrhus answered Tarentum's call, however, because he saw in it an opportunity to build an empire for himself in the Western Mediterranean that he could then use to recover the Macedonian throne. Pyrrhus controlled a world-class army of professional infantry, skilled cavalrymen, and elephant-mounted shock troops that seemed likely to easily overwhelm the citizen levies of the barbarian Romans. This would, he expected, eliminate the Roman threat to Tarentum, cause the defection of Rome's allies in Italy, and enable Pyrrhus to build a large army of allied forces to help him in further campaigns. Once he overwhelmed the Romans, a later author reported, Pyrrhus expected that Italy would become a base from which to mount additional campaigns against Sicily, Carthage, Libya, and, ultimately, Macedonia and Greece.[2]

The Tarentines, Pyrrhus, and the Greek cities of Southern Italy that were closely watching his campaign probably imagined that the war would end with a Roman defeat and withdrawal. The Romans had only recently established a military presence in Southern Italy and, if they behaved like any other Italian power, they would simply pull back from Tarentum and other Southern Italian cities when faced with the disciplined, well-equipped, first-world army fielded by Pyrrhus. Pyrrhus himself seems to have expected that he could induce a Roman retreat without even fighting a battle. The historian Dionysius of Halicarnassus preserves a letter that Pyrrhus supposedly sent to Rome offering to arbitrate the dispute among Rome, Tarentum, and Tarentum's Italian allies so that no side would need to fight. But the Roman consul Lavinius answered curtly that if Pyrrhus had determined to make war on them, he would do well to "investigate those against whom he would be fighting." Lavinius even sent a captured spy back to Pyrrhus with the instruction that the king himself should come "openly so as to see and learn the might of the Romans."[3]

Lavinius had given Pyrrhus fair warning. When Pyrrhus got his first glimpse of the Roman forces, he was said to have remarked with some astonishment that "the discipline of these barbarians is not barbarous." The Romans made an even greater impression when the forces clashed. Although Pyrrhus was able to attack an exposed Roman army as it crossed a river, the Romans nevertheless held their ground against a cavalry assault led by Pyrrhus himself. Pyrrhus's horse was killed beneath him yet he emerged victorious when a charge by his elephants broke the lines of Roman soldiers who had never before fought the animals. Pyrrhus won the battle, but at an alarming cost. He had lost somewhere between one-sixth and one-half of his best troops and, because these were highly trained professional soldiers, the dead and wounded were not easily replaced. Although the Tarentines had fought well and some neighboring Italian communities provided Pyrrhus with additional troops following the battle, these reinforcements were inferior to the men that Pyrrhus had lost. In the meantime, the Romans "lost no time in filling up their depleted legions and raising others," a fact that Pyrrhus supposedly noted with "consternation." His dream of Italian domination now seemingly out of reach, Pyrrhus sent an embassy offering peace and a military alliance to the Romans if they would in exchange agree to free the Greek cities in Southern Italy they had recently come to control.[4]

Pyrrhus sent Cineas of Thessaly to Rome to lead the negotiation. A gifted orator and student of the famous Athenian statesman Demosthenes, Cineas could be so persuasive that Pyrrhus once remarked that his words had conquered more cities than the king's armies. Negotiations between states in the ancient world consisted largely of emissaries making public demands that the other party either accepted or declined. This meant that, even if a victor offered lenient terms, acceptance required the vanquished to publicly admit their defeat and take a hit to their international prestige. Substantial power could be preserved but humiliation could not be avoided.[5]

When Cineas arrived in Rome, he brought with him expensive presents for the families of individual Roman senators and extremely lenient terms for the Republic. Rome could have peace, the return of its captured prisoners, and even Pyrrhus's help in future campaigns if only Rome allied with Pyrrhus and pardoned Tarentum. The Senate, later sources say, was inclined to accept these terms until an old, blind senator named Appius Claudius was carried into the senate house by his sons. The speech this respected senator gave would become legendary. The chamber became quiet as he entered and, when he finally stood to speak, he chastised his younger colleagues. "I have previously borne the unfortunate state of my eyes," he began, "[but now I wish that my ears had been afflicted so that I could avoid] hearing about your shameful deliberations." He recalled how, in his younger days, Romans spoke about Alexander the Great and the defeat they would have inflicted on him had he turned west instead of east. Pyrrhus, however, is a mere shadow of Alexander. The thought of bowing to him, Appius continued, "diminishes the glory of Rome." Although Pyrrhus promises an alliance, the Senate should not suppose that any agreement with him can end the trouble that he brought. Instead, his success will attract others and "they will despise you as men whom anyone can easily subdue if Pyrrhus leaves without his hubris being punished." Indeed, the cost Rome will bear is its willingness to allow other Italians "to mock the Romans."[6]

Appius Claudius's speech did more than point out that humiliation lurked beneath Pyrrhus's generous terms. It also emphasized that this humiliation was dangerous. Every senator in the third century understood that Roman domination of Italy was precarious. At the time of Pyrrhus's arrival, nearly all of the three million Italians living south of the Po River were either Roman citizens or citizens of cities bound by alliances that required them to provide Rome with troops whenever it asked. These allied cities were still autonomous, and their politics more regularly focused on conflicts between local families and tensions with regional rivals than on their relations with Rome. As the most powerful polity on the peninsula, Rome could referee these disputes if necessary, but it largely stood back from them when it could to avoid inciting resentment unnecessarily. It was the universal recognition of Rome as Italy's dominant power that ultimately held this structure together. If Rome refused to fight to maintain this primacy and avoid humiliation at the hands of an outsider like Pyrrhus, the alliance structure on which its power and security depended could rapidly fall apart. Indeed, this likely seemed an existential threat to a city that only three years before had seen a Gallic army advance within forty miles of it before a combined force of Romans and their Italian allies pushed the barbarians back.[7]

Appius Claudius's speech convinced the Senate that Pyrrhus's offer was sweetened poison that they must refuse. Cineas returned to Pyrrhus not just with news of Rome's surprising refusal of his offer of alliance but also with a report detailing "the excellences of their form of government," the impressive nature of the Senate, and the huge number of Romans and allies who were capable of bearing arms. When Cineas's experiences in Rome joined with Pyrrhus's own failures to capture the allegiance of any significant Roman allies in Southern Italy, Pyrrhus finally gained a full appreciation of the Republic's tremendous ability to build political consensus among its citizens and allies. It became clear to him that, once the Republic and its allies decided on war, they would remain resolute until a victory without humiliation was achieved.

If Pyrrhus now knew the power of the Roman Republic as a governing system, he did not yet understand how strongly the Republic's ideals shaped the behavior of its individual citizens.

He would learn this only when a Roman embassy led by Gaius Fabricius Luscinus arrived to negotiate an exchange of prisoners. Pyrrhus had heard from Cineas that Fabricius was a good soldier and respected politician who was also relatively poor.[8] Thus, when Fabricius arrived, Pyrrhus offered him "so much silver and gold that he would be able to surpass all the Romans who are said to be most wealthy."[9] Fabricius, we are told, responded to Pyrrhus by informing him that his assumption was incorrect. Though he did not possess great material wealth, Fabricius told Pyrrhus, he did hold the highest offices in the state, he was sent on the most distinguished embassies, he was called upon to publicly express his opinions on the most important issues, and he was praised, envied, and honored for his uprightness. The Roman Republic, he continued, provided everyone who goes into public service with honors more splendid than any possession. It also regularly made an account of the property of Romans and could easily find anyone who had become wealthy dishonorably. What good would it do, Fabricius supposedly concluded, for him to accept gold and silver when this would cost him his honor and reputation? How could he endure a life in which he and his descendants were wealthy but disgraced?[10]

Pyrrhus now understood precisely what sort of society he had decided to fight. The Roman Republic was simultaneously a powerful state and a frightened one that recognized it could not afford to lose any war it fought. It had a unique ability to build political consensus among leading Romans and Roman allies as well as a great capacity to mobilize armies of citizen soldiers to fight to defend it. It also possessed a powerful system of incentives that rewarded loyalty with honors that the Republic alone could generate. This was a state quite unlike anything that Pyrrhus had ever encountered—and quite unlike anything the world had ever seen. Its citizen armies looked inexhaustible, its aristocracy appeared indivisible, and its leaders seemed unbribeable. Pyrrhus had failed to beat the Romans quickly and he now understood that he could not defeat them through treachery. He had no choice but to fight on.

Pyrrhus would advance within a two-day march of the city of Rome in 280. He would win another costly battle against the Romans in 279. And he would then depart Southern Italy. As he left, he supposedly commented: "If we should win one more battle against the Romans, we will be totally destroyed."[11] He would return to the Italian mainland and suffer a defeat at the hands of the Romans in 275 before leaving Italy for good and abandoning Tarentum to its fate. With the fall of Tarentum to the Romans in 272, the Republic finally and fully answered Appius Claudius's call for vengeance.

The two speeches supposedly delivered by Appius Claudius and Fabricius to Pyrrhus and his envoys together illuminate the foundations of the Roman Republic. On its most basic level, the Republic provided a legal and political structure that channeled the individual energies of Romans in ways that benefited the entire Roman commonwealth. By the turn of the third century BC, the structures of the Republic had also evolved so that members of leading wealthy families (the *nobiles,* or, in English, the nobles) directed many of the collective and individual ambitions of the Roman people. The nobles usually came from famous families, but talented "new men" could break into their ranks as well. Regardless of their family background, these Roman nobles of the early third century agreed that virtue lay in service to Rome and that dishonor fell upon those who put their private interests above those of the Republic.[12]

As Appius Claudius understood, the dedication and achievements of Roman elites had made the city extremely powerful, but Rome sat uneasily atop the rest of Italy. The city did control nearly all of the peninsula south of the Po, but this control was based on an intricate web of alliances and military levies that provided Rome with its floods of soldiers. Allies continued to provide troops and citizens continued to turn up for military levies in large part because they believed that the Republic would win the wars it entered and would punish those who failed to fulfill their obligations to Rome. Any sign of weakness, however, would rebalance the equation. Allies might peel away, citizens might refuse to serve, and, because Rome lay on the western Italian coastal plain, an enemy that arrived in Italy could quickly advance on the city. Once fighting began, the structure of Roman power demanded that Rome fight until it won.

But Appius Claudius seems to have also understood that individuals are rarely moved by such larger strategic considerations for very long. This is why his appeal to his fellow Roman senators hinted at a much more powerful reason to resist Pyrrhus. Bravery in war defined a Roman man in this period and was often conspicuously displayed. A man who saved the life of a Roman citizen by killing an enemy was awarded the *corona civica,* a wreath of oak leaves that he could wear for the rest of his life during religious processions. The spoils he stripped from an enemy he killed in battle could be displayed in his home. And these honors also helped define who he was after his death. The sarcophagus of Lucius Cornelius Scipio Barbatus, a consul in 298 BC, bore an inscription commemorating the offices he had held as well as his courage in capturing two Italian cities, subjugating the region of Lucania, and bringing back captives. The epitaph of his son, consul in 259, parallels that of his father by mentioning his own consulship as well as the fact that he "took Corsica and the city of Aleria."[13]

This sort of honor did not just come from the conquest of cities. A eulogy given in 221 after the death of Lucius Caecilius Metellus celebrated him for being "the first to lead elephants in a triumphal procession" following his capture of them in the First Punic War. As Rome's military victories spread beyond Italy, it became something of a custom among Roman elites to display impressive war spoils publicly in triumphs and semiprivately in the reception areas of their houses. Surrender to an adversary such as Pyrrhus simultaneously robbed individual Romans of the opportunity to excel through military service and diminished them all as cowards unwilling to do what was necessary to defeat an opponent. For individual Roman senators, these painful stings were more consequential than surrender's implications for Rome's grand military strategies, but the men who led the Republic in the third century also understood that their personal achievements had meaning only when they served the larger goals of Roman policy.[14]

The speech supposedly delivered by Fabricius highlights a different source of Roman strength. The wars of the early third century provided an arena for men to display their military virtue, but Rome offered far more to its citizens than simply a venue for military service. The Republic effectively monopolized the rewards that leading Romans most craved. Wealth mattered in Rome as it has in most societies before and since, but, as Fabricius suggested, it was not the most important factor in determining a person's worth in Republican Rome. Romans of the third century instead judged each man's merit by the offices he held, the honors he earned, and whether his achievements equaled those of his ancestors. The measure of a man was then largely a product of his activities in the military and political lives of the Roman state. Service was repaid with honor and, by the 280s, the Republic had come to completely control both sides of this exchange. The Republic dictated what sort of service an individual gave, it determined what sorts of rewards he would receive, and it paid these rewards out in a form of social currency that it alone controlled. Although the heirs of a figure like Fabricius would inherit a patrimony full of honors, a single dishonorable action could destroy all of the social capital that the family had spent generations building. And, as Fabricius reminded Pyrrhus, this particular form of Roman currency was not like gold or silver. It could only be earned through service to Rome.

The Republic's ability to inspire political consensus and monopolize the rewards that mattered to Roman citizens grew out of a shared understanding that the Republic was a political system subject to no one but the community as a whole. Its decisions and rewards did not reflect the whims of a single master but the

sentiments and decisions of the Roman community.[15] This view of
Roman political life was a relatively new thing in the 280s. Rome
had only recently reached the end of a centuries-long political evolution that historians have come to call the Conflict of the Orders.
The Conflict of the Orders was the process through which the patricians (a group that largely comprised Rome's hereditary aristocracy) and the plebeians (a social order made up of everyone who
was not a patrician) arrived at a system of government that preserved some patrician social and political prerogatives while also
making plebeians eligible for the state's highest offices.

The system arrived at by the 280s BC featured a complicated
but elegant set of offices and procedures designed to protect this
shared Roman liberty by encouraging political compromise,
building durable consensuses, and ensuring the shared governance
of the Republic. No written constitution governed it. The Republic instead functioned according to a combination of codified procedures and long-standing conventions that enabled influential
patricians and plebeians to run public affairs with the approval
of assemblies of citizens. The interaction between the elites who
sought the highest magistracies in the state and the voters who
elected them powered political life in the Republic, but the system
had developed a set of checks and balances to make sure that neither elite ambition nor popular empowerment went too far. With
the exception of the emergency office of dictator, only filled during
times of acute crisis, all of the offices in the Roman state were
paired—that is, occupied by two or more men simultaneously—
and term-limited. The consulship, the highest regular office in the
Republic, was held by two men for a one-year term. The consuls
both had *imperium*—the authority to command armies. They also
consulted the gods on behalf of the state, presided over three of
Rome's four assemblies, and called elections for the magistrates
who would hold office the next year. Each consul had the power
to veto the actions and initiatives of his colleague, a power that
pushed consuls toward cooperation and consensus building.[16]

Roman nobles competed for other offices that ranked below the consulship. These included the praetorship, the next most esteemed regular office in the Republic and one that enabled its holder to perform judicial duties within the city of Rome.[17] Praetors could exercise imperium outside of Rome as well, but they were required to give way to a consul in the event of a conflict. Below them were aediles, magistrates who monitored Rome's markets and roadways, as well as quaestors, junior magistrates who managed the accounts. Like the consulship, these offices were held by both patricians and plebeians and offered notables from both orders the opportunity to prove themselves as they built a public career.

One major office was quite unlike these. The tribunes of the plebs had to be plebeians and were elected by the *concilium plebis,* an assembly made up exclusively of plebeians. The tribunate was a very old office whose origins perhaps date back to the very beginning of the Republic. The earliest tribunes claimed a sacrosanctity that made their person inviolable, and they used this inviolability to protect plebeians from patrician abuses by, in theory at least, physically standing between an abusive patrician and his plebeian target. As the Republic matured, tribunes came to function primarily as political agents who intervened for plebeians by opposing the actions or threats of patrician magistrates. The number of tribunes eventually grew from two to ten and their powers expanded to include a broad veto that could be exercised against other tribunes, any magistrate other than a dictator, and even the decrees of the Roman Senate. In addition to these powers to obstruct political actions, tribunes had the power to propose laws before the *concilium plebis* that bound all Romans, call assemblies, and schedule debates on policy issues. It is, then, not at all surprising that a number of noble plebeians used the tribunate as a launching pad to build popular support for eventual bids for higher offices.

The Republic had no formal political parties and, aside from tribunal vetoes and injunctions by high-ranking magistrates that prohibited more junior colleagues from acting in a certain way, the system had no easy way to discipline the ambition of nobles serving it in key offices.[18] Whereas a government populated by ambitious nobles empowered to obstruct one another might seem like a recipe for permanent dysfunction, the assemblies and Senate, the other essential components of the Republican system, ensured that magistrates were indeed accountable if they proved ineffective or unresponsive. The Republic technically had four different assemblies, but one, the *comitia curiata,* had become effectively ceremonial by the third century. Its vestigial functions included tasks such as confirming adoptions and ratifying wills.

The other three assemblies played important and diverse roles in electing magistrates and passing legislation. The *comitia centuriata* had two main functions. It elected consuls and praetors and it was called to vote on declarations of war. Voting took place by polling the members of 193 centuries, each of which was made up of a class of people who had roughly the same amount of property. These divisions originated in the pre-Republican period, were based on the military equipment a citizen could afford to provide for himself, and gave the most votes to centuries made up of the *equites* (the Roman knights) and the wealthiest infantrymen. Those two groups together controlled nearly 100 of the 193 votes in the assembly, and the men belonging to the lowest property class in Rome all fell into a single century with a single vote. This meant that magistrates could not be elected in the *comitia centuriata* unless they commanded substantial support from Rome's wealthier citizens. This presented a substantial barrier to third-century politicians who aimed to dramatically disrupt Roman political life.[19]

From the late third century until the end of the Republic, Rome's two other assemblies, the popular assembly (which included all citizens) and the *concilium plebis* (in which only plebeians could vote), made legislation and elected aediles, quaestors, and tribunes. The main difference between the two assemblies seems to have been who summoned them. Consuls and praetors summoned the popular assembly, and tribunes summoned the *concilium plebis.*[20] Voting in both the popular assembly and the *concilium plebis* occurred according to tribes. By 241 BC, there were thirty-five tribes. Four of these were made up of citizens whose families were enrolled in the city of Rome. The other thirty-one rural tribes each represented a geographic area and were created as Roman control and citizenship expanded across Italy. Each tribe had a single vote in each assembly. The assemblies' votes were held in Rome and, because there were four urban tribes and many more rural tribes, the votes of the few rural citizens who could travel to the city to vote as a part of their tribe were disproportionately important. In the early third century, these people were more likely to be wealthy, so, again, the voting system provided important structural buffers against political disruption by poorer Romans.[21]

Although the membership of the popular assembly and that of the *concilium plebis* largely overlapped, only plebeians could attend the *concilium plebis*. This gave it distinctive powers that the popular assembly lacked. Each year the *concilium plebis* elected the ten tribunes of the plebs who proposed the laws on which the assembly would vote. The tribunes also had the power to call public meetings (*contiones*) in which legislation was discussed. There was no discussion of policy when votes were actually cast; in the third century, voting in assemblies consisted simply of a citizen approaching the official recording the vote and announcing his choice either for a candidate in an election or regarding a proposed piece of legislation. The votes were then tallied according to tribe, and the majority within the tribe dictated that tribe's one vote. The decision was then carried on the basis of what a majority of the tribes had chosen.

The laws approved by the *concilium plebis* were called plebiscites and, after 287 BC, they bound all Romans, even though only plebeians had a formal say in making them. In the third century, however, the plebeians who guided discussion and carried most votes tended, again, to be the same sort of reasonably wealthy establishment figures who naturally privileged stability and gradual reform over radical political change. The *concilium plebis* had the potential to push radical reforms onto all Romans, but, in the early third century, the nobles ensured that this potential remained largely unrealized.[22]

The Senate represented the place from which most of the actions taken and laws made in the Republic originated. It officially served as a purely advisory body made up of former high-office holders, defined as "the best men of every order,"[23] and its formal powers were limited to conducting foreign policy and approving public expenditures of money. The Senate nevertheless exercised informal power over all major political, military, financial, and religious matters. Its words did not have the force of law, but these influential former magistrates could deploy tremendous social capital that gave current magistrates and everyday voters great pause before they defied its advice. Magistrates and assemblies usually acted as the Senate advised.

This combination of offices and assemblies created a finely balanced political system that promoted political consensus and punished those who disrupted it. Magistrates were notables who were elected by assemblies that, in the third century, were effectively controlled by their peers. Once in office, these noble magistrates were charged with implementing policies set by the Senate, a body populated by their older and more experienced peers, and by assemblies dominated by the men who had just elected them. At the end of their one-year term, they were also required to give account of their actions to the bodies that had elected and empowered them. If he wished, a magistrate could spend his entire term obstructing others or trying to disrupt the political system, but, at the end of the year, he would then be compelled to publicly acknowledge his lack of accomplishment before his social equals. He would also have to answer to a disappointed electorate should he ever decide to stand for office again.

The power of popular and senatorial expectations created a culture of compromise and cooperation among officeholders that prevailed in Rome for much of the third century. Consuls and tribunes seem to have taken office with a set of goals they wished to accomplish, but they also understood that they were unlikely to accomplish all (or even most) of what they hoped. The trick to a successful tenure in office was to quickly understand what one's colleagues wanted, what the assemblies were willing to approve, and what the Senate would consent to authorize. An officeholder then had to figure out how to balance all of these different agendas with his own to create a set of policies and actions that came closest to satisfying all parties. Ideally, no one got everything they wanted, but everyone got something. As a later author marveled, there was no political conflict but "only differences of opinion and contests that were resolved by legislation, and these laws were established with mutual respect and concessions to one another."[24]

Perhaps the most famous ancient discussion of the functioning of the Republic of the nobles comes in a history written in the mid-second century by the Greek author Polybius. Polybius wrote in part to explain to a Greek audience how the Romans, who did not fit neatly into a world divided categorically between Greeks and barbarians, had managed to defeat and conquer Carthage, Macedon, Sparta, Corinth, and many of the other old city-states on the Greek mainland by the 140s BC. And at the heart of his explanation was the idea that Rome succeeded because the consensus-building checks and balances of its constitution "made it irresistible and certain of obtaining whatever it determines to attempt."[25]

Polybius also argued that the true strength of a constitution became evident only in times of crisis. "The true test of a perfect man," he wrote, "is his ability to bear violent changes of fortune with highmindedness and dignity. It is essential to examine the Republic in the same way." For Polybius, military threats represented the clearest moments when quick and dramatic misfortune threatened Rome's political equilibrium. Indeed, although Polybius's narrative begins in the 260s BC with the outbreak of the First

Punic War, he waited until after he described the Battle of Cannae (the third and greatest of Hannibal's victories over the Romans, in 216 BC) to speak about the nature of Roman political life. Polybius claimed that he had not ever seen "a sharper or greater reverse than that which happened to the Romans at that moment."[26]

Although one can debate whether military defeats really offer the best tests of the resiliency of a political system, there is no denying Polybius's basic premise that the threat of annihilation can amplify the positive or negative tendencies of a state's political life. And Polybius is also generally right that, when faced with such reverses, the Roman Republic of the third century tended to rally together and remain resolute. Rome's experience before, during, and after Hannibal's march into Italy proves his point.

In the First Punic War, a conflict that began in 264 BC and that lasted for nearly a generation, Rome faced off on land and sea against a powerful Carthaginian adversary that it was initially uneager and ill equipped to fight. Carthage, a city in modern Tunisia roughly on the site of modern-day Tunis, sat on a natural harbor on the western edge of the narrow Strait of Sicily, which divides the Eastern and Western Mediterranean. Founded by Phoenicians as a trading colony, Carthage commanded one of the Mediterranean's most advantageous commercial and strategic positions and soon grew into a prosperous and powerful city. By the third century BC, Carthage possessed the region's most formidable navy, powerful mercenary armies, and an empire that extended from Spain to Sicily.

Historically, relations between Rome and Carthage had not been particularly tense. The two cities had long respected each other's distinctive spheres of influence and, on occasion, had even cooperated militarily. This made the First Punic War something of a surprising development. In fact, this was a war that Rome seems almost to have stumbled into, with the Senate declining to recommend hostilities before the consuls asked the *comitia centuriata* to vote on going to war. Most of the fighting in the First Punic War occurred on Sicily and the seas around it. This put Rome at a significant disadvantage. Carthage not only controlled the eastern part of the island but also had a fleet of warships nearby. Rome, on the other hand, had no military presence in Sicily before 264 and, crucially, lacked both a significant navy and extensive experience fighting by sea. Indeed, the first large fleet of 120 ships that the Romans put to sea was built based on a prototype created by reverse-engineering a Carthaginian warship that had run aground in 261, well after the fighting had begun.[27]

Having cutting-edge naval vessels and being able to fight with them were two different things, however. Naval warfare in the 260s involved hundreds of rowers, often manning five banks of oars, working in concert to maneuver a ship until it could smash a metal ram on its prow into the hull of an enemy vessel.

It took extensive training for the rowers of one ship to work effectively as a team; it was exponentially harder to get a fleet of 120 ships to work together when the sailors and commanders were inexperienced. The Romans responded creatively to this challenge by attaching a spiked gangplank to their ships that could grab onto an enemy ship, hold it in place, and allow Roman marines to board it. Although this innovative tactic enabled the Romans

2.1. Roman coin minted during the Second Punic War showing the prow of a warship and the bronze ram used to attack enemies (#41/11 in the standard catalog of M. Crawford, *Roman Republican Coinage* [Cambridge, 1974]). Private collection. Photo by Zoe Watts.

to win a major sea battle in 260 BC, the Carthaginians quickly found ways to blunt the effectiveness of this Roman technique. This compelled the Romans to expand their fleet until, in 256 BC, they were able to put 250 ships together to send an invasion force to Africa. The new ships allowed Rome to land an army in Africa, but the Roman invaders were repulsed and a storm off of Sicily destroyed nearly all of Rome's ships in 255. When news of this disaster reached Rome, it "was taken greatly to heart," but the Romans "did not decide to withdraw from the war but instead determined to build another 220 ships."[28]

This new fleet was built in less than three months and put to sea in the summer of 254, but 150 of its ships were lost in another storm in the summer of 253. Another fleet that was built and equipped in 250 BC was destroyed by the Carthaginians at the Battle of Drepana in 249. Much of the fighting after Drepana consisted of inconclusive land battles in Sicily, but, by 242, it had become clear to Romans that the war could not be won unless their navy cut Carthage's ability to resupply its forces in Sicily by sea. Polybius writes that "there was no money in the public treasury" to fund construction of a new fleet, in large part because the people would not consent to pay more taxes to build ships. Instead, "the ambition (*philotimia*) and patriotism of the leading men" provided the funds to pay for the fleet. Some backers were individuals, others were teams of a few men, but all paid as much as their means permitted to build and outfit a ship, with the promise that they would be repaid only if the expedition succeeded. Roman elites would gain the glory for this victory and, in 241, they did. The new Roman armada decisively defeated the Carthaginian fleet. Seeing that it lacked the resources to continue fighting, Carthage sued for peace.[29]

In the First Punic War, Rome lost far more men and ships than Carthage, but the war ended when Carthage, which was much wealthier than Rome, found itself unwilling to bear the financial and military costs of continuing the fight. Rome's incredible resilience in this conflict came from many sources, but one of the most potent was the way that Roman nobles competed to exceed one another in the service they provided their home city. The men who personally paid for ships in 242 BC did so because they were patriotic, but they also did so because the Republic repaid them handsomely with honor, the exclusively Roman currency whose value Fabricius had described to Pyrrhus. The resolution of the Roman nobles to keep putting resources into the fight against Carthage in the 250s and 240s, then, grew out of the same collective steadfastness and personal ambition that Appius Claudius urged and Fabricius described in 280.

The elite political consensus that prevailed during the final stages of the First Punic War seems to have frayed somewhat by the 230s. In 232, Gaius Flaminius, a tribune of the plebs, ignored senatorial and consular objections and pushed a law through the *concilium plebis* that distributed individual lots of land in Northern Italy to Roman citizens. Probably in part because of the popularity this earned him, Flaminius was elected consul for 223. The Senate tried to negate the election by arguing that it had occurred despite unfavorable omens, sending Flaminius a letter to this effect, but Flaminius refused to open the letter until after he defeated a Gallic tribe in battle. When the Senate then refused to vote him a public triumph in honor of the victory, the popular assembly did this instead. Flaminius was compelled by his opponents to resign his consulship before the end of the year and return to private life, but his supporters remained so influential that Flaminius was elected as censor in 220. It was while holding this office that Flaminius arranged for the construction of a racetrack (the Circus Flaminius) and the Via Flaminia, a major road linking Rome to its Northern Italian possessions.[30]

Flaminius was a *novus homo* (a new man) whose ancestors had never held high office in the Republic. Many among the group of nobles who competed with one another for the consulship saw his populist appeal as an unseemly attempt to take honors and offices that were rightfully theirs. His ambition stressed the system, but he did not break it. And, despite the powerful reactions many nobles had to Flaminius's behavior, the Republic provided a space in which he could nevertheless make meaningful and lasting contributions to the welfare of the city and its territory. The Republic was flexible enough to enable the nobles to powerfully and unequivocally express their disapproval of Flaminius while also permitting the people to enact his proposals and award him the offices and honors he desired.

This resiliency served Rome well as it again stumbled into war with Carthage in 218 BC. Whereas the First Punic War pushed Rome to its military and financial limits, Rome's second war with Carthage posed a far greater threat to the Republic. The war began when the Carthaginian general Hannibal captured a Spanish city that had put itself under Roman protection, but Hannibal had been preparing for war with Rome for years before it came.[31] Hannibal had learned both from the First Punic War and, in all likelihood, from the campaign journals that Pyrrhus had published after his encounter with Rome decades earlier. Hannibal understood that Rome would again outlast Carthage in war unless he was able to demoralize Romans and peel away Roman allies to such a degree that Italian unity shattered. Hannibal also understood that the only way to accomplish this was to take his army from Spain, march it into the heart of Italy, and defeat Romans on their home turf.[32]

The Republic was slow to realize how much of a threat Hannibal's plan posed. Rome never anticipated that Hannibal would take the fight to Italy, and its initial strategy involved mobilizing armies under the command of the two consuls, to be sent to Sicily and Spain. These armies were made up of levies of Roman citizens and allies. This process took time and, while Rome assembled its forces, Hannibal marched through what is now southern France. He crossed the Rhone before Roman forces could march to meet him, moved into the Alps, and appeared in Northern Italy by the late autumn of 218. Abandoning their plans to fight outside of

Italy, the consuls of 218 instead fought two battles with Hannibal's forces in the north of the peninsula, with Rome absorbing a serious defeat at the Battle of the River Trebia in December of 218 or January of 217.

Hannibal's early victories created an odd dynamic in Roman political life. His forces were in Italy and represented a clear threat to Roman control of the Italian north, but they did not yet seem to pose an existential danger to the Republic. Indeed, it seems that Romans did not yet realize that they were facing one of history's most gifted military tacticians. Instead of crediting the Carthaginian victories to Hannibal's skill and, in particular, the tactical superiority of his cavalry, the Roman electorate blamed the incompetence of the noble consuls who had led the armies and, implicitly, the political consensus they represented. Consequently, in the consular elections for 217 BC, the disruptive populist Flaminius was voted into office for a second consulship.

Rome's victory in the First Punic War made clear that the Republic of the third century BC had a remarkable ability to build and maintain political consensus during military emergencies. But neither Flaminius nor the Senate yet believed that Hannibal's advance represented such an emergency. Both instead saw this situation as something similar to the Gallic advance that Flaminius had checked during his first consulship in 223. Indeed, Flaminius assumed that he would follow the same script. He therefore left Rome to join his armies before the Senate could again invent a religious objection to his taking control of them, a step that prevented Flaminius from performing the vows and sacrifices that a consul normally did on his first day of office.[33] Flaminius was betting that, as in 223, he could outrun domestic political opponents and neutralize them with a quick military victory over Hannibal. As a result, he again ignored a senatorial summons to return to Rome and led his forces north toward Hannibal.[34]

Short-term domestic political competition seldom breeds good military strategy and, on a foggy morning during the spring of

217, Hannibal took advantage of Flaminius's impatience. He lured the consul and his army into a trap beside Lake Trasimeno in Umbria. Hannibal had found a spot along the lake's eastern shore where the hills receded slightly and formed a sort of natural amphitheater that trapped the spring fog that rose off of the lake. As Flaminius advanced along the narrow lakeshore, the thick fog prevented him from seeing that most of Hannibal's forces waited in the hills above. When the consul led his army onto the flat lakeshore below, Hannibal pounced. Hemmed in by the hills to their north and the lake to the south, the Romans and their allies saw fifteen thousand men die in this battle, including Flaminius himself. Another ten thousand soldiers were taken captive and a reinforcement of four thousand cavalry was killed soon afterward.

The Romans responded by suspending the normal offices of the Republic and appointing Quintus Fabius Maximus as dictator. Although consuls normally appointed dictators, the Senate and assembly agreed that the situation was so dire that they could not wait for Flaminius's colleague to return to the city and do what custom demanded. Subsequent events would show that this was the right decision. A comfortable fixture of the political establishment, Fabius did not share Flaminius's need to prevail quickly over Hannibal. Instead of confronting Hannibal, he began a strategy of shadowing the Carthaginian forces, attacking only when small detachments could be isolated from the main group, and rebuilding Roman morale. Although Fabius succeeded in preserving his forces, his strategy of delay not only earned him the unflattering nickname *Cunctator* (Delayer) but also permitted Hannibal to burn and pillage territory in Campania that belonged to Roman citizens. This unwillingness to act began to generate criticism within the army as well as popular discontent in Rome. As Fabius's six-month term ended, a consensus again emerged that Hannibal must be confronted and defeated.[35]

This led to catastrophe. Gaius Terentius Varro, a popular consul who had won election to the office by rallying people against

Fabius's strategy of delay, took the field in 216 with the largest army of Roman citizens and allies ever assembled. Perhaps numbering more than eighty thousand, these soldiers met Hannibal's much smaller forces outside of the town of Cannae in the Southern Italian region of Apulia.[36] Recognizing that he could neutralize the Romans' superior numbers by drawing them into a fight in close quarters, Hannibal created a crescent-shaped formation in his line of infantry that drew the Romans into a confined space. The rest of his forces then surrounded the Roman army on three sides, pushing the soldiers so close together that they could not move. The result was mass slaughter. Varro survived, but tens of thousands of Romans and allies died, including Varro's co-consul Lucius Aemilius Paullus, the consul who had been selected to replace Flaminius following his death at Lake Trasimeno (Gnaeus Servilius Geminus), and Fabius's former master of the horse (Marcus Minucius Rufus). With most of its troops dead or scattered, Rome itself now seemed vulnerable to attack by Hannibal.[37]

Total panic enveloped the Republic. Working off of a contemporary report written by a senator who lived through these terrifying moments, the first-century historian Livy speaks of a frantic and chaotic scene in which patrician commanders talked of leaving the city to find refuge with a foreign king, the Senate met to organize a final defense of the city, and everyone struggled to get accurate information about what remained of the Roman army. Amid all of this, Fabius Maximus again stepped forward to calm the state. He ordered that any information about the surviving Roman forces and what Hannibal intended to do should be brought first to authorities in Rome. Families who wondered about the fate of loved ones were to wait in their homes for news and, if the news was bad, their mourning was to be done privately. He also ordered guards posted at the gates of the city so that no one could flee and suggested that it be made clear to all citizens within Rome that their best hope for survival was to remain behind its walls. Not long afterward, Roman religious authorities even tried to propitiate the gods by sanctioning the sacrifice of four people, an extraordinary ritual only repeated once more in the next seventeen hundred years of Roman history.[38]

These radical measures would have attracted significant resistance under normal circumstances, especially since Fabius had proposed nearly all of them despite the fact that he held no office. But these were not normal circumstances. Fabius's relative success in containing Hannibal during his dictatorship generated "unanimous support" for all of his proposals. The Senate then appointed a dictator and immediately began the extraordinary process of building four new legions and a thousand cavalry out of a mix of very young citizens, slaves purchased from their masters, convicts, and debtors. It also sent a message to Rome's allies to marshal more troops to support Rome's war effort.[39] Roman military policy would no longer be determined by time lines and objectives tied to the ambitions of individual consuls. Instead, the state had now come to a broad agreement that Fabius's deliberate approach to Hannibal's presence in Italy was the only viable response to Cannae.

Unfortunately, the defeats at Trebia, Trasimeno, and Cannae also upset the delicate balance that kept regional powers from challenging Rome. Over the next two years, the Roman system of alliances, colonies, and direct political control of Italian territory shattered. The perception of Roman weakness induced a number of cities in Central and Southern Italy to join Hannibal's cause, in some cases by overthrowing pro-Roman local governments. Although many of these cities were in Southern Italy, the defection of Capua, Italy's second largest city, stung particularly. Not only was Capua a mere hundred miles from Rome on the peninsula's west coast but also, unlike many of the Southern Italians who turned to Hannibal, Capuans were Roman citizens. Capua's embrace of Hannibal reflected a combination of frustration at the number of soldiers the city had lost in the recent fighting and a hope that Capua could fill the power vacuum in Italy that Rome's seemingly imminent defeat would create.[40]

The idea that Rome had now been dramatically weakened also encouraged non-Italian states to challenge it over the next two years. In 215, Hannibal persuaded King Philip V of Macedon to agree to a military alliance against Rome, a pact the Greek king signed in part because he hoped to take Roman possessions along the east coast of the Adriatic. Earlier that year, a force of Gallic invaders also entered Italy, killed the consul-elect, and destroyed his army. Then, in 214, hostilities with Macedon began and the great Sicilian city of Syracuse overthrew its pro-Roman king to side with Carthage.[41]

In these dark days, Rome again embraced the sentiments that Appius Claudius had so forcefully expressed before Pyrrhus's envoys. It would not accept defeat in any theater of this sprawling war. Within Italy, the Fabian strategy of limiting Hannibal's movements would be combined with a steady and withering effort to recapture and punish those cities that had defected to him. Though some significant Italian communities had joined Hannibal, many Roman allies still believed that Rome could prevail and relished the chance to take booty, territory, and privileges from Italian rivals whose loyalty had wavered. This meant that Rome still had a decided manpower advantage over the Carthaginians. And, whereas Hannibal needed to keep his army together to avoid being overwhelmed, Rome could field multiple armies, allowing them to attack a number of Italian cities at once.

What really distinguished the Roman response to these crises, however, was the Republic's willingness to shift to what amounted to an ancient version of total war. While Rome fielded, on average, about four legions a year for most of the fourth century, the threats from so many fronts at once prompted a radical expansion of the number of men at arms. By 211, the Republic had filled twenty-five legions and deployed armies in Italy, Spain, Sicily, and Greece as well as two fleets positioned to guard against crossings of troops from Africa and Greece. This meant that perhaps 70 percent of the entire citizen population between the ages of seventeen and thirty had enrolled in the army. They did not sign up for a short stint either. Many of these recruits would remain in the army for the duration of the war; in the case of the survivors of Cannae, they were obliged to serve until Rome's final victory. The Mediterranean world had never before seen a state with so large a population mobilize its citizens so completely.[42]

Even more impressive than the Republic's ability to form and supply such large armies of citizens was its ability to maintain political support for a war that required this level of sacrifice. And yet, for nearly a decade after Cannae, Romans allowed their sons to serve and entrusted the highest offices in the state to a narrow group of well-established generals. Fabius Maximus held three consulships between 215 and 209; M. Claudius Marcellus held three between 214 and 208, Q. Fulvius Flaccus was consul in 212 and 209. The gamesmanship that allowed Roman initiative to bounce from Flaminius to Fabius to Varro had ended. In its place stood an elite united in their desire to vanquish Hannibal, even if doing so meant subordinating their own political ambitions so that more experienced and capable men could command.[43]

This unity of purpose made the Republic of the 210s uniquely adaptable. Traditionally, either consuls or praetors commanded armies, but, with twenty-five legions fighting across the Mediterranean, there were now more legions than magistrates who could command them. Furthermore, the distance from Rome to the battlefields in Spain or Greece was significant enough that a magistrate serving a one-year term would have little time to do much, after traveling to meet his armies, before his replacement would be selected. And, to make matters even more dire, the Roman economy, which was somewhat backward by Mediterranean standards before the war, had been profoundly shocked by Hannibal's victories.[44] It was unclear both how Rome could continue to pay for so many armies and, in a world in which information moved only as fast as a human messenger, how it could organize commands across so many different regions. The old Republican conventions

linking officeholders to specific commands could not be followed
when Rome fielded so many armies in such far-flung places.

The Republic evolved rapidly to meet the needs of this sprawling war. The Senate coordinated military strategy and adjusted
Roman political and financial processes so that its strategy could
be executed properly. Consuls and praetors whose terms had ended
were empowered by the Senate to continue to command armies far
afield from Italy, taking on the titles of proconsul and propraetor.
In some cases, private citizens also were given commands as proconsuls or propraetors.[45] Their terms were also extended to enable
them to divine and respond to the particular situation in the military theater assigned to them. When money was short after the
defection of many Roman allies after Cannae, the Senate relied on
credit extended by its own members and other wealthy Romans
to pay for the war. It also devalued Roman coinage in an effort to
stretch what resources it did have. Then, after Rome began receiving influxes of precious metal from the capture of Syracuse in 212,
the Senate pivoted again and remade the Roman monetary system
so that it was based around a silver coin called the denarius; this
addressed the inflation problem devaluation had caused. When
this influx of precious metal proved inadequate to meet the expenses of the war, the Senate agreed to the sale of land confiscated
following the reconquest of disloyal Italian allies.[46]

Rome's adaptability in these practical matters combined with
a steadfast commitment to the broader military strategy it adopted
after Cannae. The armies operating in Italy gradually peeled allies away from Hannibal, meting out draconian punishments for
cities like Capua that resisted. Although Rome did make shows
of force in Greece between 211 and 207, most of the fighting in
Greece was outsourced to Greek allies like the Aetolian League.
Although Rome tried to prolong the war, the Republic ultimately
signed a peace treaty with Macedon in 205 after its allies lost their
appetite to continue the fight. The campaign in Spain originally
served merely to keep Carthaginian forces bogged down so that

they could not reinforce Hannibal. As the campaign ground on, however, Roman successes under the young proconsul P. Cornelius Scipio undermined and ultimately eliminated Carthaginian control of the peninsula altogether.

The first serious questioning of Rome's post-Cannae strategy occurred after Scipio victoriously returned from Spain in 206. Denied a triumphal procession on a technicality, the charismatic commander won the consulship for 205 with the unanimous support of all 35 tribes. Scipio then began pushing to be given a command to end the war by taking a Roman army to Africa, a proposal that attracted wide and enthusiastic support. But Scipio's proposal seemed incredibly reckless to Fabius and the group of experienced senators who had managed the war since Cannae. Hannibal remained undefeated in Italy and, with no Carthaginian presence remaining in Spain, and Rome in control of the seas, the architects of the strategy to contain him cautioned that Scipio's planned invasion seemed like another reckless attempt by an upstart to win glory for himself. When the Senate seemed inclined to accept the argument of Fabius and his allies that Hannibal should be defeated in Italy before anyone considered attacking Africa, Scipio hinted at the possibility of bringing the question before the popular assembly.[47] Ultimately, Fabius and his allies realized that they could not block Scipio from attacking Africa without unpredictably disrupting Roman political life. They relented, but on the condition that the disgraced veterans of Cannae (who the Senate seems to have viewed as essentially expendable) form the core of the army that Scipio would command. Then, as Scipio trained these men in the new and complicated tactics he had perfected in Spain, senatorial opponents sent a commission to investigate their fitness. Although the commissioners apparently expected that these troops could never be suitably prepared for battle, they instead left deeply impressed by their discipline.[48]

Even as they erected obstacles to Scipio's planned invasion, the Roman elite remained conscious of the need to project Roman unity during the last years of the war. As Scipio gathered and trained his invasion force, the Sibylline Books, a collection of prophecies that the state consulted in times of emergency, produced an oracle indicating that the foreign foe who had landed in Italy could only be dislodged if Rome brought the cult of the Anatolian goddess Cybele to the city.[49] The introduction of a foreign goddess could have been a source of major social friction, but the Roman nobles made sure that all factions of the city came together to greet Cybele—including, most notably, people connected to both Scipio and those in the Senate who opposed him. When the goddess's statue arrived at the Roman port of Ostia, Scipio Nascia, a relative of the general, and Claudia Quinta, a member of a family whose long-standing hostility to the family of the Scipiones was well-known, both greeted it. They led a crowd of young women belonging to the city's leading families who escorted the statue into the city. And, although Cybele represented a goddess who came from Asia Minor, the first priest of the cult, Marcus Porcius Cato, would later gain a considerable reputation for his fierce advocacy of Roman tradition. The introduction of the cult of Cybele was, then, a very public statement of Roman unity after the argument about Scipio's planned African invasion.

In the end, Scipio's invasion of Africa succeeded in ending the war. Hannibal was recalled to Africa after Scipio won a series of victories in 204, and Scipio ultimately defeated him when the two squared off at Zama in 202. Scipio then negotiated a peace treaty. Rome would retain the territory it took from Carthage in Spain, though Carthage itself would remain independent, ungarrisoned, and in control of the territory it possessed in Africa at the war's outset. It would become a Roman ally, the size of its military would be severely restricted, and it could wage war only if Rome approved. Carthage was also required to pay an immense annual tribute in precious metals to Rome for the next fifty years.

This peace treaty helped to set the parameters of Roman public life for much of the next half century. When the war with

Hannibal started, the Republic controlled territory only in Italy and its surrounding islands. It fielded perhaps four legions in any given year, its economy was underdeveloped, and agriculture depended heavily on small-scale cultivation. And the Republic had only minimal involvement with political affairs in Spain, Greece, or Africa.

The Second Punic War changed all of this. It required Roman soldiers to fight in theaters across the Mediterranean, and the conduct of such an expansive war compelled Rome to fundamentally alter both its relationship to other polities and the operations of its own government. Roman armies had campaigned on the eastern coast of the Adriatic, in Gaul, in Spain, in Sicily, and in Africa. Roman commanders and senators built military alliances with tribes in Spain, a league of city-states in Greece, and the kingdom of Numidia in North Africa. The number of legions under arms increased dramatically, as did the number of magistrates the Republic empowered to command armies. The rampant inflation during the early years of the war also forced the Republic to completely remake the Roman monetary system into one stabilized by the creation of the denarius that was supported, at least initially, by plunder taken from the capture of cities during the war. Once the fighting ended, however, Rome could neither demobilize nor dismantle the political and economic systems it had created to win it.

Rome could not pull back from the areas its forces had entered and it needed to maintain the economic, military, and political structures that allowed it to exert influence over them. The conquest of Carthaginian Spain meant that Roman administrators and soldiers now had to secure and govern territory on the peninsula. The need to protect this territory from attack by other Spanish tribes set off a series of grinding campaigns that led ultimately to the brutal conquest and pacification of the entire peninsula. Philip's surprising declaration of war against Rome, the alliance Rome made with the Aetolian League, and the Republic's failure to punish Philip drew Rome into Greek affairs and made the Republic extremely sensitive to any geopolitical changes that might increase the Macedonian threat. And, finally, although Rome maintained no military presence in Africa, the relationship with Carthage that the treaty had created ensured that Rome would remain involved in political affairs there as well.

Within Rome, the elite of the Republic continued to take to heart Appius Claudius's idea that Rome must fight until it wins the wars it enters. They also embraced Fabricius's notion that Roman ambition should be channeled toward honorable service as an officeholder and general rather than to the accumulation of wealth. Whereas the significance of these ideals seemed clear to Romans living through the war with Pyrrhus, their application became much more blurry in a world where wars did not always end, administrative appointments dragged on for many years, and conquest brought wealth as well as glory. As the second century dawned, leading Romans gradually grew to realize that elite ambition and competition were growing ever more heated at precisely the moment when the Republic was beginning to lose its monopoly on the social currency that mattered to these elites. The unity that the Republic displayed so prominently upon the arrival of Cybele would seem ever more illusory as the second century progressed.

CHAPTER 3

EMPIRE AND INEQUALITY

WHEN ROME BEGAN THE SECOND Punic War, its leading citizens seem to have imagined that they were embarking on a fight that would proceed along many of the same lines as Rome's first fight with Carthage. This war, too, would be fought first in Sicily and Spain and then in Africa itself. Rome would follow established procedures for recruiting armies, assigning commands, and allocating resources. And, in the end, victory over Carthage could be won without substantial challenges to the basic functioning of Roman government and the long-standing arrangements through which Rome controlled Italy.

By 202 all of these expectations must have seemed absurdly naive. The war had fundamentally and permanently changed the economic, political, and military life of Romans and, as the second century dawned, Romans came increasingly to understand that a state that reconfigured itself to project power across wide distances during a war would never return to its previous form. (The United States would reach a similar realization after World War II.) Not only would Rome need to fill the power vacuums left by the defeats of Carthage and its allies but the internal transformations that enabled Rome to survive Hannibal also could not be easily undone. Still, no one in Rome or the wider Mediterranean could yet imagine how profoundly Rome's evolution during the Second Punic War would change their world.

The first sign that the Mediterranean had entered a new era came just two years after Carthage's surrender in 202. The entry of Philip V into Rome's war with Carthage had, in the end, made little difference to Hannibal's campaign. Rome quickly built an alliance with the Greek Aetolian League, with the Aetolians conducting most of the fighting against Philip. The war petered out when the Aetolians came to terms with the king, and, for the first time in recent history, an adversary had challenged the Romans only to emerge essentially unpunished.

Although Rome had gained no new territory in Greece or its environs during the conflicts with Philip and Hannibal, the fighting compelled Rome to cultivate relationships with Greek states in the Eastern Mediterranean. The Aetolians, of course, were the Greeks with whom Rome had dealt most closely, but other Greek states had also cooperated closely with the Republic as it struggled to defeat Carthage. Around 213 BC, for example, the Ptolemaic kingdom of Egypt had helped Rome stave off bankruptcy by sending a large quantity of gold bullion to the Republic that could be minted into distinctive coins. Then, in 208, Ptolemaic ambassadors had tried to mediate an end to Rome's war with Macedon. And Rome had also developed deep ties with the kingdom of Pergamum in Asia Minor. Not only had Pergamum participated for a time in the war against Philip but it had also facilitated the transfer of the goddess Cybele to Rome as the Republic prepared for the invasion of Africa.[1]

Rome had withdrawn somewhat from the Greek world after the peace treaty with Philip, but, after the experiences of Pyrrhus's invasion earlier in the century and Philip's alliance with Carthage, the Senate was now very much aware of the need to follow Greek developments. And, as the new century dawned, Rome became greatly troubled by an alliance that threatened to overturn the balance of power in the Eastern Mediterranean. A series of volcanic eruptions between 210 and 205 BC dramatically affected food production in Ptolemaic Egypt and, in 207 or 206, the kingdom was hit by a serious rebellion that nearly toppled the dynasty. As Egypt seethed, the rest of the Greek world sensed an opportunity. Philip V and Antiochus III, the leader of the Seleucid Greek dynasty based in Syria, reached an alliance through which they would work together to dismember the Ptolemaic kingdom and split the spoils among themselves. Although neither kingdom immediately moved decisively, the threat that such a pact posed to the balance of power across the region could indeed seem frightening to Rome. The threat of an even more powerful Macedonian kingdom seemed particularly serious given that Philip had tried to expand his kingdom to the west by exploiting Rome's preoccupation with Hannibal in the 210s. Romans could not be faulted for thinking that he might try something similar in the future.[2]

By 200 BC, alarmed reports from Roman allies in Pergamum, Rhodes, the Aetolian League, and Athens reached the Senate. All of them detailed Philip's aggressive actions and described the territorial divisions supposedly outlined in his agreement with Antiochus. The Senate voted to declare war on Philip conditionally, with war to be avoided if Philip were to cease his attacks on the Greek states that had complained to Rome. While Philip deliberated, the consul P. Sulpicius Galba was allotted the command against Macedon. Galba had already fought against the forces of Philip during Rome's earlier conflict with Macedon and had become somewhat familiar with both the region in which the fighting would occur and the tactics of the enemy. Crucially, Galba had also become aware of the riches and honors that he could gain for himself if Rome decided to fully and energetically prosecute this war.[3]

Though the Senate could propose a course of action, the Republican system required the *comitia centuriata* to endorse any senatorial recommendation for war. And it was here that Galba and the other members of the Senate hit an unexpected problem. Fatigued by the effort Rome had put in to defeat Hannibal and apparently egged on by a tribune of the plebs who complained that the Senate refused to allow the people to enjoy the fruits of peace, the assembly voted overwhelmingly against a second war with Macedon. "The senate," a later historian observed, "could not tolerate this behavior." Individual senators took turns abusing the tribune of the plebs and urging Galba to schedule another public discussion of the issue as a prelude to a second vote.[4]

Although Galba's exact words are now lost, the speech that he delivered in this public meeting probably drew powerfully on Romans' traumatic memories of Hannibal's recent invasion of Italy. Livy records that Galba pointed out to the populace that Rome would have to fight Philip somewhere, and the wars with Pyrrhus and Hannibal had shown that it was better for Rome to confront adversaries abroad rather than in Italy. Lurking beneath this claim was perhaps also a realization that Rome had failed to impress either Macedon or other Greek states with its conduct of its last war with Philip. Galba may have felt the need to assert Roman power forcefully to avoid another military challenger coming from the east. The assembly seems to have been swayed by Galba's speech and voted for war, though with the condition that no one who had served in the African campaigns of the Second Punic War would be compelled to serve in the war with Macedon.[5]

Galba got his war, but the fighting proved much more difficult than he had anticipated. Both Galba and his successor found themselves blocked from advancing into Greece by Philip's energetic defense of mountain passes. It was not until 198 that Roman forces, under the command of the consul T. Quinctius Flamininus, broke through Philip's defenses. When Philip sent messengers to try to negotiate a peace, Flamininus found himself in a difficult position. His term in office was nearly over and, though he could conceivably declare the war won if he accepted Philip's peace offer, he had the chance to gain far greater honors if his command were to be extended. After three days of negotiations, Philip proved willing to grant a number of territorial concessions as a price for peace, but Rome's Greek allies were unsatisfied with the deal he offered. Philip then proposed that the impasse could be broken if he sent an embassy to appeal directly to the Roman Senate. Before the issue could come before the Senate, however, Flamininus learned that his command against Philip had been extended. Recognizing that Flamininus now had time to decisively defeat Philip and serve as the architect of the peace, Flamininus's officers sabotaged the senatorial discussion.[6]

In 197 BC, Flamininus's Roman legions met Philip's phalanx on a ridge in Thessaly called Cynoscephalae (literally, the Dog's Head) where they outmaneuvered the Macedonian forces and put the king to flight. After a second round of negotiations, Philip and the Senate agreed to a treaty by which Philip would pay a massive war indemnity, evacuate all of the territory that he controlled in central and southern Greece, and disband his fleet. In 196, Flamininus used the occasion of the Isthmian Games in Corinth to announce that all Greeks in Greece would be free from all foreign garrisons and tribute payments. The Macedonians would leave, the Romans would not replace their garrisons with Roman troops, and no other Greek kingdom or city-state was to try to fill the vacuum the departure of these great powers would leave. It was then communicated separately to representatives of Antiochus III that the Greek cities of Asia Minor once controlled by either Philip or the Ptolemies were to be free as well.[7]

Antiochus was unmoved and, in an interview with Roman representatives a few months later, reportedly told the Romans that they had as much business with affairs in Asia as he did with those in Italy. And, in the immediate term, this settled things. Flamininus and the Roman commissioners sent to sort out Greek affairs spent most of 195 and 194 implementing the agreement with Philip before withdrawing their forces. But almost immediately after this withdrawal, Rome began receiving reports from its Greek allies in Asia Minor about Antiochus's moves to fill the vacuum left by Philip's humiliation. In 192, Rome's former allies in the Aetolian League convinced Antiochus to make the much more provocative move of landing a force of ten thousand infantry, five hundred cavalry, and six elephants in Greece, a step that challenged Flamininus's declaration that Greece should remain free of foreign control.

The troops and elephants alarmed Rome far less than who accompanied them: Antiochus had chosen to challenge the freedom of Greece with an army led by Hannibal. Whatever restraint Rome might have felt about campaigning against a king whose domains stretched from the Aegean to India disappeared once the Senate learned of Hannibal's presence. This was now a war that Rome was determined to prosecute fully. Once Roman forces landed, Antiochus made a show of fortifying the famous mountain pass at Thermopylae before retreating to Asia, leaving the Aetolians to face the Romans alone. He seemed to imagine that the Romans would again cede Asia as his sphere of influence if he stayed out of Greece.

He was wrong. The consul for the year 190 assigned to confront Antiochus was Lucius Cornelius Scipio, the brother of Scipio Africanus, and Lucius was eager to match his brother's achievement at Zama with his own resounding victory over Hannibal. Roman forces under Lucius's command crossed into Asia, turned down a series of peace proposals from Antiochus, and defeated Hannibal, the king, and his full army in 188. Scipio then dictated that peace would depend upon Antiochus evacuating all of western Asia Minor, paying an indemnity of 15,000 talents (fifteen times what Rome had compelled Philip to pay), and surrendering Hannibal. If he complied, Antiochus could keep his throne and control over the rest of his territory. The territory he and his allies ceded would fall under the control of four regional powers: the Achaean League of Greek cities, the Macedonian kingdom of Philip (which had ingratiated itself to Rome by allowing Scipio's army to pass through its territory safely), the kingdom of Pergamum, and the Republic of Rhodes. After an additional year of campaigning in Greece and Asia Minor by the Romans, the consuls for the next year compelled the Aetolians to become subject allies of the Republic. Rome again withdrew from Greece.

This arrangement, through which Rome farmed out the stabilization of Greece and Asia Minor to allies, proved only slightly more enduring than Flamininus's "freedom of Greece." Everyone in the Greek world knew that distant Roman power supported these four regional hegemons, but the states were bound in alliance only to Rome and not to each other. This meant that Rome alone would have to guarantee the stability of the system amid the friction resulting from changes in the leadership of those states, challenges to their control of territory, and regional rivalries. These issues had emerged already in the 180s, and Rome's unwillingness to involve itself forcefully in the politics of the Greek world meant that the system neared collapse as the 170s dawned.[8]

Philip's death in 179 further destabilized Greece. After sanctioning the murder of one son with whom the Senate had particularly good relations, Philip passed the Macedonian kingdom to his son Perseus. Perseus in turn began to fill the leadership void that Rome had left. He built up close ties with the cities of southern and central Greece, married a member of the Seleucid royal family, and received honors from Rhodes. Rumors soon reached Rome that Perseus had begun rebuilding the Macedonian military into a force that could again threaten the peace. Rome reacted, however, only when the king of Pergamum came to Rome and, speaking before a closed meeting of the Senate, detailed a series of real and imaginary offenses committed by Perseus.[9]

Hostilities began in 171 and, surprisingly, Rome suffered a series of defeats in the first two years of the war. When Perseus's victories combined with the fact that a Roman fleet had sacked a number of allied Greek cities, Rome soon faced a serious crisis. Not only were Greek states rallying to Perseus but also the consuls for the year 169 ran short of enough volunteers to assemble an army willing to go to Greece. The war was won following a decisive battle in 168 that saw the Roman commander Aemilius

Paullus defeat Perseus's phalanx and, not long afterward, capture the king himself.

After Paullus's victory, Rome again sought to build a structure through which Greeks could govern themselves in a fashion that would enable it to again withdraw from Greece. The kingdom of Macedon was broken up into four republics that were forbidden from cooperating with one another and required to pay taxes to Rome. The Achaean League was compelled to send Rome 1,000 hostages (including the historian Polybius) to guarantee its good behavior, and the Aetolian League saw 550 of its leading citizens massacred as punishment for being a disloyal ally. Even Rhodes, which had only tried to mediate the conflict, saw Rome strip it of all territory on the Asian mainland. And, finally, although the Seleucids had played no direct role in the war, a Roman emissary confronted the king Antiochus IV in 168 while he was attacking the Ptolemaic capital of Alexandria in a separate conflict. He presented Antiochus with a senatorial decree ordering him to retreat, drew a circle in the dirt around the king, and told him to decide whether to obey the Roman order before he stepped out of the circle. Antiochus wisely called off the attack.

The punishments that Rome meted out and the political reforms it compelled following the third war with Macedon did not work any better than Rome's previous two attempts to regulate Greek affairs. Rome was drawn back into Greece yet again in 150 BC when a Macedonian pretender reunified the kingdom and the Achaean League fell into civil war. The Romans responded with fury. The Macedonian pretender was defeated in 148 BC and Macedon was made into a Roman province governed by a Roman governor. It would not fall out of direct Roman control again for more than a millennium. The Achaean situation was suppressed even more brutally. In 146 BC, Roman armies completely destroyed the ancient city of Corinth, looting everything of value and enslaving those of its population who survived before razing its buildings.

Rome did not manage to handle affairs much better in any of the other theaters where fighting occurred during the Second Punic War. It took nearly a decade of intense fighting in the 190s, for instance, for Rome to reestablish its dominance over the territories in Northern Italy that Hannibal's Gallic allies had overrun. There was then another forty years of regular campaigns before Rome fully established control over Liguria in northwestern Italy.

Resistance to Roman control in Spain lasted even longer and was even more intense. Although it seems that the Senate may have been looking to draw down the Roman presence in Spain after the last Carthaginian forces there had been defeated in 206, obligations to Spanish allies and the possibility of Carthage reestablishing itself on the peninsula prevented this. Military operations continued with such regularity that, by 197 BC, the Senate created two Spanish provinces that would be governed by Roman officials with command of armies. This administrative shift prompted a massive rebellion by Rome's new Spanish subjects, with fighting that lasted until the early 170s. Conflict broke out again in the 150s with a series of attacks across the provincial frontiers by raiders based in western Spain. These small episodes of violence metastasized into a general revolt when a Roman governor ordered the residents of the city of Segeda to stop building fortifications. As in Greece in the same period, Roman commanders in Spain responded by shifting from a method of control dependent upon cooperation with existing political entities to one in which local resistance was brutally suppressed. Unlike Greek states, however, Rome's Spanish adversaries regularly resorted to guerilla tactics that prolonged conflicts at terrible cost. It was not until 133 that Romans ended this wave of Spanish resistance with the capture and destruction of the city of Numantia.[10]

Rome's most significant failure came in its relationship with Carthage. The peace treaty that Rome signed with Carthage after the Second Punic War proved far more enduring than any of the treaties Rome signed with Greek kingdoms or Spanish groups.

Indeed, North Africa was the one place where Roman military disengagement did not quickly lead to a breakdown in order during the second century. Rome mediated conflicts between Carthage and the neighboring kingdom of Numidia in 195, 193, and 181–180 and even refused to listen to Numidian charges that Carthage sought to collaborate with the Macedonian king Perseus during the Third Macedonian War. But as Greek and Spanish events pushed Romans to reassess the larger policy of disengagement from areas where it had once fought, Rome's attitude toward Carthage began to change as well. By the 150s, the prominent Roman senator Cato took to ending all of the speeches he gave on any topic whatsoever with the phrase "Carthage must be destroyed."

Rome continued to try to goad Carthage into war, but it was not until the year 149 that Carthage proved unable to endure Roman provocations. A series of border disputes with Numidia in the mid-150s led to a Numidian attack to which Carthage responded militarily without Roman approval. Although completely understandable, Carthage's actions constituted a violation of the peace treaty with Rome. When Roman commissioners arrived to investigate the situation, Carthage preemptively undertook the public ritual of submission that all defeated Roman adversaries performed even though Carthage had not actually fought Rome. By right, the Roman ambassadors could dictate any conditions they wanted on a defeated adversary, but, when they ordered the seafaring Carthaginians to abandon their coastal city and move inland, Carthage resolved to fight. The war proved far more difficult than the Romans anticipated. Carthage held out until 146 BC (the same year that Rome destroyed Corinth), but, when Roman forces finally stormed Carthage, they took a horrible vengeance on their most formidable historical adversary. The Romans razed the city and enslaved its inhabitants. The general responsible for this victory, Scipio Aemilianus, was the son of the victor over Perseus and the grandson by adoption of the Scipio Africanus who had defeated Hannibal. Even in victory, he was said to have shed tears and publicly lamented the fate of the enemy by reciting a passage from Homer's *Iliad*.

Many contemporary observers openly questioned the morality of Rome's actions in 146 BC. Polybius even saw the destructions of Corinth and Carthage as the culmination of a deeply rooted social degradation that had taken hold in the Republic since its great triumph in the Second Punic War.[11] Whatever Rome's moral trajectory, it is clear that the failure of the Roman system of indirect control of the Mediterranean in the first half of the second century profoundly changed the Republic. The nearly endless warfare of the period had profound demographic and economic consequences that combined to shatter the politics of cooperation and consensus that had long governed Roman political life.

The demographic consequences are perhaps the most surprising. There is no doubt that Hannibal's invasion of Italy, the attacks of his Gallic allies, and the Roman reconquest of the parts of the Italian peninsula that had defected together killed many Romans and Italians. The activities of these armies also severely damaged the agricultural infrastructure of Central and Southern Italy, a situation best demonstrated by Rome's repeated appeals for food from allies in Sicily and Egypt in the 210s. Rome's policy of confiscating large amounts of territory from Italian cities that had defected to Hannibal further disrupted food production on the peninsula. The large numbers of Roman military deaths in the early years of the war, the enslavement of civilians during the years of Roman reconquest of disloyal allies, and the food shortages caused by agricultural disruption caused the number of male citizens registered in Roman censuses to fall from 270,713 in 234–233 BC to 137,108 in the census taken in 209–208.[12]

Widespread death during war is not unusual. What is remarkable is how quickly the population recovered over the subsequent decades, even as Rome continued to fight in Greece, Spain, and Africa. The nearly constant warfare of the second century killed perhaps as many as 358,000 soldiers.[13] Despite these horrific losses, the first census figures that we have following the destruction of Carthage and Corinth count 328,442 male citizens, nearly double the population counted at the height of the war with Hannibal.[14] This massive increase in Roman census numbers tracks the broader growth in the overall Italian population in the period. It seems that a few factors combined to make the Italian population so resilient. Although Roman military service was difficult and often took young men away from their families and farms for multiple years, these soldiers tended to be men in their late teens and twenties, who had not yet reached the age at which they would normally marry. Although Roman soldiers came from families that met a basic property qualification, they usually had either older or younger family members who could help with the farm labor. These factors meant that constant warfare neither delayed Italians from marrying at the usual age nor depressed long-term agricultural production. At the same time, Roman families seem to have responded to the number of casualties sustained in war by having more children.

The Republic could absorb this rapidly growing population in the years immediately following the end of the Second Punic War. The new births initially served merely to replace the two hundred thousand or more Italians who had died in the war with Hannibal. As they came of age, these new Italians found lots of economic and agricultural opportunities available to them. The Republic had confiscated large tracts of land following its conquest of the Italian cities that had allied with Hannibal. This land belonged to the Republic, but it was in no one's interest to allow it to lie fallow; everyone remembered well the food shortages that Italy had endured during Hannibal's campaigns. To ensure an adequate food supply, Rome allowed Roman citizens and allies to farm this public land in exchange for a rent payment. The booming postwar population also had the option to settle in the colonies that Rome set up following its conquest and pacification of Northern Italy and to farm this newly incorporated Roman territory.

At a certain point, however, the growth in the Italian population outstripped the Republic's land resources. The problem
was not simply that parents were having more children but also,
as time passed, that the young men coming of age began to exceed
the casualties in war by ever-increasing numbers. In time, these
larger families caused a real problem for rural Italians. Inheritance
in second-century Italy involved dividing the family property
evenly among all sons and, when there were too many living sons,
farms would be divided into plots too small to support a family.
Some of this excess population could join the colonies set up in
Northern Italy, but, once Roman control was firmly established in
Italy south of the Alps, the Republic effectively stopped sponsoring
colonies. Families were left to deal with the problem of limited
land as best they could using their own resources.[15]

To be sure, rural families were not being reduced to starvation
or forced to abandon their lands en masse. In fact, archaeological
evidence shows that small farms remained the norm throughout
Italy until the massive political upheavals of the 80s BC. There
was instead a noticeable decline in relative wealth, as younger rural
Italians grew up understanding that they would have less of everything than their parents did. For poor families, this meant perhaps not being able to pay the dowry that a daughter would need
to marry. But declining relative wealth did not just affect poor
Romans. Even larger, well-established families sometimes found
multiple generations living together in a small house as their once-
ample wealth was divided across generations. For example, in the
middle second century, sixteen members of the prominent Aelii
family all lived together on the same small farm. And, crucially
for the Roman state, many members of these large rural families
saw their land divided into such small parcels that they no longer
qualified for military service.[16]

As the rural population continued to grow, it seems that many
young Romans decided to make a fresh start for themselves by
moving from the countryside into Italian cities. Cities across the

peninsula grew during the second century, but none grew as large
or as quickly as the city of Rome itself. The city population grew
from around two hundred thousand people at the end of the war
with Hannibal to perhaps five hundred thousand by the mid-130s
BC.[17] Most of this population growth consisted of immigrants.
Livy records that, as early as 186 BC, "the city was burdened by
a multitude of people born abroad," by which he means primarily
Italians from outside of the capital. Although Livy's view reeks of
xenophobia, chemical analysis of tooth enamel of people buried in
cemeteries around Rome confirms the picture he paints. Between
29 percent and 37 percent of these remains bear chemical markers
indicating that the person moved to Rome from another location.[18]

The relative decline in living standards of many Italians that
resulted from population growth occurred even as some elite Romans and Italians accumulated unprecedented amounts of wealth.
In the early years of the second century, this wealth derived directly
from the spoils of Rome's imperial expansion. There can be no
doubt that the wars in Greece and those against Carthage transferred massive amounts of booty back to Rome. Scipio Africanus,
for example, brought 123,000 pounds of silver to the treasury following his victory over Hannibal at Zama, and Lucius Cornelius
Lentulus brought 43,000 pounds of silver and 2,450 pounds of
gold taken from Spain in 200 BC.[19] The sums taken in the Macedonian and Syrian wars seem to have dwarfed even these hauls. In
addition to precious metals, these wars brought substantial numbers of slaves, including a reported 150,000 captured by Aemilius Paullus in 167 BC worth the equivalent of 141,000 pounds of
silver.

Although the early years of Hannibal's invasion had effectively bankrupted the Republic, two developments made Rome's
medium-term state finances more predictable by the 180s, even as
the Republic continued to be almost constantly at war. The war
indemnities that Carthage, various Greek states, and Antiochus
III all agreed to pay Rome provided a steady revenue stream that

collectively nearly matched the amount of plunder brought home by Scipio Africanus following Hannibal's defeat.[20] After Rome transformed Spain and then Macedon and Africa into provinces, the taxes collected from these territories more than replaced the sums brought in by these fixed-term tributes. Unlike tribute payments, tax payments represented a permanent and predictable source of funds.

The development of large-scale precious metal mines in Spain (probably in the 190s) and Macedonia after 158 gave the Roman treasury another significant source of revenue. By the mid-150s, these operations combined to generate more than twice the revenue plundered from Carthage by Scipio in 201. Then, around 157 BC, the Roman state began to exploit a newly discovered source of very pure and easily extracted gold in Northern Italy. So much gold then flooded onto the Italian market that the price of the metal collapsed.[21]

All of this new revenue led to some important changes in how the Republic operated. After the consul Manlius's campaign in Asia Minor in 187, the Republic issued a wholesale refund to all citizens who had paid an extra tax to support the army's expedition. Following the victory over Macedon in 167, Rome entirely stopped collecting taxes on Italian lands held by its citizens. In addition, the scale of silver bullion coming into the treasury catalyzed an evolution of the Roman monetary system from one heavily dependent on relatively large, low-value bronze coinage to one based more prominently on lighter, more valuable silver denarii. The minting of silver denarii, which had been done in relatively small quantities in the 190s and 180s BC, increased so dramatically by the 150s that soldiers began to be paid in silver denarii rather than bronze coins.[22]

Military expenses accounted for perhaps three-quarters of the entire Roman budget in the first half of the second century, and salaries to troops paid in these silver coins helped to spread some of the wealth generated by Rome's empire to regular citizens. As the

3.1. The remains of the second-century BC Pons Aemilius spanning the Tiber. Photo by Manasi Watts.

second century progressed, the state also began to pay large sums of money to contractors who performed significant construction, infrastructure, and bureaucratic projects. Once Roman public finances stabilized in the 180s, magistrates began commissioning massive public works. These included a renovation of the city of Rome's sewer system that cost 6 million denarii, the construction of the Pons Aemilius bridge across the Tiber, an expansion and updating of the city's ports and trading facilities, and a series of major roads linking cities in Central Italy with colonies in the north of the peninsula.

Then the booty captured from Corinth and Carthage in 146 BC funded the construction of the massive Aqua Marcia. The largest and most expensive infrastructure project of the century, this aqueduct and another constructed twenty years later combined to nearly double the water supply coming to the rapidly growing capital.[23]

Though state revenues paid for these projects, the Republic lacked any sort of developed bureaucratic or technical corps that could actually execute such complicated tasks. Instead, officers of the Republic outsourced this work to contractors. Contractors handled tax collection in the provinces, mining operations in Spain

3.2. The Aqua Marcia in the modern Parco degli Acquedotti (Rome). Photo by Manasi Watts.

and Macedon, and the many infrastructure projects undertaken across Italy and the provinces. The censors and other agents of the Roman state awarded these contracts to individuals or syndicates of investors who then subcontracted parts of them to others. Polybius famously wrote that "almost everyone is involved either in the sale of these contracts or in the kinds of business to which they give rise."[24] These contracts brought paid work to the engineers, architects, tax collectors, and manual laborers ultimately employed by subcontractors, it is true, but the Roman elites who bid on the projects made far more money from them. In this way public contracts resembled the division of war plunder among the Republic's elites. Average Romans certainly benefited from them, but the disproportionate share of this wealth that went to elite Romans made many of them extremely rich.

By the 150s, the wealthiest Romans had moved beyond generating income from plunder and public contracts alone. These elites generally pursued a widely diversified investment strategy that included agricultural land in Italy, industrial properties, money-lending concerns, and shares of trade syndicates that did things like ship wine to Gaul. Cato the Elder, for example, apparently first invested much of his share of the 4 million denarii worth of precious metal plundered from Spain in 194 in Italian land.[25] Although these properties, worked by groups of slaves, were productive, neither the number of slaves nor size of the properties was overwhelming.[26] As he grew older, however, Cato developed a more sophisticated sense of which sorts of land investments could generate income in a way that was "safe and secure." A later biographer wrote that Cato "bought pools, hot springs, places given over to fullers, pitch-works, and land with natural pasturage and forests, all of which brought him a great deal of money."[27] These properties were all sources of different raw materials for industry and therefore offered a stable income. As his income grew, Cato also became a regular investor in commercial lending. Although a law from 218 BC banned senators from engaging directly in commercial shipping, Cato formed partnerships of fifty investors that backed the commercial operations of fifty ships.[28] He fronted all of the initial capital and then lent money to investors that they could each use to buy a share in the enterprise. Cato himself entrusted one share to a freed slave who acted as his agent. He then profited from the trading activities as well as the interest on these loans, while following the letter of the law and limiting his direct exposure in case the cargo was lost.

One feature of Cato's investments has often been underappreciated. Like a modern home mortgage that is packaged into a bond and resold, a wealthy man like Cato could sell the debt of his investors and then reinvest the proceeds in another venture. As long as the wealthy investor could continue to front the initial capital on a shipping voyage or public contract, he could almost perpetually loan money to other investors looking to buy shares in the venture and then either reinvest the paper profits in a new scheme or use them to buy agricultural or investment property. People with access to capital could then quickly and dramatically increase their wealth if they managed their investments skillfully.[29]

By the middle of the second century, the combined effects of military conquests and growing financial sophistication began to produce a class of superwealthy Romans. This, in turn, changed elite political competition. The days of Fabricius, in which personal qualities, honors, and family pedigree mattered far more than wealth, were receding. By the end of the third century, ambitious politicians had no doubt that money had become deeply intertwined with the pursuit of public office. This was evident already in the actions of Scipio Africanus following his victory over Hannibal. He awarded each of his thirty-five thousand soldiers 40 denarii (the equivalent to four months' military pay) and apparently convinced the Senate to award each of them an acre and a quarter of land in Italy as well. Scipio also kept 700,000 denarii worth of property for himself, enough to make him the richest man in Rome at that time. Scipio seems to have understood that this wealth could be used as a tool to further enhance his reputation. He provided lavish games following his return to Rome, and between 205 and 190, he paid for a series of public monuments commemorating his military victories. The most evocative of these was a garish arch with seven gilded statues that Scipio had erected upon the Capitoline Hill in Rome.[30]

Scipio's actions sparked an arms race through which elite Romans experimented to find even more powerful ways to use their wealth to build up their public profiles. Soldiers came to expect ever larger bonuses from victorious commanders. When Fulvius Flaccus celebrated a triumphal procession following some minor victories over the Ligurians in 179 BC, his grants to his soldiers exceeded those provided by Scipio following his victory over Hannibal. By 167, after the Third Macedonian War, Aemilius Paullus felt obligated to give his foot soldiers 100 denarii, his centurions 200 denarii, and his *equites* 300 denarii apiece.[31]

There were other ostentatious displays of wealth and power. Public spectacles and gladiatorial games put on by magistrates became larger and more impressive. A memorable gladiatorial show in 200 BC had 25 pairs of fighters. By 183, a similarly memorable gladiatorial performance required 120 fighters. Public works also by necessity became larger and more impressive. By the 180s, commanders were not just decorating existing temples with war spoils but building entirely new ones. Even dinner parties and feasts, which were often open to selected members of the public, became far more opulent. By the 180s, public funeral feasts for senators could stretch across multiple days and fill the Forum (Rome's most important public space) with reclining guests. Not only did these events last longer, they were also so lavish that, in 161 BC, the Senate was forced to issue a law limiting the amount of silver brought out at any individual banquet to one hundred pounds by weight.[32]

Elite competition extended to private life as well. By the middle of the second century, superwealthy Romans were building sumptuously decorated luxury villas along the seaside in Campania and importing a range of luxury products from the Eastern Mediterranean. Ancient authors remarked on what they called decadence and blamed either the generals who vanquished Antiochus III or those who beat back Perseus of Macedon for introducing such luxuries to Rome. In truth, however, the rapid sophistication of Rome's economy had simply enabled some people to become far wealthier than their ancestors could ever dream of being. Scipio Africanus, for example, was likely both the richest Roman of his time and the richest Roman who had ever lived at the time of Rome's victory over Antiochus III in 188. Crassus, the richest Roman a little more than a century later, at one point controlled a fortune worth nearly forty times what Scipio possessed. The natures of their fortunes were as different as their relative sizes. Scipio's fortune largely consisted of tangible things of value taken from Carthage and Spain that remained in his possession. Crassus's fortune, by contrast, largely existed on paper and not as physical objects contained in a vault. It was much more liquid than the fortune of Scipio and, because of this, it could be easily invested in ways that would enable it to grow much more rapidly.[33]

Rapid wealth creation like that experienced by Romans in the first half of the second century can be profoundly destabilizing to a social order that relies upon elite political competition. Some of the families that dominated Republican political life in the third century remained important into the second century, but the scale of military operations, the impressive victories that resulted from them, and the wealth that military success and economic sophistication generated all far surpassed what Rome had ever seen before. The ancestral honors and public offices that a man like Fabricius could proudly claim mattered more than private wealth seemed quaint in this sparkling new Roman world of seaside villas, bronze couches, and overseas conquests. The political structure of the

Republic still managed to channel the ambitions of elite Roman men toward offices and honors that only the state could offer. But second-century elites were also becoming increasingly enamored with advertising their wealth and business acumen, areas of achievement over which the Republic had much less control. The Republic's monopoly on the rewards that leading Romans sought was beginning to loosen. As it did, some of the established families who were falling behind economically became increasingly concerned that they could not compete effectively in this new environment.

As consequential as these divisions within the aristocracy were, the emergence of this class of superwealthy Romans opened an even more dangerous chasm between Roman elites and the ordinary Romans who fought the Republic's wars. The wars of the second century, the infrastructure projects within Italy, and the growth of industry in both Italian cities and rural estates that required seasonal labor all created jobs for Roman citizens. But, as we saw earlier, population growth within Italy meant that the economic outlook of many Romans in the mid-second century was bleaker than that which faced their parents. Many of the rural Italians who were forced to share small homes and farm small plots of land with members of their extended families were just barely making it. These were the seasonal laborers employed at the olive groves and vineyards of the rich during harvesttime.[34] These were also the dockworkers and craftspeople who moved to Rome and other cities to find steady work. They knew that their lots were worse than their parents'. They also saw firsthand how their relative poverty compared to the unprecedented opulence that the richest Romans now enjoyed. The new economy produced great wealth for a few winners, but the frustration of the newly poor and the fear that some of the old elite were losing their grip on power created conditions in which a fierce populist reaction could occur.

The men who governed Rome for much of the half century following Hannibal's defeat generally avoided cultivating this sort of populism. The Republic remained stable despite massive economic and social changes in large part because of their relative restraint. But the generation of politicians coming of age at the end of the 140s took notice of the growing inequality in Roman and Italian society and, unlike their elders, they did not refrain from exploiting the anxiety it produced as they competed for Rome's highest offices. Their choices would set the Republic on a very different, very dangerous course.

CHAPTER 4

THE POLITICS OF
FRUSTRATION

THE DESTRUCTION OF CARTHAGE AND Corinth in the year
146 BC affirmed Roman domination of the Mediterranean
world. Macedonia and North Africa, the homes of Rome's two
great rivals in the wars of the late third and early to mid-second
centuries, were now controlled by Roman governors appointed by
the Senate. The taxes their residents paid now supported the Roman army and fueled a rapidly developing Roman economy. The
explosion of Roman power and individual Roman wealth over the
five decades between Hannibal's defeat at Zama and Carthage's
destruction revolutionized both the Mediterranean world and
Rome itself. In one lifetime, Rome had shifted from a relatively
poor regional power into the state at the political and economic
center of the Mediterranean world.

The deliberative and consensus-based political culture of the
Roman Republic was designed to prevent revolutions, not to manage them. And, though the first half of the second century saw relatively little political turmoil within the Republic, the economic,
demographic, and military changes that occurred during this period were indeed revolutionary. Their effects needed to be managed,
but change came too quickly for the slow and deliberative Roman

political system to manage it effectively. An empire like the one Rome now possessed required a permanent administration that could collect taxes, promote commerce, and convey information from its far-flung domains back to the capital. The city at the center of the empire also required dedicated attention to ensure that it grew sustainably and provided the basic necessities for its population.

By the middle of the second century, Rome had become the place in which the business of empire was conducted, through which much of its wealth passed, and to which increasing numbers of the empire's population gravitated. But instead of meeting these changes by rapidly expanding the size of its administration and the scope of its political activities, the Republic stumbled into a system in which the maintenance of the infrastructure of the growing capital and the essential elements of the Roman imperial project were effectively outsourced to private contractors. Roman contractors, not Roman government officials, ran the mines, built the roads, and collected the taxes that fueled the empire. These legitimate activities could be lucrative, but lax monitoring by magistrates in Rome enabled contractors as well as provincial governors to corruptly pocket even more.[1]

The outsourcing of empire brought huge profits to those who had enough money to bid for these new government contracts. It also proved a boon to the elected magistrates who moved on to provincial governorships when their terms in office ended, a fact that vastly increased the amount of money candidates were willing to spend to get elected. The large majority of Italians, however, could not afford to join the scramble. They certainly could not afford political campaigns, and, as large families divided their lands among many heirs, many Italians found their holdings slipping below the property qualification that enabled their sons to serve in the military.

Even for those still wealthy enough to serve, the nature of military service and the rewards it offered began to change in the mid-140s. The wars in Africa and Greece had been, relatively speaking, conventional affairs in which armies met each other on battlefields. The areas in which fighting occurred also had been relatively wealthy. When the Romans emerged victorious in those wars, there was plenty of plunder for soldiers to take home as a reward. Service in these campaigns was not easy, but soldiers embarking on them fought with the reasonable expectation that the fighting would, at the very least, earn them more than simply the basic military pay the state provided. The Republic continued to fight after 146, but the nature of the campaigns changed. Now military service was required in places like Spain, where warfare was asymmetrical and the plunder was modest. Whereas recruits for some of the Roman armies sent to Greece in the mid-second century had been easy to find, Romans rioted to avoid being conscripted into the armies sent to Spain.[2]

By the end of the 140s, it was clear that significant portions of the population living under Roman control felt frustrated at the Republic's inability to police the corruption and inequality resulting from Rome's rapid economic and military expansion. One of the first signs of this discontent came in 149 BC with the creation of a standing criminal court, manned by senators, that was charged with trying cases involving extortion and other misuses of power by Roman governors in their provinces.[3] Although Romans had articulated the principle that provincials had the right to bring charges against the magistrates governing them since at least the 170s BC, this is not what motivated the creation of a permanent court for trying corrupt governors.[4] It seems instead that senators had become concerned that excessive wealth gained from provincial service could allow political rivals to gain an advantage over their competitors in future elections. As money became a crucial factor in one's ability to win the offices and honors that determined the success of the Roman elite, the incorruptibility of Fabricius now looked increasingly like a relic of a much different Rome.

Other signs of discontent appeared in a series of laws designed to change the way Romans voted. Before the 130s, Romans voting in elections or as members of a jury did so by personally approaching an election official and announcing their vote aloud. Although efforts to intimidate voters were rare, there was nothing to prevent someone from "observing" how the votes were cast, and there was no written record of the breakdown of the votes against which one could check the tally.[5] In 139, a tribune named Aulus Gabinius pushed to change the election of magistrates so that voters placed a clay tablet bearing the name of their chosen candidate into a basket. Then, in 137 BC, the tribune Lucius Cassius Longinus Ravilla backed a law extending the use of secret ballots to juries presiding over trials for every offense but treason. Then, in 131, a third tribune, Gaius Papirius Carbo, extended the use of secret ballots to votes on legislation taken within assemblies.[6]

No contemporary literary sources survive that describe what prompted this outpouring of support for secret ballots, but later Republican authors make it clear these reforms proved to be quite controversial, especially among members of the senatorial elite. Gabinius was later criticized as an "unknown and sordid man" whose law was thought to have disrupted political affairs by estranging ordinary citizens from the Senate. The Cassian reform prompted even more vocal opposition at the time it was proposed. Although Cassius came from a noble family, the extension of the secret ballot

4.1. Denarius minted by P. Licinius Nerva in 113–112 BC showing Roman citizens walking across a platform to cast their votes (Crawford 292/1). Private collection. Photo by Zoe Watts.

to trials was seen as a populist measure that brought shame to his family because it courted the "fickle praise of the mob." One of Cassius's fellow tribunes worked alongside one of the consuls to block this law. Scipio Africanus the Younger finally broke the impasse by persuading the tribune to withdraw his veto. Carbo, for his part, is called "a seditious and wicked citizen" who elite audiences apparently viewed as a particularly craven opportunist.[7]

Such criticisms notwithstanding, the introduction of secret ballots responded to at least two genuine political problems. First, secret ballots made voter intimidation much more difficult. Although people could (and, apparently, did) still physically position themselves in ways that might allow them to see what was written on an individual ballot, no figure now could stand nearby and listen to how each individual voted. Second, this reform also made it much more risky to try to influence an election through the distribution of political favors or bribery. There was now no way for a corrupt candidate to determine whether the people he paid actually delivered the votes they promised.[8]

The introduction of secret ballots also coincided with some clear evidence that new paths were emerging through which politicians could build a career for themselves by seeming like they were advancing the cause of good governance amid tremendous economic inequality. Though Gabinius, the author of the first secret ballot law, does not appear to have parlayed this achievement into any higher offices, another Gabinius, who may have been his grandson, served as consul in 58 BC.[9] Both Cassius and Carbo were rewarded more promptly. Cassius's status as a champion of voting protections propelled him to a consulship in 127 and the censorship in 125. Carbo, for his part, built his early career as a populist around the voting reform he sponsored, although upon winning the consulship for 120, he turned dramatically against other populists.

The impact of these reforms extended beyond the careers of the tribunes who sponsored them. They helped to catalyze the emergence of a personality-driven, populist politicking through which ambitious politicians sought out ways to define and disseminate their own individualized political brand. Nothing shows this better than the rapid evolution of the design scheme for the silver denarius. Every year the Republic selected three relatively junior members of elite families to preside over the Roman mint. These moneyers superintended the minting of the coins and often signed the coins minted under their supervision. Initially, these signatures served essentially as a quality control mechanism that forced the moneyer to acknowledge any inferior design or poor execution. The denarius had maintained a more or less consistent appearance across the nearly eighty years since its creation during the Second Punic War. Like Greek civic coins, early denarii usually had a standard design, with a helmeted head of Roma (a female deity who personified Rome) on the front and either an image of the divine twins Castor and Pollux (the Dioscuri) on horseback or an image of a divine figure in a chariot on the reverse.[10]

Almost immediately after Gabinius introduced the secret ballot for the election of magistrates, however, the behavior of moneyers changed. In 139, one decided to replace the customary divine figure in a horse-drawn chariot on the reverse of the coin with an image of Hercules in a chariot drawn by centaurs. The following

4.2. Denarius of 133 BC showing the head of Roma and Jupiter in a four-horse chariot (Crawford 248/1). This iconography reflects the standard design of the denarius in the early and mid-second century BC. Private collection. Photo by Zoe Watts.

year saw two different moneyers issue denarii with new adaptations of this standard iconography on their reverse. One coin showed Juno drawn in a chariot by goats, and the other depicted a warrior drawn in a chariot. Although the significance of these particular images remains unclear, it is assumed that all three of these moneyers chose these specific designs because they communicated something about themselves while remaining broadly consistent with the historical iconography of the denarius.

In 137 BC, two of the moneyers chose to break away completely from the traditional design of the denarius.[11] Whereas Roma remained on the front of the coin, one chose to depict on the reverse a scene from Rome's founding mythology in which the shepherd Faustulus found Romulus and Remus suckling from the she wolf (see figure 4.3). The other moneyer, Ti. Veturius, broke completely with precedent. The front of his coin depicted Mars, not Roma, and the reverse shows a scene in which two warriors take an oath while standing over a kneeling figure (see figure 4.4). Apparently a reference to a historical incident in which the Romans honored an unfavorable treaty with the Samnites, this coin seems to weigh in on a contemporary political controversy over whether or not the Romans should abide by a treaty that a relative of the moneyer had helped to negotiate in Spain.[12] Then, in the years 135 and 134, two brothers descended from the Minucia family each issued denarii showing two of their ancestors who had once served as consuls standing beside a monumental column that had been erected to honor a third ancestor, L. Minucius, for paying for a public distribution of grain to the poor in 439 BC (see figure 4.5).[13] These coins, issued amid a period of growing discontent among Rome's poor, branded the contemporary Minucii family as benevolent figures who had historically served as protectors and champions of Rome's vulnerable.

Veturius and the Minucii brothers understood that high-value denarii offered an ideal platform to build a political brand among the soldiers who received them as military pay. Soldiers worried

4.3. Denarius of 137 BC showing the head of Roma and a scene with the she wolf suckling Romulus and Remus, an iconographic evocation of Roman traditions (Crawford 235/1). Private collection. Photo by Zoe Watts.

4.4. Denarius of 137 BC showing Mars on the obverse and two warriors taking an oath while standing over a kneeling figure, a probable reference to a Roman-Samnite treaty (Crawford 234/1). Private collection. Photo by Zoe Watts.

4.5. Denarius of 134 BC showing an ancestor of the moneyer giving grain to the poor (Crawford 243/1). Private collection. Photo by Zoe Watts.

about the financial pressures felt by Italian farmers or the status of a treaty suspending fighting in Spain would see these coins and might understand that the moneyers responsible for them shared their concerns. And with Romans now able to vote by secret ballot, appeals like these suddenly had the possibility of swinging elections toward populist candidates and policy ideas that elite Roman politicians may once have been able to hold back. The innovative moneyers and reformist tribunes of the early 130s BC tried to build support for themselves by seizing on the growing popular discontent with the directions of Roman political and economic life. They broke with precedent to use their offices in ways that defined them as champions of particular reforms and that developed individual political brands. But none of them had done anything to threaten the stability of Rome's republican government.

It would not take long before a tribune would decide that reform required him to disrupt the basic norms governing the Republic. The author of this challenge was a man named Tiberius Gracchus. Tiberius came from one of the plebeian families that had fared best in the competitive arena of elite Roman politics. His great-grandfather held the consulship in 238 BC and was the Roman general responsible for conquering Sardinia. His great-uncle had held two consulships during the height of the war against Hannibal and had served as the deputy commander to Fabius Maximus. And Tiberius's father, Tiberius Sempronius Gracchus, served as consul in 177 and 163 BC, secured two triumphs for his service in Spain and Sardinia, served as an augur, and helped to fill the ranks of the Senate through his service as censor in 169.[14]

Tiberius's mother, Cornelia, came from even more prominent stock. She was the younger daughter of Hannibal's conqueror Scipio Africanus and his wife, Aemilia, who was herself a member of the old patrician family that also produced Aemilius Paullus (the victor in the Third Macedonian War). Cornelia's marriage to Tiberius Sempronius Gracchus represented the consummation of a great political alliance between the Gracchi and the Scipiones.

Historical rivals, the two families had come together in 184 when Tiberius Sempronius Gracchus (who was then serving as tribune) twice used his veto to prevent the imprisonment of Scipio Africanus and Scipio Asiaticus while they were being tried for improperly taking money secured from Antiochus III. Cornelia then arranged for Sempronia, the only one of her daughters to survive into adulthood, to marry Scipio Aemilianus just before he captured and destroyed Carthage. This marriage again reinforced the bonds among the families of the Gracchi, the Scipiones, and the Aemilii.[15]

Tiberius Gracchus was born, then, into one of the most enviable positions imaginable. He bore the name of a famous consular family and his mother descended from two of the second century's most successful clans. These connections ensured that he would receive some of the most promising lower offices the state had to offer, but Tiberius was also well prepared to excel once he took office. Tiberius was an intellectually talented youth and Cornelia ensured that he had a world-class training in public speaking and philosophy so that he could develop the skills necessary to command the attention of both voters and soldiers.[16]

Tiberius's first public service could not have been better chosen. He served under his brother-in-law Scipio Aemilianus in the Third Punic War, sharing a tent with him and earning an award for bravery when he was the first Roman soldier to successfully get over the wall of an enemy town. Following the war, Tiberius married Claudia, the daughter of the former consul and censor Appius Claudius and the great-great-granddaughter of the Appius Claudius who once had urged Rome to resist Pyrrhus of Epirus. The Claudii were another one of Rome's oldest and most outstanding elite families, with nearly twenty different members of the family holding a consulship in the century and a quarter between the First Punic War and the 140s. Although he belonged to one of the clans on which the Republic had historically depended most heavily, Tiberius's father-in-law Appius Claudius also had a bit of a rogue streak. After provoking a battle so that he might give himself the pretext to celebrate a triumph, Appius Claudius celebrated it without authorization. One of his daughters had to intervene to prevent him from being dragged from the triumphal carriage by a tribune.[17]

Tiberius's talents and family alliances marked him as a rising star in Roman politics by the time that he next entered office. In 137 BC, Tiberius was chosen to serve as quaestor, the lowest office that qualified one for membership in the Senate. Assigned to assist the consul Gaius Hostilius Mancinus while he campaigned in Spain against the city of Numantia, Tiberius almost certainly assumed that his father's experiences in the region and the connections his family had developed with local leaders would help Tiberius succeed there much as he had in Africa. Unfortunately, Mancinus's military incompetence proved nearly as great as Scipio's genius. After a series of battlefield reverses forced him back into his fortified camp, Mancinus panicked and tried to retreat at night. By morning, the Roman army was completely surrounded and Mancinus sued for peace. Because of the reputation of his family, the Numantines demanded that Tiberius negotiate the agreement. The treaty they agreed upon permitted the thousands of surviving Roman forces to withdraw, but their Spanish captors kept all of the plunder they had taken.[18]

When he returned to Rome, Tiberius was shocked to see that some senators, including his brother-in-law Scipio Aemilianus, had denounced the agreement he had negotiated "as a disaster and disgrace" to Rome. Members of the Senate called for the entire army, including its leaders, to be returned in chains to Numantia. Scipio in particular wanted the treaty nullified because he hoped to continue the war and to secure a command for himself that would enable him to subdue Numantia as he had earlier subdued Carthage.

The popular reaction to the treaty was far different from that of the elites in the Senate, however. A later author writes that "the relatives and friends of the soldiers, who formed a large proportion of the citizen body, came flocking to Tiberius, blamed the general for everything, and insisted that it was through Tiberius' efforts that the lives of so many citizens had been saved." Average Roman citizens had no enthusiasm for yet more fighting in Spain. The wars there had been long, unpopular, and draining. Sensing this popular mood, the Senate compromised. It disavowed the treaty and sent Mancinus to Numantia, but it permitted the rest of Mancinus's soldiers and staff to remain in Rome. Scipio would soon get his war, but, bowing to the sentiments of the war-weary populace, he assembled his army from "volunteers sent by [other] cities and kings as personal favors to him." By the time that he set out in 134 BC, the gulf between his world and that of the many ordinary people who had flocked to Tiberius as the savior of their friends and family members could not have been larger.[19]

Tiberius recognized that his fortunes had changed dramatically since his return from Spain. No longer the golden child of the establishment, he had instead become a polarizing figure who believed that Scipio and his allies had attacked his reputation unjustly.[20] He now faced a significant dilemma. It would be seen as a terrible failure if a man of his talent and pedigree did not attain a consulship. His shame would only be compounded by the fact that most male relatives on both sides of his family and his wife's family had served as consul. The break with Scipio, however, had blocked the inside path to the consulship. Tiberius confronted the choice of either trying to rebuild his reputation within elite circles or capitalizing on his new popularity among the Roman citizenry. He chose the second option.

After Scipio set off for Spain in 134, Tiberius stood for election as a tribune of the plebs. His brother Gaius would later write that Tiberius was motivated in part by the sight of a countryside populated not by hearty Roman small landowners but by large estates and pastures tended by barbarian slaves. Although archaeological evidence shows clearly that the Italian countryside was neither deserted nor filled with large estates in the 130s BC, there can be no doubt that the growing inequality between wealthy figures like Scipio and the men he commanded in the armies had become a serious problem. This economic inequality provided Tiberius with a potent issue that simultaneously inflamed the anger of ordinary Romans who felt that the new imperial economy had left them behind and emphasized how Tiberius would continue to fight for their interests against the entrenched Roman elite.[21]

Surviving sources do not say whether Tiberius campaigned on the issue of land reform, but it is clear that, once he was elected, he began to work immediately on a land reform bill that could provide farmland to some of Rome's poorer citizens. Inspired, we are told, by slogans and pleas written by his supporters on walls all over the city, Tiberius gave an impassioned speech in which he lamented the impoverishment of the people of Italy and, alluding to a recent slave rebellion in Sicily, spoke dramatically about the consequences of farms manned primarily by slaves.[22]

This speech set the stage for a reform that Tiberius then proposed. He focused on the publicly owned land that Rome had taken from cities that opposed it in war. These parcels of land were scattered across Italy, and the state had rented the land out to farmers, shepherds, and herdsmen. A law from 367 BC forbade people from working more than 500 *iugera* (about 300 acres) of this public land, with additional restrictions placed on the number of animals that one could pasture on it. The law originally tasked freed slaves with observing activities on the land, but, as the public properties grew to include land spread across all of Italy, monitoring and enforcement both slackened. People came to occupy more than the maximum 500 *iugera,* they began making improvements to the land, and they grazed more than the permitted number of cattle.[23]

Tiberius proposed a law that required those who held more than 500 *iugera* to surrender any land above that threshold back to the state in return for fair compensation. They would also be allowed to keep an additional 250 *iugera* for each son to farm. Any land that came back into the possession of the state would then be redistributed in lots of 30 *iugera* (around 20 acres) to the poor or landless by a commission of three men. Those receiving the land would take possession of it, but they could not sell or transfer the land to people looking to piece together larger portfolios of property. Although many of those who held the public lands at present were not Roman citizens, it seems the law proposed to redistribute land only to Roman citizens.[24]

This modest reform addressed popular interest in land redistribution while simultaneously offering compensation to those who would lose use of public property. Indeed, something like it had been proposed in 140 BC by Scipio's friend the consul Gaius Laelius, though Laelius ultimately withdrew the proposal when elite Italians loudly objected to it. The climate was different in 133, however. Scipio remained in Spain, and one of the two consuls for the year was in Sicily dealing with a slave revolt. The consul remaining in Rome, Publius Mucius Scaevola, favored Tiberius's proposal, as did Tiberius's father-in-law, Appius Claudius, and Scaevola's brother Crassus, who would be named *pontifex maximus,* the head of the college of priests in Rome, the following year. This looked like a reform that could gain broad support and quickly be voted into law.[25]

Despite Tiberius's prominent supporters and the moderation of his measure, however, the Senate refused to endorse the proposal. At the same time, opponents began waging a public relations campaign to convince people that Tiberius aspired to take over the state. The accusation seemed absurd. But Tiberius was indeed proposing something novel: that the Republic play a role in balancing the distribution of the wealth of empire that Rome's citizens, both rich and poor, had created together. What alarmed Tiberius's opponents in the Senate was not the practical effect of the law but the principle behind it. A further cause for alarm lay in the reaction of non-Roman upper-class Italians, many of whom rented this public land and would have been adversely affected by the redistribution. Tiberius had then effectively proposed to take property used by Rome's Italian allies without their consent or their input.[26]

After the Senate refused to endorse the proposal, Tiberius decided to break with custom and bring his motion directly to the *concilium plebis*. This was neither illegal nor entirely unprecedented, but it was also not at all ordinary. And Tiberius's action only prompted an even greater senatorial backlash. Tiberius's opponents took their fears to Octavius, one of his fellow tribunes, and persuaded Octavius to veto the measure before it could come up for a vote. It was, of course, Octavius's prerogative to veto any law he wanted, and it was also common for the Senate and the tribunes to work together to ensure that no measure strongly opposed by the Senate became law. In all likelihood, Octavius and his backers hoped that Tiberius would follow the example of Laelius seven years prior and simply withdraw his bill. But Tiberius was not Laelius. Unlike Laelius, Tiberius was not a consul and, if he backed down, he could probably not expect to become one. And, perhaps just as importantly, Tiberius had no intention of bowing to the demands of a tribune who acted on behalf of the same senators who had turned on him after the peace treaty with Numantia—especially when the law he had authored enjoyed enthusiastic public backing.

Sensing that he could not succeed politically if he played by the existing rules, Tiberius responded to Octavius's opposition with fury. In Plutarch's words, "These tactics angered Tiberius. He then withdrew his conciliatory law and introduced one which was more gratifying to the people and harsher to the illegal owners of the land. It demanded that they should vacate the land which they had acquired in defiance of the earlier laws, but this time it offered no compensation."[27] Tiberius then called a series of public debates in which he and Octavius discussed the merits of the law. He pointed out that Octavius, as a holder of large tracts of public land, had a clear motivation for opposing the law. Tiberius even offered to pay Octavius out of his own funds for the property he would lose, an offer intended to both emphasize Octavius's conflict of interest and insulate Tiberius from the charge that he had personal animosity against Octavius. When none of this worked, Tiberius then decreed a ban on all public activity until a vote could be taken on the new law. He made sure that this ban was observed by sealing the Temple of Saturn so that no money could be withdrawn from the public treasury. And yet Octavius still refused to yield.[28]

Tiberius then called for a vote again. On the day the ballots were to be cast, however, the voting urns disappeared, leaving the supporters of Tiberius on the verge of rioting. When the Senate proved unable to mediate the dispute, Tiberius resorted to some political stagecraft. He announced that he saw no way out of the impasse with Octavius and claimed that the people could justly take away the power of office that they had bestowed on Octavius when they elected him tribune. He then proposed that he and Octavius should each submit to a vote in which the people could decide whether or not they should continue in office. Knowing full well that the voters would support him in these circumstances, Tiberius offered to go first. Octavius also understood the political dynamics of the moment. He refused the offer and, on the following day, the assembly voted to strip him of his office. Despite Tiberius's calls for calm, Octavius barely escaped an angry mob outraged by his obstruction and eager to take vengeance on him now that his person was no longer protected by the sacrosanctity of the tribunate.[29]

Octavius's deposition fell into a legal gray area. Other officials had seen their terms of office end prematurely, as we saw earlier when the Senate effectively rescinded the consular power of Flaminius in the third century. But Tiberius had done something quite different and much more dangerous. Resentful of the obstacles that had been thrown in the way of his proposals, Tiberius fanned the flames of popular resentment against the narrow group of elites who blocked the state from responding to the needs of ordinary Romans. He did not actively encourage violence from his followers, but, by potentially touching everyone in the city, the threat of physical violence that now rippled through Rome spread more fear than even an actual riot could. The volatility of Tiberius's followers constituted a potent political weapon that could fire anywhere, at any time, and for unpredictable reasons.[30]

The deposition of Octavius removed the threat of a veto and ensured the passage of Tiberius's reform. Tiberius, his brother Gaius, and Appius Claudius were then chosen as the three commissioners who would redistribute the public land. Tiberius now faced another very real problem. The unusual political procedures and threats of violence that he had used to pass the law creating the land commission had intensified the opposition of those who had sought to derail his reform. Their alarm only increased when it became clear that Tiberius intended to use the commission as a vehicle to advance his own career and those of his family members. The Senate could not rescind the law authorizing the land commission, but it could refuse to fund the commission's operations. Land redistribution would, at the very minimum, require teams of surveyors and other skilled people to determine plot boundaries, assess whether people actually were using more than five hundred *iugera* of land, and set new property lines within the parcels of land that were redistributed. Those to whom the land was redistributed also required assistance to buy agricultural equipment, seeds, and other start-up materials. The Republic had a significant role to play in ensuring that this reform succeeded—and the Senate controlled the funds on which all of these actions would depend.

The Senate unsurprisingly refused to provide any money for Tiberius's land commission. Under ordinary circumstances, this would end the matter. The land commission would continue to exist legally, but, without funds, it was effectively dead. The Senate pushed even further, however. Under the influence of Tiberius's cousin Scipio Nascia, the Senate refused to approve even a tent for

Tiberius to use while conducting land commission business, and it set his per diem at an absurdly low amount. Helped in part by a rumor that his opponents had poisoned one of Tiberius's friends, the tribune remained popular, but it was clear that he would have to foot the bill personally for his land commission if he wanted it to do much of anything at all.[31]

Fortune then intervened spectacularly. Attalus III, the king of Pergamum, died and left his kingdom and its treasury to "the Roman people." While there was no exact precedent for a bequest like this one, the Republic had clear procedures for dealing with situations of this sort. The Senate handled foreign relations and the disbursement of public funds. By rights, the Senate would be expected to accept this bequest and administer the distribution of the unexpected windfall. Tiberius, however, saw in the language of Attalus's bequest a further opportunity. Because the will marked the beneficiaries as the Roman people, Tiberius claimed that the *concilium plebis,* not the Senate, should decide how to disburse Attalus's money and determine the fate of the territory he left to Rome. He then proposed that the money should be used to pay for the land commission and provide supplies to the small landholders the committee would resettle. The assembly would also vote at a later time about how to handle the territory that Attalus left to Rome.[32]

Tiberius now pushed the Roman political system in a new and troubling direction. He was advocating for a sort of mediated direct democracy in which the old institutional balances between the Senate and the *concilium plebis* would be stripped away. In Tiberius's conception, the assembly would become the dominant force directing all facets of Roman policy. Led by assertive tribunes and protected by secret ballots that enabled plebeians to vote anonymously for the first time, the assembly could legislate as the popular will demanded. It would also depose at will any tribunes who tried to work with senators to block the proposals the assembly wanted to pass. Beneath this empowerment of the tribunes and the assembly lay a revolutionary new idea that true liberty for Romans existed only when popular voices and votes overcame the distorting forces of the Senate and elites.[33]

First, Tiberius had proposed that the Republic assume a new role in redistributing property to Rome's poorer citizens. Now he had effectively advocated for a rebalancing of power between the key Republican institutions of the Senate and the assembly in a way that again empowered Rome's less wealthy by challenging the authority of the city's elites. Both of these steps proved disturbing to senators and their wealthy Roman and Italian allies, but what perhaps troubled them most of all was Tiberius's own role at the center of these transformations. With his masterful command of the public mood and his skill at conjuring the threat of violence, Tiberius stood to benefit most directly from the institutional revolution that he was advocating. Many senators began to fear that, if Tiberius succeeded in empowering the assembly while marginalizing the Senate, his talents and popularity might result in a brand of personal rule constructed around his ability to manage popular moods.

The public discussion concerning Attalus's bequest featured a series of powerful attacks against Tiberius from some of the Republic's most distinguished men. A number of former consuls rose to charge Tiberius with aspiring to absolute power in the state. One of them, who lived near Tiberius, even claimed that a diadem and royal purple robe had been taken out of Attalus's treasury so that it could be given to Tiberius when he became king.[34] Another challenged Tiberius to explain why senators should not expect that other tribunes who sided against him and with the Senate would not, like Octavius, also be deposed.[35] Tiberius responded the next day by explaining that he did not deprive Octavius of his tribunate. The people did. And it was then and remained now their right to bestow and withdraw the power of that office as they saw fit.

After this tumultuous public discussion, the *concilium plebis* again voted to follow Tiberius's direction. Attalus's treasury would fund the land commission and provide supplies to those settled by it. Land reform could move forward. But it would soon become clear that the constitutional damage that Tiberius had done far out-weighed any benefits the law might have created. Despite the threats of violence and the radical political steps that Tiberius had taken to create and fund his land commission, the commission itself had a rather limited remit. It could indeed redistribute land worked in parcels larger than five hundred *iugera*, but only in certain parts of Italy. The rich farmland of Campania, for example, seems to have been largely left alone.[36] Even if the commission had redistributed all of the public land in Southern Italy, however, it is estimated that perhaps fifteen thousand poor families could then have been resettled—out of an Italian population then numbering several million. The reform would do even less damage to the wealthiest Italians. Although those holding large tracts in areas the commission proposed to redistribute would undoubtedly take a financial hit, landholdings represented only a part of the diversified investment portfolios of Italy's wealthiest families. Few (if any) of the very richest families in Rome or Italy would be ruined by this reform. But many Romans would eventually be harmed by the breaching of institutional norms that it took to get land reform put in place.[37]

Tiberius made two crucial and ultimately fateful choices that ensured this controversy would become far more explosive than past moments of political discontent in Rome. For the 150 years that had passed since the end of the Conflict of the Orders, the Republic had avoided political violence because Romans had largely respected the unwritten customs that determined how the Senate, magistrates, and assemblies divided power. Politicians understood the damage that could be done if one used the full legal authority that the assembly could technically claim as a tool to overturn the customs that shaped these patterns of interaction between different parts of the Republic. For more than a century, they had voluntarily held back from doing this. Tiberius's decision to openly challenge both the Senate and a sitting magistrate by direct appeal to the *concilium plebis* deeply upset these norms. It was suddenly unclear which rules now governed political disputes and which mechanisms, if any, continued to check the power of the Republic's various institutions.

Tiberius's strategic use of the threat of force at moments of political confrontation made the situation even more dangerous. As tensions surrounding the land commission grew, Tiberius fanned the flames of public anger by encouraging rumors that political opponents had threatened him and poisoned one of his friends. This sometimes led crowds of angry supporters to accompany him through the city.[38] Tiberius's household attendants physically removed Octavius from the Rostra, and a mob of his supporters threatened to assault Octavius after his removal. Tiberius never ordered or even condoned violence, but he did make regular use of the threat of it.

This flirtation with violence put Tiberius in a precarious position as the end of his one-year term as tribune approached. Tribunal sacrosanctity had protected him as long as he was in office, but he would have no such sacred safeguard once he was again a private citizen. Amid rumors that his opponents would target him the moment he left office, Tiberius decided to seek a second consecutive term as tribune. Standing for a second term was not illegal, but it was nonetheless without precedent. Tiberius himself understood that this extraordinary decision required public justification. He again drew upon his skill as an orator. Summoning his followers, he told them that his safety depended on him continuing to hold office. When his rural supporters did not come to the city in large enough numbers to ensure that Tiberius would win the votes of the rural tribes, Tiberius even resorted to canvassing personally among some of the urban poor in the city of Rome. After the first two of the thirty-five tribes had cast their votes, an objection was raised about the legality of Tiberius standing for a second consecutive term. In this procedural chaos, the assembly adjourned for the day.[39]

Tiberius appealed directly to his followers for protection. He told them that he feared "his enemies would break into his house at night and kill him." Many of his supporters camped outside of his home, spending "the night there on guard." Whereas Tiberius had previously used threats of mob violence quite skillfully, never before had he confronted such a real threat to his safety. He lost his deft touch in this climate of fear and uncertainty. When the people assembled again the following morning to continue casting votes, a scuffle between supporters and opponents of Tiberius broke out on the margins of the crowd. Meanwhile, the Senate convened to discuss a response to the situation. The consul Scaevola pointedly refused to agree to use force to put down any disturbances connected to the election, but Tiberius's cousin the *pontifex maximus* Scipio Nascia led a group of senators and attendants out of the Senate to where Tiberius stood. At first, the crowd parted, perhaps out of respect for Rome's chief religious officer or out of fear of the men he led, and then began to flee, breaking benches as they ran. Some of Nascia's mob carried clubs. Those who did not picked up broken pieces of benches and began attacking the members of Tiberius's entourage who did not flee fast enough. In the mayhem, Tiberius was grabbed by the toga, pulled to the ground, and clubbed to death. He was one of perhaps two hundred or three hundred Romans killed that morning.[40]

Romans understood that the Republic changed irreversibly on that day in 133. Centuries later Plutarch would write that this was the "first outbreak of civil strife in Rome that resulted in the bloodshed and murder of citizens since the expulsion of the kings."[41] Cicero, writing just a lifetime after the events of that year, claimed that "the death of Tiberius Gracchus, and even before his death, the whole manner of his tribunate divided one people into two factions."[42] And Appian portrayed Tiberius both as "the first to die in civil strife" and as a figure whose death polarized the city between men who mourned him and those who saw in his demise the fulfillment of their deepest hopes.[43] Appian also noted that Tiberius "was killed on the capital while still tribune, because of a most excellent design he pursued violently."[44]

Appian understood the most destructive aspect of Tiberius's tribunate. Fortified by his deep personal conviction that land reform was essential, Tiberius normalized the use of threats and intimidation as tools to advance a political program that he believed to be just. Although Appian agreed with the excellence of Tiberius's proposal, he understood that one courted danger by using violence instead of regular political means to pursue even the most admirable goal. The Republic was based on compromise and competition guided by a set of political norms that could be unfair but that were nevertheless recognized by all elites. They allowed themselves to be bound by the rules of the Republic in exchange for the chance to compete for the rewards it offered. Appian likely speaks for himself when he writes that some of those who mourned Tiberius's death also mourned for themselves and for that moment when his murder revealed that there was "no longer a Republic but the rule of force and violence."[45]

These authors all wrote with the considerable advantage of hindsight. Though shocking, it is unclear how quickly Romans understood the profound damage that had been done to Republican institutions and norms of conduct in 133 BC. Perhaps in an attempt to turn the page on the entire episode, the Senate allowed the land reform to proceed even though its author was dead. Attalus's bequest continued to fund its operations, a new commissioner was appointed to replace Tiberius, and the land commission began judicial inquiries against those who refused to document their landholdings. The Gracchan commission would continue to work until perhaps 118 BC, though other land reform measures continued even after that date.[46] There was also a swift reaction against those involved with Tiberius's death. Scipio Nascia was sent to Asia after he was threatened with impeachment for murdering a tribune. He died soon after leaving Rome.[47] Crowds once even shouted down Scipio Aemilianus when he indicated before the assembly that he disapproved of Tiberius.[48]

But, as the 120s dawned, it became clear that the Roman political system had not stabilized. Italian allies whose farms were
affected by the investigations and lawsuits of the Gracchan land
commission had no direct ability to change policies created by and
for Roman citizens. They first tried to seek redress through political allies who had influence in Rome, with Scipio Aemilianus
serving as a particularly vocal advocate of their interests. In 129
BC, Scipio seems to have argued that land use issues involving
Italian allies were essentially matters of international relations that
should fall under the authority of the Senate, not the assembly or
agents appointed by it. Popular anger against Scipio grew as rumors flew that he intended to abolish the land commission, but his
efforts came to an abrupt end when he turned up dead under mys-
terious circumstances. Whispers that Scipio's wife Sempronia and
Tiberius's mother Cornelia had poisoned him soon flitted about
the city.[49]

After Scipio's death, Italian allies began to wonder whether
the Republic really wished to protect their interests. A measure
in 126 BC to expel non-Roman citizens from the crowded city of
Rome deepened distrust between Romans and their Italian allies.
Then, in 125, two events made clear the depth of the problem.
The consul Fulvius Flaccus, who was also one of the Gracchan
land commissioners, proposed extending citizenship to those Italian allies who asked for it, but the law failed to receive approval.
Perhaps because of the measure's failure, the Latin colony of Fregellae, which had remained loyal even during Hannibal's presence
in Italy, revolted against Roman authority. This touched off wider
anti-Roman unrest and resulted in the destruction of the city by a
Roman army.[50]

Even greater uncertainty gripped both Rome and its Italian
allies when Tiberius's brother Gaius held the tribunate in 123 and
was reelected for the year 122. Gaius came into office defined
in large part by his brother's land reform program and violent
death. Not only did Gaius have the Gracchan name but he had

also served for ten years on the Gracchan land commission before standing for election. Gaius enhanced his association with his late brother by claiming that he decided to seek the tribunate only after Tiberius appeared to him in a dream. This made him popular with the people who had supported his brother but scorned by those in the Senate who had once opposed Tiberius.[51]

Once elected, Gaius undertook a legislative program that far exceeded anything his brother had imagined. Tiberius had forcefully argued for the principle that the magistrates of the Republic should do something to improve the economic situation of the rural poor. In practice, however, Tiberius's vision of the state's role was relatively modest. Gaius, however, extended this principle much more widely. He passed a law creating a publicly funded grain distribution that sold grain at below-market rates to all Roman citizens who needed or wanted it. He also reformed the process by which land was distributed by the land commission, apparently exempting some of the land farmed by Italian allies. He backed a law requiring the state to provide military equipment and clothing to soldiers free of charge, while setting a minimum recruitment age of seventeen years. He then restarted the process of founding colonies for landless Roman citizens, with a colony planned for the site of what once had been the city of Carthage.[52]

To pay for this growth in government expenditures, Gaius also revolutionized the process of tax collection in the province of Asia.[53] What had in the past been a piecemeal effort, in which small bidders worked district by district under the supervision of the governor, was transformed into one in which the censors at Rome awarded one contract for the entire province. This centralized approach was designed to simultaneously maximize the revenue collected by the state and minimize the opportunity for corruption among provincial governors. Gaius then paired this new tax-collecting scheme with a judicial reform that ended the senatorial monopoly on acting as judges in civil cases and serving as jurors in criminal cases. An allied tribune also pushed through a law requiring that only *equites* (the members of the second high-est social class in Rome, after members of the Senate) serve on juries deciding cases of extortion. This key reform ended a system in which senatorial juries sat in judgment of their elite peers, and thereby made convictions for corruption more likely. Although all of these measures attracted vociferous senatorial opposition, there was no repeat of the procedural gridlock that Tiberius encoun-tered. Not only did Gaius's popularity and rhetorical skills sur-pass those of his brother, but senators understood that obstruction would only lead to a recurrence of the violence of 133.

Gaius's second year as tribune proved less successful. When Gaius spent two months of 122 in Africa supervising the plan-ning of the new colony at Carthage, his opponents decided to take advantage of his absence. Instead of arguing against his popular reforms, they elected to outbid him. Tribunes opposed to Gaius began proposing (but apparently never passing) even more elab-orate measures, like the creation of twelve new colonies in Italy that would provide land for perhaps thirty-six thousand families. Where Gaius pushed the idea of extending citizenship to all Ital-ian allies, they instead raised the alternative that no Italian should be subject to flogging as punishment, while simultaneously push-ing back against Gaius for too freely granting citizenship to non-Romans. This proposal, too, never passed, but that seems to have been beside the point. It succeeded in painting Gaius as an ex-tremist while simultaneously allowing his opponents to appear willing to compromise. Whereas Gaius accomplished a great deal in 123, his rivals' efforts to better his every proposal in 122 soon made him seem ineffective and out of touch.

The efforts of the Gracchan opponents in the 120s proved far more effective than the confrontational tactics used against Tibe-rius in 133. Gaius found himself out of office in 121 and, when he no longer held a position, one of the consuls for that year then moved to defund the colony that Gaius had hoped to found at Car-thage. While one of the tribunes led an official public discussion of the issue, Gaius and an ally appear to have called for a rival, un-sanctioned public discussion of policy. Their followers mixed with those attending the official event and violence broke out, leading to the death of an attendant of the consul. The Senate responded forcefully, reverting to the sort of aggressive measures it had taken in response to Tiberius. It declared an unprecedented emergency and voted to allow the consul Lucius Opimius to take any actions he deemed necessary to defend the Republic, including the killing without trial of Roman citizens. Lucius, in turn, called all senators and *equites* to arms, marched on Gaius and his supporters, and ultimately killed Gaius, Flaccus, and as many as three thousand of their followers. When Tiberius was killed by Nascia's mob, per-haps three hundred other Romans died with him. A little more than a decade later, thousands died alongside Gaius as the Senate empowered the consul to use the resources of the Republic against a Roman citizen and his followers. Political violence had quickly moved from the fringes of Roman politics to become a senatorially sanctioned tool. And, to certain Romans, the use of this violence against the Gracchi made the brothers symbols of a political order willing to use any means (including murder) to block reformers.[54]

Later historians picked up on this idea by highlighting the inevitability of the murders of Tiberius and Gaius Gracchus. Plutarch, for example, began his *Life of Gaius Gracchus* by describing a dream in which Tiberius appeared to Gaius and told him: "There is no escape. Fate has decreed the same destiny for us both, to live and die in the service of the people."[55] Gaius mentioned this dream often and understood that it committed him both to serve the Roman people and to suffer a violent, premature death. But, in truth, it was not Fate but Tiberius himself who condemned Gaius to this death. Frustrated by a system that had first shut down his expected path to the consulship and then obstructed the legislative program he pursued as an alternative, Tiberius chose to attack the patterns of political behavior that had promoted deliberation and compromise in the Republic for the previous 150 years. And he did so with an air of menace. Though his political creativity and the threats of violence from his crowds of supporters did enable Tiberius to get his land reform measure passed, they also removed the restraints that had long defined how Roman political controversies unfolded. No one could now be sure that disputes would play out peacefully. Any violent incident, however small, could now seem like a threat to the Republic. Although Gaius took pains not to use threats in the same way that Tiberius had, it did not matter. Once violence and intimidation became political tools, any disturbance at all provided an excuse for overreaction. The Gracchi brothers were the first victims of this new world Tiberius created. They would not be the last.

CHAPTER 5

THE RISE OF THE OUTSIDER

The murder of Gaius Gracchus and his supporters in 121 BC changed the dynamics of Republican political life. Control of the state fell to men like the senator Opimius, the consul responsible for the massacre of Gaius and his supporters. These men seem to have decided to leave the conflicts of the 130s and 120s in the past. They refrained from openly challenging or rolling back the reform programs of the Gracchi. The land reform commission continued to operate, Roman citizens remained eligible to claim subsidized grain, and Roman *equites* still presided over extortion trials of senators. Indeed, Opimius even paid for the construction of a temple to the goddess Concordia, a structure designed to emphasize to all that the disturbances of the 130s and 120s grew out of factionalism and the violent climate cultivated by the Gracchi.[1] Many senators seemed to believe that the populist appeal of the Gracchi lay in the tangible benefits and privileges they delivered to Roman citizens. These senators believed that the people would remain quiescent as long as these benefits remained intact and, with luck, the peaceful functioning of the Republic could return.

Many of those who supported the Gracchi did benefit from their reform programs, but the true appeal of Tiberius and Gaius lay in what their attacks on the wealthy and well-placed symbolized. This their opponents could not co-opt. The brothers' violent deaths, meanwhile, had made them martyrs. Their examples resonated whenever the corruption or the arrogance of the elite surfaced in particularly notable ways. And, perhaps most crucially, their model of political confrontation remained available to any politician who was ambitious enough to wager his life in a bid to win political power.

No politician proved so desperate in the 110s. The decade instead saw a narrow group of families dominating the highest offices of the Republic. Between 123 and 109, four families held nearly half of all consulships. Six different members of one family, the Caecilii Metelli, held the office in this period, including one year in which M. Caecilius Metellus served alongside his brother-in-law M. Aemilius Scaurus.[2] A later author wrote of these years that this consolidation of power by the elite brought about "unlimited and unrestrained greed that invaded, violated, and devastated everything, respecting nothing and holding nothing sacred."[3] Indeed, by the middle of the decade, Rome was shaken by a series of lurid scandals involving members of these and other senatorial families. In 114, three of the six Vestal Virgins were charged with violating their vows of chastity.[4] The Vestals all came from elite families and were the priestesses who served as ceremonial housekeepers for all of Rome by preparing food for religious rituals and maintaining the fire sacred to Vesta, the goddess of the hearth. As part of their religious role, the Vestals all pledged to remain chaste for thirty years.

Allegations of sexual impropriety by half of this college of priestesses had potentially serious religious consequences for all Romans. But the three Vestals were treated differently based not on their sexual misconduct but on the social status of the men with whom they had engaged in it. One Vestal, who had been involved with a Roman *equite,* was convicted in 114 and buried alive. The two others, both of whom were accused of relations with men of senatorial families, were initially acquitted in a trial before the Roman priests, who were themselves all senators. Amid popular outcry at the perception that the priests had held senators and *equites* to different standards, one of the tribunes entering office in 113 proposed a law establishing a special independent commission to investigate the case. Headed by Lucius Cassius Longinus Ravilla, the sponsor of the law that had established the secret ballot for jury trials in 137 BC, this commission convicted both Vestals and their paramours. It also dealt a serious blow to the prestige of L. Caecilius Metellus Dalmaticus, the *pontifex maximus* who had presided over the previous trial. Other trials of senators followed that year, including one in which the former consul C. Porcius Cato was convicted of extortion by a jury of Roman *equites* following the defeat of an army he headed in Thrace.

These investigations occurred in a climate of growing popular discontent. A series of Roman military defeats combined with a set of ominous religious portents in the later 110s and early 100s to suggest to many Romans that elite arrogance, incompetence, and impiety had angered the gods and led the state astray. Priesthoods remained dominated by members of Rome's most powerful families and, with evidence of divine displeasure all around, Romans began seeking ways to placate the gods. The execution of the three Vestals in 114–113 was soon followed by the ritual sacrifice of Greek and Gallic prisoners and, in 109, the first-ever criminal conviction of a member of the Roman priestly college for misconduct. Politicians from outside the charmed circle of senatorial families soon sensed an opportunity to shift attention from the religious problems of a few elite priests to the more pervasive political corruption of entrenched senatorial families.[5]

An objective observer would likely question why so many Romans felt such alarm. Roman military victories still outnumbered Roman defeats and, unlike the situation a century earlier when Hannibal's armies roamed the Italian peninsula, Rome itself was never remotely threatened in the 110s. The economy continued to grow much as it had for much of the previous century, with the very rich accumulating wealth at levels unimaginable even a few decades before. At the same time, there is no doubt that a growing consensus was emerging among lower-class Romans, Roman *equites,* and even some Roman senators that something was profoundly wrong with the Republic.

The sense of unease that loomed over the Republic for much of the second half of the 110s began to shift Rome's political geography profoundly following a series of episodes involving Jugurtha, the savvy king of Numidia in North Africa. The illegitimate grandson of Masinissa, the Numidian king who had fought alongside Scipio Africanus at Zama, Jugurtha had been sent by Masinissa's heir Micipsa to serve alongside Scipio Aemilianus during the final stages of Rome's war against the Spanish city of Numantia in 134–133. Jugurtha proved both capable and amiable, impressing his commander Scipio with his skill as a soldier and building friendships with a host of influential Romans. Fortified by a commendation from Scipio, Jugurtha returned to Numidia and soon was adopted as a son by Micipsa. When Micipsa died in 118, Jugurtha was supposed to share his kingdom with the king's two legitimate sons, Hiempsal and Adherbal.[6]

The arrangement quickly fell apart. Jugurtha soon rebelled—encouraged, the historian Sallust writes, by "many new men and nobles in the [Roman] army for whom riches were more powerful motivators than honor and virtue" and by Jugurtha's sense that everything in Rome could be bought.[7] By 116, he had killed Hiempsal and defeated Adherbal in battle, forcing him to flee to Rome and appeal for the intervention of the Senate. Amid furious lobbying and, Sallust says, outright bribery by Jugurtha, the Senate elected to send a commission to Numidia that divided the kingdom between Jugurtha and Adherbal. Emboldened by the Senate's decision and, Sallust alleges, the ease with which he had bribed members of the senatorial commission, Jugurtha reopened hostilities rather than observing the commission's division of the kingdom. His forces trapped Adherbal in the city of Cirta and killed him in 112. They also killed a number of Roman and Italian merchants when they captured the city.[8]

Although some of Jugurtha's associates argued that the Romans should not intervene further in an internal Numidian struggle, the massacre of the Roman and Italian businessmen in Cirta proved too powerful a slight to ignore. One of the incoming tribunes, a man named Gaius Memmius, informed the Roman people that a small faction within the Senate sought to pardon Jugurtha's crime. Pressure from the *concilium plebis* then compelled the Senate to assign the Numidian conflict to one of the men who won the consular election in 112. So, in 111, the consul Calpurnius Bestia led a Roman army to confront Jugurtha. Rumors already circulated in Rome that Jugurtha had bribed members of the senatorial commission sent to mediate the earlier conflict with Adherbal, and, when Bestia concluded a hasty peace treaty with Jugurtha after a short campaign, these suspicions of elite corruption erupted into open outrage. But, despite a general outcry against the deal, the Senate could not reach a consensus about how to respond.[9]

The tribune Memmius sensed that this senatorial hesitation offered an opportunity to exploit the growing popular anger. In a series of public meetings, Memmius "urged the people to take vengeance" and "warned them not to forsake the Republic and their own liberty." Speaking before the Temple of Concordia, a structure that had been erected by Opimius as a monument celebrating the goddess for her supposed restoration of political harmony after the crushing of Gaius Gracchus, Memmius supposedly reminded his audience that they have been "a plaything for an arrogant cabal" of elite senators and that their protectors, the Gracchi, "have fallen unavenged."[10] Memmius then called for his listeners not "to resort to arms" but instead to use the courts to punish the senatorial corruption that had led to both a lackadaisical prosecution of the war and a quick treaty to end it. The assembly then decided to send the praetor Lucius Cassius to Numidia so that he might bring Jugurtha to Rome to testify before the Senate. When Jugurtha arrived, however, one of Memmius's fellow tribunes (who Jugurtha again may have bribed) prevented the king from testifying and effectively killed the investigation.[11]

The failure of Memmius's investigation prompted a renewal of the war. But the war under the new consul went poorly, prompting a Roman surrender and retreat. This defeat further fueled popular anger in Rome. C. Mamilius Limetanus, one of the tribunes in 109, set up a tribunal investigating the possible corruption of the Roman officials involved in various negotiations with Jugurtha. The tribunal worked suspiciously quickly and convicted four former consuls (including Opimius, who had served on the initial commission sent to Numidia) and one sitting priest. Even Sallust, who evinces no doubts about the guilt of these men, conceded that the investigation was conducted with "bitterness and violence based upon rumor and irrational passion of the people."[12]

The military situation in Numidia began to improve gradually under Q. Caecilius Metellus, the consul of 109. After retraining what remained of the Roman army that had retreated from Numidia the year before, Metellus began a slow but deliberate advance back into Jugurtha's territory. His steady progress in 109 earned him an extension of the command for a further year. By 108, however, many Romans had tired of the domination of the Republic's highest office by what seemed a closed and corrupt cabal of senatorial families. Although Metellus had changed the course of the war with Jugurtha, Roman defeats elsewhere in fighting against the barbarian Cimbri to Rome's north meant that Metellus's success had done nothing to improve the general mood.

Gaius Marius, an ambitious member of Metellus's staff in Numidia, saw this as a moment when he could launch a bid for the consulship. Marius, who Sallust described as possessing every attribute a consul needed "except for the antiquity of his family," had once heard from a soothsayer that he would become consul.[13] Marius genuinely believed that this was his destiny, but even a few years earlier, the consulship would have seemed an impossible ambition for a man like him. For one thing, Marius was a "new man," a member of a family of Roman *equites* whose ancestors had never before been members of the Senate.[14] He also had not always shown the best political judgment. He began his career as a client of the house of Caecilii Metelli and may have earned election to the tribunate for the year 119 with their help. While tribune, Marius proposed a law that would narrow the pathway leading to the voting urns in which ballots were placed so that no observers could see the ballots as voters carried them forward. This had provoked a public dispute in the Senate, during which Marius threatened to have both consuls arrested, one of whom was L. Caecilius Metellus Dalmaticus. In the short term, this public embarrassment of a relative of Marius's patron proved damaging to his political fortunes. After serving as tribune in 119, Marius lost elections for both aedileships and then got the least votes of all successful candidates seeking the praetorship in 116. Then, after serving a term as praetor, Marius faced a prosecution for bribery.[15]

Times and attitudes had changed by 109, however. Marius appears to have rebuilt his relationship with the Cecilii Metelli sufficiently so that he earned a position on Metellus's staff in Africa. But, if Marius and his old patrons did reconcile, Marius felt no enduring loyalty to the family. By the early 100s, Marius's public confrontation with the now-discredited L. Caecilius Metellus Dalmaticus looked increasingly like a stroke of political good fortune that he could exploit. Rome was gripped by an antiestablishment fever and no one was more representative of the corrupt and ineffective Roman establishment than the Metelli clan that had dominated the consular lists for much of the previous decade and a half. Even though he presently served on the staff of a Metellus, Marius's history with the family meant that he could still brand himself as the anti-Metellus candidate. If necessary, he could enhance this status by offering critical reports of his commander's conduct on campaign. Indeed, there was no more perfect foil to this political dynasty than a new man running a campaign that was explicitly hostile to Metellus and his family.

It is not clear whether other members of the Caecilii Metelli clan saw the danger in Marius's candidacy when he announced it in 108, but the Metellus who commanded Marius in Numidia certainly did not. He felt sure that Marius's descent from a nonsenatorial family was automatically disqualifying. This was, Metellus believed, a moment when no "new man" "was so famous or illustrious for his achievements that he was considered worthy of that honor."[16]

Metellus said as much to Marius when Marius asked his commander for leave from the army to campaign for the consulship. After some initial shock and polite attempts to dissuade Marius, Metellus warned him not to "entertain thoughts above his station" because "not everyone ought to aspire to everything, but they ought instead to be satisfied with what is theirs."[17] When Marius continued to press for leave, Metellus finally responded with exasperation: "Wouldn't it be better to wait until you can stand at the same time as this son of mine?"[18] The son he mentioned, a boy of about twenty, would not be eligible to stand for the consulship for another twenty-three years—at which point Marius would have been over seventy years old. It seems certain that Marius ensured that many people in Italy quickly learned of Metellus's condescension; Metellus's dismissive reaction appears in a range of later sources both favorable and unfavorable to Marius.

Metellus's response to Marius's request changed the tenor of the campaign he was to wage. Marius could now run explicitly as the popular antidote to the corruption, arrogance, and entitlement of the aristocratic Metelli. Marius also understood how to get this message across to voters in Rome. He spoke often with Roman businessmen who had traveled to North Africa. Marius told them that Metellus was deliberately prolonging the war so that he could hold on to power as long as possible, and Marius promised that he could end the war quickly if he were to be put in charge of the army.[19] He also talked to the wealthy and well-connected Roman *equites* serving in the army—the group most frustrated by the incompetence and moral corruption of the entrenched senatorial elite—about how he would manage the war differently. Marius then encouraged these businessmen and soldiers to write to their friends and associates in Rome, tell them how Metellus was mismanaging the war, and demand that Marius be chosen as consul and given the Numidian command.

These equestrian surrogates helped Marius quickly build a popular movement in the capital. Elected officials who supported Marius filled public meetings with accounts of Metellus's treachery and corruption as well as praise for Marius's virtues. Although the initial enthusiasm for Marius came from the *equites* and their associates, crowds of landless workers and craftsmen joined these *equites* to greet Marius when he returned to Rome to officially announce his candidacy for the consulship. Marius repeated his attacks on Metellus and promised a swift victory over Jugurtha once he won power.[20] It seems, though, that the enthusiasm that greeted Marius was as much for what he represented as for what he could actually deliver. The crowds of supporters, Sallust would later write, were influenced less by the good and bad qualities of Marius and Metellus than they were by their feelings about the segment of society each man represented.[21] Marius had the good fortune to be the change candidate in an election in which Romans who had soured on the old families that had recently dominated public life now craved a new political direction.

Marius won the election, a result that demoralized his opponents as much as it excited his supporters. Although the Senate had conferred command of Numidia to Metellus for another year before the consuls for 107 were elected, Marius's victory prompted one of the tribunes to put the question of who should command in Numidia before the *concilium plebis*. The people then overwhelmingly voted to give the command to Marius and strip it from Metellus, despite a series of recent successful engagements against Jugurtha. Marius celebrated this decision loudly and publicly, calling his consulship "the spoils" that the people "seized" from the "nobles" they "had conquered." He then set to the task of building an army that could go and reinforce the troops Metellus already had in Numidia.[22]

Marius requested permission to raise a large number of new troops, a measure that the Senate eagerly approved. The senators felt confident that Marius would fail to find willing soldiers. Rome still had not found a solution to the problem of decreasing numbers of citizens meeting the minimum property qualification for military service that Tiberius Gracchus had raised a generation before. And recruitment of eligible soldiers was made even more difficult because the Republic already had an army in Numidia (an army that was itself a reinforcement of another army sent earlier) while other Roman forces continued to fight in southern Gaul. Marius's opponents thought that he would fail to build an army to lead against Jugurtha and that this failure would permanently undermine his credibility. Perhaps sensing the problem, Marius elected to break with precedent and build his army with recruits drawn from classes of Romans that other commanders had ignored. Some of Marius's most eager supporters came from the Roman poor, who saw in him a military genius and who believed that their service under him would lead to easy victory and substantial plunder. Marius elected to build his army around these poorer men, both because they were among his most enthusiastic backers and because they had the most to gain from service under him.[23] Like Tiberius Gracchus a generation before, Marius decided to put his own personal ambition ahead of his fidelity to the Republic's norms. Enrolling the landless in his army was not illegal, but it was nonetheless a significant break with recent Roman precedent.

Metellus refused to receive Marius when he and his army arrived in Africa, instead electing to have his deputy hand over control of the Roman forces to his replacement. Once he took official control of the army, Marius set to the task of building confidence and capability in his new recruits. Marius possessed exceptional skill as a military leader. He intentionally directed his forces to undertake easy engagements against poorly defended forts and settlements so that they might become accustomed to fighting together. Marius also gradually increased the difficulty of the objectives he set, and the combination of the growing skill of his forces and a series of fortunate events allowed Marius to progressively reduce Jugurtha's strength. In 105, Jugurtha was betrayed by his father-in-law and taken captive by Marius's subordinate, a man from an old, distinguished family named Sulla.

Marius's victory over Jugurtha validated his claim that men outside of the political establishment offered the Republic better and more effective leadership. A series of military reverses along Rome's northern frontier during those same years further strengthened his case that the Republic needed fresh leadership. The Germanic Cimbri tribe bested one of the consuls of 109 in battle, and, in 107, Marius's consular colleague died when a confederation of Alpine tribes defeated his army. The most severe blow, however, came in October of 105, when the Cimbri annihilated Roman armies headed by one current and one former consul outside of the city of Aurasio, what is now Orange in southern France. As many as eighty thousand soldiers are said to have been killed. This defeat, the worst sustained by Roman forces since Hannibal's victory at Cannae more than a century before, came amid reports that the ex-consul Quintus Servilius Caepio had refused to cooperate with his superior, the serving consul Gnaeus Mallius Maximus. Caepio was a member of the old patrician Servilia clan that had populated the consular lists since the first decade of the fifth century BC. As consul, he had burnished his conservative credentials by reversing recent legislation that placed Roman *equites* on juries for extortion trials. When this creature of the establishment bickered with Mallius, who was the first in his family to hold the consulship, his destructive condescension seemed to embody the rottenness of the closed order of traditional Roman elites. Anger at elite arrogance and incompetence now mingled with alarm at the threat Italy faced from German invaders. Romans looked for a savior. Although Marius had not yet returned to Rome, he was elected in absentia to a second term as consul and tasked with saving Italy from barbarian invasion.[24]

Other politicians also sought to ride the tide of popular indignation that had carried Marius to such heights. Seen by some as the political heirs of Tiberius and Gaius Gracchus, the men following in Marius's wake often shared more of Tiberius's talent for provocation than Gaius's gift for programmatic thinking. They had also learned from Marius's attacks on Metellus that personal assaults on the integrity of leading senators offered a potent formula for winning these coveted rewards. Among the most prominent of these young guns were the noble Gnaeus Domitius Ahenobarbus, the son of a consul who nevertheless made his first political splash by prosecuting a former consul, and Gaius Norbanus, a tribune who prosecuted Caepio for the loss of the army at Arausio. These actions eventually propelled both men to the consulship.[25]

No one more brazenly took advantage of this political climate, however, than Lucius Appuleius Saturninus. Saturninus first appears in the historical record as the quaestor supervising the import of grain to Rome in 104 BC, but he was removed from that office before his term ended. He then won election as a tribune for the year 103 and quickly tried to build an alliance with Marius, who at that point was seeking election to his third consecutive consulship (and his fourth consulship overall). Saturninus built trust with Marius by pushing forward a law assigning land to the veterans of Marius's African campaigns as a reward for their service. He and Marius then orchestrated a spectacle in which Marius feigned reluctance to stand again for the consulship while Saturninus disingenuously branded Marius a traitor to Rome for failing to step forward and serve the Republic in a time of peril. Marius then deigned to run, and was reelected overwhelmingly, returning north to serve as consul and oversee the fighting there for the year 102.[26]

Fortunately for everyone concerned, the year of Marius's fourth consulship saw a string of significant Roman military victories, including two defeats of large armies of Germanic invaders near modern Aix-en-Provence. Marius was awarded a triumph for this but decided not to celebrate it. Instead, he returned to Rome long enough to win his fifth consulship (an unprecedented fourth consulship in a row), which covered the year 101. Joining forces with Quintus Lutatius Catulus, the other consul of 102 whose command had been extended, Marius inflicted a massive defeat on the Cimbri and their allies the Teutones, killing tens of thousands of their soldiers and enslaving as many as sixty thousand others. Although both generals shared credit for the victory and jointly celebrated a triumph, in the popular mind it belonged primarily to Marius. Indeed, a coin issued in 101 seems to show Marius and his eight-year-old son riding in the triumphal chariot—the first-ever representation of a living figure on a Roman coin. But Marius, who was now hailed as the third founder of Rome because he was believed to have saved the city from destruction, seemed to many Romans to have earned this unique honor.[27]

Marius had become Rome's preeminent politician through a unique blend of political opportunism, creativity, and military skill, but the political climate and the military circumstances of the 100s had enabled his rise. With Jugurtha and the Germanic invaders defeated and the elite monopoly on the consulship a thing of the past, it was unclear where Marius now fit. Populist politicians had become increasingly radical in the years since Marius's

5.1. Coin showing Marius, the first living Roman to appear on a Roman denarius, and his son in triumphal chariot (Crawford 326/1). Private collection. Photo by Zoe Watts.

first consulship. The attacks on Metellus that won Marius the office now looked tame.

Marius confronted an uncomfortable choice. After his return to Rome in 101, he could have collected his many honors and stepped into the role of an elder statesman. His military victories and multiple consulships had ensured that he would long be mentioned among the most honored and accomplished of all Romans. Judging by the measures of Roman virtue that Fabricius had described to Pyrrhus almost two hundred years before, Marius could hope for nothing more. He had proven himself, bettered the lot of his family, and given his descendants the standing to match his accomplishments, if they were at all capable. Marius, however, was not Fabricius. He did not simply look to collect his share of the honors distributed to Roman notables. He greedily wanted to remain at the center of Roman political life for as long as he could.

This desire would perhaps have been understandable if, like Gaius Gracchus, Marius had authored a program of broad policy reforms that he wanted to implement. But Marius was not a reformer at heart. Though he backed reforms put forward by figures like Saturninus (and may even have genuinely thought some of them to be good ideas), in the end he did not advocate for any policy that did not benefit his political standing. Gaius Gracchus stood for a set of principles. Marius stood for Marius. This was not a problem on a military campaign, where Marius's personal success and that of the Republic were bound together, but Marius had much more trouble figuring out how to maintain his stature once his triumph concluded. As Plutarch noted more than two hundred years later, "in war, supreme power came to him because he was needed, in civilian life his supremacy was restricted" and subject to challenges he was no longer accustomed to face.[28] Unwilling to retreat from the public eye, Marius instead decided to stand yet again for the consulship, for the year 100.

Writing centuries afterward, Plutarch commented on how Marius "set his heart on his sixth consulship with all or more than the enthusiasm of a man standing for office for the first time," a notable comment given the scorched earth tactics Marius had used to win in 108.[29] Other authors speak about a massive campaign of bribery undertaken to shore up Marius's vote. Although Marius may indeed have pandered to voters during the term of his sixth consulship, his decision to remain closely aligned with Saturninus would prove to be his most dangerous choice. Saturninus too seems to have been a victim of the shifting political norms of the later 100s. His conduct as tribune in 103 had seemed outrageous to many, but he became even more brazen in subsequent years. In 101, Saturninus was again selected as tribune after violence during the voting caused the death of one of the newly elected tribunes. Although it is unclear what role he played in fomenting this violence, Saturninus appears to have been working together with C. Servilius Glaucia, a serving tribune who won election to the office of praetor for 100.

Glaucia and Saturninus came to office eager to pursue an agenda. In 102, Marius's old foil Metellus had been selected as censor, serving in that office alongside one of his cousins. The two Metelli tried to expel Saturninus and Glaucia from the Senate. Though they ultimately failed, their attempt greatly angered Saturninus and Glaucia. Marius too continued to hold a grudge against Metellus. Some of this went back to the condescension Metellus had shown Marius in 109, but Marius also resented the fact that some Romans had given Metellus credit for the Roman victory over Jugurtha. Metellus had even been awarded the honorific title "Numidicus" upon his return from Africa. More recently, Metellus had also imposed restrictions on a temple that Marius proposed to build and may even have tried to mount a consular campaign in 101 to thwart Marius's election. All of this made Marius perfectly willing to help his allies ruin Metellus.[30]

The three men embarked on a legislative strategy that simultaneously marginalized Metellus and rewarded some of their own most important supporters. As tribune in 100, Saturninus

proposed a law that would divide the land taken from the Cimbri among the Roman and Italian veterans of Rome's recent wars.
This law addressed a problem that had been created by Marius's recruitment of soldiers who failed to meet the property qualification
and expected rewards for their successful service. These soldiers
had served honorably under Marius and, like the veterans of his
African campaigns, they would now be provided with land and
the security that came with property ownership. This distribution
also served the strategic imperative of settling Romans and loyal
Italian allies in the Gallic lands that war and the mass enslavement
of the Cimbri had depopulated.

The proposal proved extremely popular among Marius's veterans. Although many in the city objected to the benefits it provided
to Italian allies in addition to Roman citizens, Saturninus's law
was likely to pass overwhelmingly once Marius mobilized his veterans and supporters in the countryside to come to Rome to vote.
Understanding this, Saturninus added a provision to the law that
required all senators to take an oath swearing to uphold the law
within five days of its passage.[31] Those who refused were to be expelled from the Senate and fined. This upset members of the Senate and generated considerable unease among some of Saturninus's
fellow tribunes, but partisans of Saturninus drove those tribunes
away from the Rostra when they attempted to impose their veto.
Urban residents opposed to the law then claimed that they had
heard thunder, which would trigger a religious requirement that
voting stop—but Saturninus ignored this as well. With these legal
and religious provisions ignored, some of the law's opponents then
turned to violence. They attacked partisans of Saturninus with
whatever weapons they could find, but Saturninus's supporters
had come to the voting in the Forum equipped with clubs. Beat-
ing back the assault, they then passed the law.

Initiative then passed to Marius. As consul, he proposed to the
Senate that it should consider whether to swear the oath the law
required. Though oaths like this had been required in previous

laws, the violent cloud under which the law was passed posed a particular problem for certain senators. If they publicly swore to uphold a law passed in this way, they would legitimate the tactics that led to its passage.[32] Saturninus, Glaucia, and Marius had guessed from the outset that Metellus could be induced to refuse to swear the oath. When senate debate began, Marius then sprung a trap designed to ensnare Metellus. Marius spoke before the Senate and stated forcefully that he opposed the section of the law that required senators to swear an oath. He claimed that he would not do so and urged others to do the same. After Metellus spoke in agreement, Marius adjourned the Senate.

On the fifth day after the law's passage, the quaestors summoned the senators to publicly swear the required oath. Marius came forward and swore to uphold the law "insofar as it was a law,"[33] a statement that left open the possibility that Marius could later claim that the violence and the breach of religious customs that colored the law's passage had invalidated it from the outset. When other senators saw Marius's fudge, they too swore the oath. Metellus, however, refused to do so on principle. Saturninus then apparently had agents go to the senate house the following day to remove Metellus. When other tribunes objected, Saturninus offered a motion charging Metellus with violating the new law and requiring him to be tried directly before the *concilium plebis*.[34] Rather than subject himself to this trial (and the violence that would likely result from Saturninus's further manipulation of his followers), Metellus decided to go into exile. The assembly then voted to ban any Roman from providing Metellus with water and fire, a step that gave Metellus's voluntary exile the force of law. Metellus could only return to Rome if another law was passed that annulled the exile.[35]

As the year progressed, politics turned even darker. Marius had clearly lost whatever political initiative he once possessed. The year instead belonged to his allies Saturninus and Glaucia. At some point during the year, Saturninus passed a law criminalizing the "diminution of the majesty (*maiestas*) of the Roman people," a deliberately vague legal concept that in practice may have been intended to punish foolish military decisions by commanders.[36] The tension within the city grew as the elections for the magistrates who would take office in 99 approached. Although Marius decided not to seek another consulship, Saturninus secured reelection to the tribunate and also managed to get two allies into office alongside him. One of those allies, not coincidentally, claimed to be an illegitimate son of Tiberius Gracchus. Glaucia, for his part, hoped to use the strong-arm tactics he and Saturninus had practiced to jump from praetor to consul. When the election for consul took place, however, Glaucia looked to be in danger of losing. After the first consul for the year was chosen, Glaucia found himself facing off against Memmius, a more impressive and more qualified opponent, for the second position.[37] Perhaps reprising the electoral violence of the year before, Glaucia and Saturninus sent a gang of supporters armed with clubs into the *comitia centuriata* while the voting was going on. These men attacked Memmius and clubbed him to death in front of all of the assembled voters.

Chaos ensued. Opponents of Saturninus armed themselves and set out to kill him the following day, but the armed supporters of Saturninus and Glaucia battled them in the streets before eventually being pushed back to the Capitoline Hill. While they fortified their position on the hill, the Senate passed a Senatus Consultum Ultimum, a legal step that empowered the current consuls to do whatever was necessary to prevent harm coming to the Republic. This measure, which had given Opimius the legal authority to attack and murder Gaius Gracchus a generation before, now compelled Marius to deal with a new crisis of violence involving a leading populist politician. Marius, a populist darling only a few years before, had to decide how to handle a situation in which he was expected to use force or the threat of force against men who had recently been his closest allies.

Marius found himself in an impossible position. He had built his public profile around the idea that only he could save the Republic from a combination of external threats and internal aristocratic hubris. But the Senate had now set a trap for Marius that was as perfectly designed as the one he had used to ensnare Metellus just months earlier. Marius could either save the Republic or fight alongside the champions of the veterans and dispossessed who formed his core political constituency. He could not do both.

Forced to decide, Marius accepted the senatorial decree and reluctantly summoned troops under his authority. Perhaps hoping that the situation might resolve itself, Marius did not hurry to the Capitoline Hill. As he delayed, however, the water supply to the Capitoline temple where Saturninus and his associates had barricaded themselves was cut. While some of those besieged alongside Saturninus apparently advocated setting fire to the temple and martyring themselves, Saturninus and Glaucia instead trusted that Marius would help them and recommended surrendering to Marius in exchange for safe passage off of the hill. Marius agreed to their proposal. Later sources suggest that a crowd demanded that, like Gaius Gracchus, Saturninus, Glaucia, and those of their supporters who had taken refuge in the temple should all be put to death immediately and without a trial. Marius had enough sense not to do this. Instead, he imprisoned his former allies in the senate house, presumably so that they could safely be held until a trial could be conducted.[38]

Marius's attempt to promote law and order failed dramatically, however. Saturninus's supporters in the city had scattered and his opponents had no interest in waiting for a trial. None of the middle ground Marius hoped to occupy remained. Once Saturninus and his associates entered the senate house, a crowd of angry people began tearing the rooftiles off of the building and hurling them at the politicians within. Saturninus, Glaucia, and a number of other officeholders were killed in the assault—many of them, Appian notes, while still wearing the insignia of their office. Other associates of Saturninus were then attacked and killed around the city over the course of the next few days, including the incoming tribune of the plebs who claimed to be Tiberius Gracchus's illegitimate son. After that day, Appian writes, "no one had any hope of protection from freedom or democracy or the laws or honors or offices" because even the tribunes, traditionally sacrosanct, had participated in and been victims of horrible acts of mob violence.[39]

Marius could not stop the carnage and, in the minds of many of his former supporters, he bore some responsibility for the deaths of Saturninus and Glaucia. Even worse, in those erstwhile supporters' eyes, he now seemed to serve the same senatorial establishment against which he once fought. After his actions against Metellus, however, this establishment could never trust Marius. And, perhaps most importantly, this spasm of violence undercut Marius's claim that he alone could serve as Rome's savior. The murders in the senate house showed most definitively that Marius could perhaps save Romans from invaders—but he could not save Romans from each other.

Marius's fall came swiftly after these events of early December 100 BC. His term as consul ended a few weeks later and he slipped into an unwanted semiretirement. He was unable to prevent the return of Metellus from exile in 99. The following year, he could not prevent a mob from murdering the tribune who had worked with him to try to keep Metellus away. Then, later in 98, Marius decided not to stand for selection as censor because he feared that he would be passed over for the honor.[40] He instead elected to leave Rome and travel to Asia Minor, ostensibly so that he could make sacrifices at cults there. When he returned to Rome, he built a house for himself near the Forum, hoping that his physical proximity to the political life of the city might reinvigorate his career. It appears not to have worked. Marius was largely left at the political margins for much of the rest of the decade, wanted by neither the aristocrats with whom he had clashed nor the people he had claimed to champion.

Marius's downfall was a personal defeat, but the manner in which it occurred had profound consequences for the political life of all Rome. In his heart, Marius craved the same combination of honors and offices that had long motivated Roman notables. The Republic of the 110s restricted these rewards to so narrow a group of elites that Marius decided that he could win the consulship only by attacking Metellus, a figure who seemed to embody an increasingly arrogant establishment. Marius's attacks were personal, but they resonated symbolically. Marius's specific charges of corruption and incompetence against Metellus were all likely false, but those lobbed by others against senators supposedly bribed by Jugurtha and the commanders who lost a Roman army at Arausio seem plausible. And, by making such charges the centerpiece of his consular campaign, Marius undercut public faith in the legitimacy of the elites who had been running the Republic for much of the past generation. Marius could then position himself as the only person who could save the Republic from this moral and institutional rot.

A delegitimized establishment helped Marius in the short run, but it seriously damaged the Republic. The political system that had encouraged compromises and generated political consensus was now discredited alongside the men who had led it. Politicians like Saturninus then took advantage of this structural weakness— and Marius's unwillingness to be satisfied with the extraordinary run of offices he had already secured pushed him to cooperate with these new, violent allies. Political violence, which had been rare in the 130s and 120s, became a tool that now played a semiregular role in the Roman political process. This began with the tacit threats posed by the presence of Marius's veterans in the city when Saturninus pushed through the law providing them with land, but intimidation regularly degenerated into outright violence as the decade progressed. It first seeped into the balloting on particular pieces of legislation and then, by 101, into murderous attacks during elections for magistracies. And Marius largely stood aside.

Marius's disengagement would prove as destructive as his initial decision to cooperate with Saturninus. Violence prevents compromise, destroys consensus, and encourages extremism. It is very hard to bargain away parts of an agenda for which followers have shed blood—but it is very easy to use such sacrifices to build still more enthusiasm for a radical cause. Even though his leadership pushed Romans toward political extremism, in his heart Marius was neither an extremist nor an anarchist. He was an opportunist who built a career as a political outsider but who failed to find a way to pivot toward the political mainstream. When Marius returned from his campaigns against the Cimbri and the Teutones, he was no longer a political outsider crusading against a corrupt and ineffective elite. He stood, instead, at the center of political life in the Republic. But the structures that had brought such stability to the Republic for nearly two centuries had become too weak to integrate Marius into the Roman political establishment. He was the most powerful man in Rome, but, because the elites whose monopoly on the consulship he had helped shatter had no interest in working with him, Marius could not reward his soldiers without depending on the violence and intimidation of Saturninus and Glaucia. And so he remained tied to them even as their tactics grew more and more destructive.

Marius's tolerance of the violence and intimidation his allies wielded served his immediate interests, but he lacked the ability to control where events would go. And, ultimately, Saturninus proved so violent that the Senate could compel Marius to choose between his most important supporters and the welfare of the Republic. Marius chose the Republic—and his supporters could not forgive the betrayal. For them, Marius's inclination to save the Republic from the electoral violence his allies had perpetrated was not a service to Rome that all could agree was necessary. It was instead an abandonment of popular champions. This showed that the politics of consensus was dying. And Marius, isolated and ignored, could only sit in his beautiful house near the Forum and watch it fade away.

CHAPTER 6

THE REPUBLIC BREAKS

THE HISTORIAN APPIAN CALLED THE death of Saturninus in the year 100 BC the "third incident of civil violence among the Romans, after the affairs of the two Gracchi."[1] He was correct, but only in the most general way. Though the murders of Tiberius and Gaius Gracchus shocked Romans, their deaths had the effect of at least temporarily resetting Roman political dynamics. When the two Gracchi died, the political violence their actions had spawned died down too. Things returned to something that seemed normal. This was not the case in 100. The alliance of Marius, Saturninus, and Glaucia revealed that the normal political rules of the Roman Republic were no match for any politician who commanded the loyalty of an army of veterans living in the countryside or a mob of urban supporters. Not only could men like these rig elections, but they could even arrange for the condemnation of innocent men who angered them. All Romans now knew that the Republic could not protect itself or its citizens from the politics of intimidation and violence.

As the year 99 dawned, it was clear to most Romans that Saturninus and Glaucia had gone too far in their use of violence. But their fate did nothing to change the obvious reality that, if used skillfully, a measured combination of threats and physical violence could serve as part of a sustainable political strategy. This is why, unlike the situations in 133 and 121 BC, the assassinations of 100 did nothing to calm Roman political life. Saturninus, Glaucia, and even, to a degree, Marius himself had used these tools to dominate the Roman state. They had come to bad ends, but, one could perhaps argue, their early successes showed that violence and intimidation tactics worked politically as long as one did not deploy them too recklessly.

This meant that, instead of the tense stability that followed the murder of Gaius Gracchus, the 90s brought chaos. In 99, a tribune named Furius proposed confiscating the estate of Saturninus while also obstructing an effort to get Metellus recalled from exile. Then, in 98, Furius was himself prosecuted by another tribune, and a mob tore Furius to pieces before a verdict could be reached. Although Metellus was allowed to return from exile soon afterward by virtue of a law that attracted great support, such moments of consensus seemed to become rarer as the 90s progressed.[2]

The biggest issue Rome faced in the second half of the 90s concerned the large population of Italians who lived in the city but who were not Roman citizens. By the year 100, Rome had unquestionably surpassed the Egyptian city of Alexandria as the world's largest. Its population would approach a million people by the middle of the first century, making it the first city on earth to reach this milestone. As the capital grew, so too did the concentration of economic activity within it. Despite the efforts of the Gracchi and their populist successors, the Republic and its Italian allies had never managed to address the economic strains on rural areas caused by the second-century explosion in the Italian population. While the small farmers in the countryside struggled, Rome boomed. This prompted waves of younger Italians from the countryside and the peninsula's smaller cities to flock to Rome in search of work that was more exciting or more lucrative than what they could find at home.[3]

Unfortunately for these new arrivals, the city of Rome in the 90s was not built to accommodate a population rocketing toward a million. The early- and mid-second-century infrastructure projects had barely been enough to meet the needs of a city of two hundred thousand. The political difficulties of the last three decades of the second century had also made it difficult to find the will and resources to construct the expensive new aqueducts, sewers, and bridges that might improve the lives of Rome's new migrants. Instead of infrastructure expansion, which required the state to spend massive amounts of money up front but which had relatively small long-term costs, late-second-century Roman politicians elected to build popular support for themselves by creating entitlement programs through which the Republic began to provide assistance to Roman citizens. These programs, which began with the subsidized grain distributions created by Gaius Gracchus, had recurring costs that grew alongside the Roman citizen population and required regular sources of revenue to fund them.[4]

This provision of ongoing entitlements, and the resulting need for reliable revenue streams, changed the way the Republic worked. The Republic that faced Pyrrhus in the 280s BC asked a great deal of its citizens and offered them little more than honor and security in return. Rome in the 90s, however, had regular obligations to its citizens. It also demanded much less of them than it once had. Soldiering in Rome's armies, for instance, was evolving from the primary vehicle through which citizens served Rome into a professional occupation, through which the state paid Romans for their service. Marius's decision to raise armies made up of soldiers who did not meet the old minimum property qualification further exacerbated this shift. While many citizens who met the property qualification still did serve, the recruitment of poorer soldiers meant that military service now touched all segments of the Roman citizen body. But the military became a paid pursuit chosen by some rather than an obligation that all citizens shared. And, after Marius's Roman veterans received land as a reward for their service, many Roman citizens began to expect the Republic to pay soldiers while they served and provide land to them upon their discharge.

All of these developments made Roman citizenship an increasingly prized privilege. By the 90s, Roman citizens had the right to
live in Rome, purchase subsidized grain, vote in the elections that
chose magistrates, and participate in the political processes that
shaped the Republic. As the Republic came to devote ever more resources to its citizens, and continued to make policy that affected
its Italian allies, the leading citizens of these allied towns and cities
became ever more conscious of their lack of a direct voice in the
Republic's decision making. Italians could influence Roman policy only by asking friendly Roman magistrates to communicate
their concerns to the Senate or *concilium plebis*. The flaws in this
arrangement had already become clear in 133 BC when Tiberius
Gracchus pushed through his land reform bill over the strenuous
objections of both the Italian allies whose farms would be affected
and their Roman advocates. By the early 90s, Rome's growing political dysfunction had made it even more difficult for sympathetic
Roman citizens to effectively advocate for Italian interests.

The growing number of Italian immigrants in Rome further
strained relations between Rome and its Italian allies. Not only
did Roman politics now affect the economic interests of wealthy
leaders of Italian cities but it also affected the lives of multitudes
of lower-status Italians living in Rome itself. In addition, the flow
of people from Italian cities to Rome reduced these cities' tax revenues. Though the Republic did pass a law in the year 95 that prevented non-Romans from avoiding taxes by pretending they were
Roman citizens, this did little to solve either the revenue problems
in Italian cities or the immigration problem in Rome. Instead, this
law only further heightened tensions between Romans and other
Italians by emphasizing the particular privileges and status that
Roman citizens now enjoyed.[5]

The men leading the Republic in the 90s needed to carefully
calibrate their policies to balance the needs of Roman citizens, Italian elites, and Italian immigrants to Rome. But they lacked the
skills to do this. Instead of calming this combustible situation, they

ignited it. A tribune named Livius Drusus threw the match in 91 BC. Motivated by a desire to return senators to the roster of potential jurors in extortion trials, Drusus concocted a complicated scheme to build support for rolling back this check on senatorial corruption.[6] Drusus understood that his proposal would be deeply unpopular with everyone but senators. To make it more palatable, he packaged his reform with an additional measure to found colonies of Roman citizens on public land in Italy and Sicily.[7] These foundations revived and expanded upon the failed colonial schemes that Drusus's father had floated when he served as consul in 122 BC. Like those initial plans, Drusus's ideas seem to have proven popular with the Roman citizens they were designed to benefit. One would expect this. In recent years, Roman colonies had been founded outside of Italy, as Roman politicians recognized the unfairness of seizing land currently farmed by Italian allies. But colonies in Italy were naturally much more desirable to Roman citizens than sites in Gaul or North Africa. Drusus recognized that many poorer Roman citizens might consent to his jury reform if doing so would also reopen Italian land to Roman colonists.

The measures passed without sufficient thought about the larger consequences these land redistributions would have for non-Romans. Drusus had bought the support of these Roman citizens with land presently farmed by Italian allies, who would not be eligible to settle in the new colonies.[8] And Drusus did not offer anything to these Italians. They had once again been excluded from a Roman political process that affected them profoundly, this time by seizing some of the land on which their economic and social status depended.[9]

Italian anger boiled as the agrarian commission that Drusus's measure empowered to redistribute Italian public land began its work. Rumors of Italian plots to assassinate the consuls and other signs of an emerging rebellion began trickling into Rome in the spring of 91. By late summer, alarmed Romans turned on Drusus and began to blame him for provoking this crisis. Drusus then tried to salvage his program by proposing a radical expansion of

Roman citizenship to include all Italian allies.[10] In one step this would have both resolved the problem of Italian political representation in Rome and, potentially, opened up Drusus's new colonies to all Italians. It just might have been enough to stop the nascent Italian revolt—if it had passed.

To many Romans, Drusus's proposal looked like capitulation. Roman citizens had come to appreciate the status and benefits that their citizenship conferred, and they did not want to see these things diluted by a citizenship expansion. They had no intention of allowing Drusus's proposal to become law. Not long after Drusus floated this idea, an assailant stabbed him to death while the tribune mingled with supporters in the atrium of his house. The assailant was never identified. The only clue to his identity was the shoemaker's knife lodged in Drusus's hip.[11]

Italy erupted. The first blows of what Romans would come to call the Social War (derived from *socii,* the Latin word for "allies") were struck in the city of Asculum soon after Drusus's murder. A crowd of people attending a local festival there murdered two Roman officials sent to investigate rumors of sedition and then killed all of the other Roman citizens in the town. This violence precipitated a wider rebellion in which large swathes of Central and Southern Italy openly turned against Rome. By the beginning of the year 90, the Italian rebels had come together into a political union, established a capital, and begun issuing their own coins showing the Italian bull trampling on a Roman wolf. Although the revolt was widespread across Central and Southern Italy, some cities in those regions remained loyal to Rome and others housed Roman garrisons that succeeded in keeping unrest at bay. Crucially, the northern regions of Umbria and Etruria (modern Tuscany) also remained in the Roman camp. For the revolt to succeed, the Italian allies needed to eliminate these Roman enclaves before Rome could mobilize the resources of its Mediterranean empire and mount an effective counterattack. Italian military operations thus targeted those pockets of Roman resistance within Italian territory.[12]

Roman political infighting gave the Italian rebels some additional time to mobilize. In perhaps one of the clearest signs of the depths of the Republic's political dysfunction, Roman politicians responded to this external threat by first looking for internal enemies. They passed a treason law, the *lex Varia,* that sanctioned the investigation of those Romans "through whose help or advice" the allies decided to rebel. The law also gave its sponsor, Q. Varius Hybrida, a weapon that he could use to punish the supporters of Drusus who had now become associated with the Italian cause.[13] Though some Romans initially saw the Italian revolt as an opportunity for internal political bloodletting, the true danger of the situation rapidly became apparent as the year 90 began. Both consuls for the year 90 were given command of armies designated for campaigns in Italy and one of the consuls for 91 had his military command prolonged. But even these measures proved insufficient to defeat the Italians. As the year dragged on, an increasingly concerned Senate summoned some of Rome's most experienced commanders out of retirement. These included Lutatius Catulus (consul in the year 102), P. Licinius Crassus (consul in 97), and, most notably, Marius.

Marius's return made an immediate difference. In the conflict's first months, Roman commanders struggled to fight effectively on the war's northern front. One consul had been killed in battle in June of 90. His replacement as commander died in an ambush later in the year. A third Roman commander was beaten in battle and then besieged in the city of Firmum. Marius changed the trajectory of the war. Much as he had done in the wars against Jugurtha, the Cimbri, and the Teutones, Marius energetically took to the field, defeated an Italian army, broke the siege at Firmum, pushed Italian forces back to Asculum, and then placed that city under siege.

Rome had less success in the south. The Samnites, one of Rome's most determined Italian adversaries in the fourth century BC, again vexed the Romans. They swept down toward Italy's west coast and captured a string of cities, including communities like Herculaneum and Stabiae that lay on the Bay of Naples. These southern areas would soon become the focus of much of the fighting.

These military reverses shifted the political dynamics in Rome. The losses in battle and the surprisingly fierce Italian armies convinced Rome that it required additional manpower. They also forced Rome into the realization that it needed to find ways to prevent additional Italian cities from breaking with Rome and joining the rebel cause. Rome's immediate response seems to have been to arm freed slaves and task them with the defense of the coast between Cumae and Rome, but the social and economic consequences of the wholesale emancipation of Roman slaves made this unworkable as a long-term defensive strategy. It then began to dawn on Roman politicians that the citizenship proposal of Drusus may not, in fact, have been such a terrible thing. Not only might the extension of citizenship to loyal allies deprive the Italian rebels of potential recruits but it would also provide Rome with a new source of loyal soldiers. In October of 90, the consul Lucius Julius Caesar oversaw the passage of a law that extended Roman citizenship to the Latin, Etruscan, and Umbrian communities that did not rebel. This was followed, probably in 89 BC, by another law, the *lex Plautia Papiria*, that extended citizenship to all individual Italians who presented themselves before a praetor and asked for it. A further law, a *lex Calpurnia*, divided the masses of new Roman citizens into voting tribes. Then, in 89, one of the consuls sponsored a law extending "Latin rights," a political status just below that of full Roman citizenship, to the non-Italian inhabitants of Cisalpine Gaul—an area that now comprises much of modern Italy north of the Po River.[14]

These political changes combined with Roman military successes to drain much of the energy out of the Italian rebellion. Although a wary Senate decided not to extend Marius's command, Roman successes continued in the north in 89 BC under other leadership, effectively ending the war there. In the south, the Samnite forces that had given Rome such trouble in 90 were pushed back from all of the cities they had captured in the west (save Nola). By the end of the year, Rome had regained dominance over the region, though it was not yet fully under Roman control.

The hero of these southern campaigns was Lucius Cornelius Sulla, an ambitious and unscrupulous member of an old, faded patrician family. Sulla's ancestors had once been wealthy and powerful, but, by the time of Sulla's birth, no member of his family had held the consulship in a century and a half. Although Sulla's father still qualified for membership in the Senate, the family no longer stood out for either its wealth or its influence.[15]

As Sulla began his political career, however, he became convinced that he could overcome the political and financial limitations that had constrained the ambition of his immediate ancestors. Sulla was a deeply religious man who came to trust a series of visions, oracles, and other divine messages that foretold tremendous good fortune and personal achievements.[16] His financial circumstances improved when he secured inheritances from his stepmother and from an older woman to whom he had attached himself romantically. Sulla also possessed remarkable good fortune in his public career. He served as quaestor under Marius during the campaign against Jugurtha and managed to be the highest-ranking Roman officer present at the capture of the Numidian king. Although Marius celebrated the triumph over Jugurtha, Sulla understood that his own role in this event had raised his public profile in Rome and could, if effectively utilized, propel him to high office. Sulla had the scene of Jugurtha's capture cut into his signet ring and repeatedly advertised his connections to Bocchus, the Mauretanian leader whose betrayal of Jugurtha led to the Numidian king's capture by Sulla. Sulla built upon these successes in Numidia when he served first as a legate and then as a military tribune in Marius's campaigns against the Cimbri and Teutones. In 102, he moved over to serve under Marius's colleague Catulus. Sulla would later claim that it was in this capacity that he saved Marius's army when it ran short of provisions during that campaign.[17]

As the 90s began, Sulla shifted his focus from military to political campaigning. He stood for praetor and ran a campaign that advertised his military achievements, but, because the public had already attributed most of the victories Sulla claimed to have won to Marius and Catulus, Sulla was defeated. He ran again the following year, seeking a praetorship for the year 97 BC. This time he won after a campaign that emphasized the quality of African animals that Bocchus would provide for Sulla's praetorian games. He may also have been helped by an aggressive effort to bribe the electorate. Following his praetorship, the Senate sent Sulla to Asia Minor and tasked him with restoring the king of Cappadocia and checking the expansion of his neighbor, Mithridates of Pontus. He seems to have stayed in the region until about 93 BC.[18]

Sulla's return to Rome was accompanied by a flurry of activity that suggests he may have been planning to stand for the consulship. In a clear move to further bolster Sulla's public profile, Bocchus erected a gilded sculpture of Jugurtha's surrender to Sulla in the Roman Forum. Sulla's political opponents, by contrast, initiated a prosecution in which they claimed that Sulla's growing wealth had been extorted from one of the Asian kings with whom Sulla had recently worked. Although the person prosecuting the case failed to show up on the day the trial was scheduled, the charge alone slowed Sulla's political momentum and held him back from the consulship.[19]

This was where Sulla found himself when the Social War began. He was a rising star but had not yet cracked the upper echelon of Roman political life. Despite his great luck, he was entering his late forties and had failed to progress to any office higher than that which his father had held. Time was running out for him to reach the consulship, and, with Italy now enveloped in war, Rome had turned back to the trusted and experienced leaders who had saved it in the recent past. But the devastation that the Social War inflicted on the ranks of these senior commanders in 90 BC opened a door for Sulla. He began the conflict in the familiar position of a subordinate to Marius, but, as the war progressed and other commanders either died or failed to have their command renewed, he moved from subordinate to commander. In this role, Sulla showed an ability to undertake "successful actions...on the spur of the moment" that seemed to demonstrate an almost supernatural talent for attracting good fortune. This nurtured in Sulla an incredible self-confidence that pushed him to consider courses of action others might have thought rash or unwise.[20]

In addition to his penchant for good fortune, Sulla possessed an innate understanding of how to motivate soldiers to create armies that were intensely loyal to him. As he matured as a commander, Sulla showed himself able to deftly manage even the most difficult armies. He expertly manipulated the emotions of soldiers. He made his armies crave combat by filling their downtime with mundane manual labor, he rewarded them generously when they prevailed in battles, and he decided whether to punish or pardon offenses based on which response would most enhance his own authority and reputation among the soldiers. During the campaign season in 89 BC, for example, troops under Sulla's ultimate authority murdered the former consul Postumius Albinus during a prolonged siege of Pompeii. Sulla elected not to punish the mutineers but instead told them to atone for their action by fighting harder against their true enemies.[21] Sulla's leniency was perhaps understandable. The Social War represented a time of profound crisis, an engagement with enemy forces loomed, and Sulla could not spare any troops—even disloyal ones. But there was also a long-term strategy at play. Sulla had pardoned troops who, by law and custom, should have been severely punished. These men owed their lives to him—and Sulla understood quite well that this was a debt he could eventually call upon them to repay.

Sulla would not have to wait long. He returned to Rome at the end of 89 to stand in the upcoming consular election. By that time, Roman military operations in the Social War were winding down. The city of Nola continued to resist, as did some Samnite communities in Southern Italy, but the extension of Roman citizenship to those Italians who wished to claim it and the military victories Sulla and other commanders had won in 89 meant that the Italian threat had largely been neutralized. The war was not yet quite over—but its outcome was no longer in doubt. And this meant that Sulla stood for election as the man seen as perhaps most responsible for Rome's victory. He was elected easily.

Sulla also understood that the year 88 offered one consul a rare opportunity to rise even higher in Roman popular estimation. While the Social War raged in Italy, the Roman governor of the province of Asia had restored the deposed kings of two neighboring kingdoms. Rome had no troops to spare, so the monarchs had been compelled to borrow heavily from Roman bankers to pay the local armies that backed their return. When one of these monarchs, a king named Nicomedes of Bithynia, ran short of funds to repay his loans, he decided to raise money by raiding territory in the kingdom of Pontus. Mithridates, the king of Pontus, had backed Nicomedes's rival, and the Bithynian likely thought that Mithridates would shrug off this raid as an aftereffect of the war that brought him back to power. But Mithridates was a powerful king who had spent much of the past generation expanding his northern Anatolia kingdom into an empire that included much of the territory lining the coast of the Black Sea. He was unwilling to ignore the provocations of a weak, indebted Roman client king.[22]

Mithridates sent envoys to ask the Romans to stop Nicomedes's invasion. The Romans refused. They instead chastised the envoys for their arrogance and cautioned them that Rome would not allow Nicomedes or any other allied king to be attacked by Pontus. Mithridates then mobilized his army. After a series of victories over Bithynian forces, Mithridates won a major battle against Roman forces in Bithynia that allowed his army to move into the Roman province of Asia. The effects were at least as catastrophic as the Social War. The Romans had controlled Asia for nearly half a century, and many Romans had significant commercial ties with the region. Tens of thousands of Romans had settled in Asia, Greece, and Aegean islands like Rhodes. Mithridates understood that the presence of these Roman settlers and businesspeople reinforced the general perception among Greeks that Roman rule served primarily as a tool for the massive transfer of wealth and resources from prosperous eastern cities to their Italian masters. The savvy king realized that a dramatic sign that he had broken Roman control over Asia might incite a broader rebellion across other Greek areas. Thus, as Mithridates took control of Asia, he ordered the massacre of as many as eighty thousand Roman and Italian merchants, businessmen, and colonists living in the area.[23]

Mithridates's brutality succeeded in inciting rebellions among Greeks living under Roman control. Much of Asia fell out of Roman political control, a loss that had serious economic implications. The death of so many Roman businessmen, the confiscation of their property, and the loss of the Asian tax revenue they had been contracted to collect collapsed the Roman financial system. The loans these dead men had taken out to finance their tax collection and business ventures would never be repaid. In addition, because these uncollectable loans had been sold to investors and the investors had in turn sold the loans to other investors, the availability of credit in Rome dried up. Defaults cascaded down the Roman financial system. In the financial panic that followed, disputes between lenders and borrowers often turned violent. Things became so dangerous that a mob of debtors even murdered the praetor Asellio when he tried to mediate their disputes through legal means. The Republic responded to the panic with a series of emergency measures that restricted the amount of debt lenders could take on, arranged for renegotiation of outstanding loans that could not be repaid, and devalued the denarius so that more physical money could enter the economy to replace the paper wealth that had evaporated.[24] None of this fixed the immense economic damage that Mithridates had caused. Though these measures helped wealthy investors recover somewhat, the economic shock caused by Mithridates's actions had

severe effects on the poor who lived in Rome. It was Asian tax revenue that had funded the subsidized grain distributions in the city
of Rome, and its loss imperiled this program on which many Romans depended for their survival.[25]

Romans now hated Mithridates with a passion reserved perhaps only for Hannibal in the past. Not only had Mithridates
committed genocide against Romans but he had also crashed the
Roman economy in ways that imperiled both the fortunes of the
rich and the survival of the poor. The glory attached to whichever
commander could defeat such a hated king would be exceeded only
by the amount of plunder he could bring back. Although Roman
commanders had already plundered some of the ancient cities in
Asia, wealthy centers like Ephesus remained untouched by Roman
armies. When these cities chose to side with Mithridates, their trea-
sures were now fair game for a Roman general and his soldiers.

The Senate had apparently already decided before the consular
election for the year 88 BC that the war against Mithridates would
be entrusted to one of the consuls chosen for that year. But, when
the Mithridates command fell to Sulla, he understood immediately that Fortune had again favored him. Sulla had already become a rich and powerful man, but the Asian command promised
to catapult him to levels of wealth and power that few Romans
ever achieved. And for Sulla's soldiers, the campaign offered precious income that could help them personally weather Rome's dramatic economic crisis.

Sulla's political rivals understood all of this as well. As the year
88 began, a range of prominent figures moved to get the Mithridates command transferred from Sulla. Marius presented the most
significant challenge. Although Marius himself held no office that
year, he was able to form an alliance with the tribune Sulpicius.
A slippery figure, Sulpicius spent the early part of 88 slithering
from the side of the established senatorial aristocracy to that of
Marius as he shopped for allies willing to back an electoral reform
proposal. Sulpicius wanted to redistribute the new citizens created

by the Social War settlement across all the Roman voting tribes, rather than grouping them in new tribes of their own. Sulpicius hoped that this move would create a powerful electoral bloc that could back him in later campaigns. But Sulpicius was not one to take chances and, when opposition to the proposal emerged from older Roman citizens who feared a loss of voting power, Sulpicius recruited a private army of as many as three thousand supporters who he armed with swords. Some of these men served as Sulpicius's bodyguards and the rest remained ready to deploy when the occasion required it. Soon the clashes between Sulpicius's armed supporters and his opponents became so severe that the consuls ordered a halt to public business.[26]

Sulpicius had begun his political career as a moderate, but the violence that accompanied his tribal reforms pushed him in a radical direction.[27] He eventually fell into an alliance with Marius. Backed by his mob, Sulpicius proposed a law to the *concilium plebis* that would take the command against Mithridates from Sulla and give it to his new ally Marius. The law itself drew upon recent precedent. Indeed, it is probably no accident that Sulpicius's law mirrored the popular votes that had stripped Metellus of his command against Jugurtha in 107 and that had deprived Servilius Caepio of his military authority during the war with the Cimbri and Teutones in 104.[28] Both of these commands, of course, also eventually went to Marius. And both of the disgraced commanders later found themselves expelled from the Senate and forced into exile.

Sulla clearly understood what passage of this law would mean. So did his supporters. As people loyal to Sulla came out to oppose a vote on the law, they confronted Sulpicius's partisans amid growing violence. In response, Sulla and his consular colleague declared an indefinite suspension of public business until tensions could be calmed. Sulpicius then summoned his armed supporters, publicly declared the holiday illegal, and roused the mob into such a frenzy that it began to call for the murder of Sulla and his colleague.

Both consuls fled, though the mob caught the son of Sulla's colleague and murdered him. Fearing for his life, Sulla proclaimed an end to the suspension of public business and then escaped to join his troops, who were still encamped outside the city of Nola. Sulpicius's mob had won Marius the Mithridates command.

Sulla then made a decision that would change Roman history. Sulpicius had used a private army to steal his command and give it to Marius. But Sulla now found himself camped among an even larger, more powerful, and more motivated group of supporters—the Roman army he commanded. If law was now made through violence and intimidation, Sulla could play this game too—and he had much more potent weapons than Sulpicius. When news about Sulla's deposition reached his soldiers, Sulla called them together and condemned the great indignity that had been inflicted on him. He asked the soldiers to affirm that they would continue to obey any orders he gave. Fearing "that they would miss the campaign [against Mithridates], they uttered boldly what Sulla desired and ordered him to lead them to Rome."[29] This horrified the officers who served under Sulla. All but one of them left the army and fled to the city "because they could not accept leading an army against their homeland." But Sulla remained undeterred. He had thousands of men willing to march on the city with him. He could ignore a few disloyal commanders.

Reports quickly reached Rome that Sulla had elected to march on the city rather than trust his fate to a political process that had eventually humiliated and exiled the last two men to have their commands stripped by a popular vote. Three embassies were sent out from the city, each more frenzied than the last, but Sulla did not slow his advance. Finally, when Sulla's forces neared Rome, he agreed to discuss the situation with Marius, Sulpicius, and the Senate in the Campus Martius, an assembly space dedicated to the god Mars along the Tiber just north of the city walls. Marius then pleaded for additional time. Understanding that Marius hoped to use this delay to prepare a defense of the city, Sulla agreed to the request and, as soon as the senatorial envoys left, resumed his march on Rome.

Sulla's armies quickly took control of two of the eastern gates of the city wall. Sulla himself advanced into the city. Marius and Sulpicius could only field an improvised defense force, which Sulla defeated on the Esquiline Hill. When it became clear that they would not prevail, Marius, and those of his supporters who could do so, fled. The only other resistance that Sulla encountered came from

6.1. The Esquiline Gate of the Servian Wall. Photo by Manasi Watts.

civilians who hurled missiles at his advancing troops. Sulla ended this by ordering his archers to aim flaming arrows at the rooftops of the wooden buildings from which the barrages originated. It was the first time in over four hundred years that a Roman army had taken the lives and destroyed the property of other Romans.[30]

His actions thus far were unprecedented, but once in control of the city, Sulla acted with surprising restraint. Although the city had been taken by force, Sulla made a point of publicizing that he punished all of his soldiers who looted or otherwise behaved criminally. He quickly called a public assembly in which he claimed to have freed the city from the control of dangerous demagogues and described his attack on Rome as a necessary step to restore the Republic. Sulla's restoration of the Republic apparently involved two steps. He first undid the damage lately wrought by the "demagogues" Marius and Sulpicius by annulling the laws of Sulpicius that had stripped him of his command and placed Marius in charge of the Mithridates campaign. He then marked Marius, Sulpicius, and ten associates as public enemies, a sentence that condemned them to death but that, in practice, forced them into exile and authorized the confiscation of their property.[31]

Second, Sulla took steps that he believed would prevent such demagoguery from happening again. He put in place new rules that limited the power of tribunes like Sulpicius to summon assemblies to pass laws, he refused to redistribute the new Italian citizens across all voting tribes as Sulpicius had promised, and he replaced the commander of the largest Roman army in Italy with one loyal to him. Sulla stayed in Rome long enough to supervise the consular elections for 87 BC and secure a public oath of allegiance from Cinna, one of the newly elected consuls. Sulla then set off for the East and the war with Mithridates.

It is unclear what Sulla thought he had accomplished. It is possible that he believed that marching a Roman army into the city against the orders of the Senate was simply an escalation of the pattern of political violence that had begun under the Gracchi.

Sulla's behavior after taking the city is evidence for this interpretation of his actions. He remained consul and, after he compelled the Senate to restore his command against Mithridates and annul the laws of Sulpicius, he and his army left to go campaign in the East as they had originally planned. It does not seem that Sulla immediately understood that he had done something quite different from what Saturninus and Sulpicius had done in recent years.

Everyone else in Rome, however, appreciated that the Republic had now entered a new stage.[32] Sulla had shown that the sort of armies of poor soldiers that Marius had debuted in the 100s would choose loyalty to their commanders over loyalty to the Republic if the commander was sufficiently inspiring and the material benefits were great enough. Whereas Roman armies had once been akin to public utilities that commanders borrowed to achieve the honors and offices by winning wars, Sulla showed that these armies could be made into private weapons that individual commanders might deploy in Rome's internal political struggles. Although Sulla might claim that he had acted to protect Rome from a demagogue, his rationalizations would not change the fact that Roman soldiers had just killed other Romans, not for the benefit of their country but for the pride of their commander. They demonstrated that Sulla's army was loyal to Sulla, not to Rome.

This lesson was not lost on Sulla's rivals. Sulpicius had been killed soon after Sulla took the city, and Sulla ordered his severed head to be mounted on the Rostra as a warning to any other golden-tongued demagogues in the city. Marius and the other exiles, however, fled Rome and regrouped, "ready to do what Sulla had done and use force to take over their homeland."[33] As soon as Sulla departed for the East, Italy again exploded. Despite his previous pledge of allegiance, Cinna turned on Sulla, took control of the Campanian army Sulla had entrusted to a loyalist, and then joined forces with an army of freed slaves and newly enfranchised Etruscans that Marius had raised in Etruria. As these two armies moved on Rome, those in the Senate loyal to Sulla sent word to

the commander of another Roman army still fighting the Samnites in Southern Italy to make peace with them and march back
to Rome. The Samnites, perhaps aware of what the Etruscans had
gained from aligning with Marius, refused to come to terms. Instead, they reached an agreement with an envoy sent by Cinna
in which they received Roman citizenship and the right to retain
any plunder they had taken in the Social War. Once the pact was
sealed, the Samnites too sent troops to support Cinna.[34]

Both Marius and Cinna had quickly learned the lessons of
Sulla's march on Rome. The Etruscans and Samnites they commanded were not agents of the Republic. The Etruscans had very
nearly rebelled against Rome just three years before, and the
Samnites had suddenly transformed from the last enemies still
fighting the Social War to Roman citizens participating in a civil
war. None of these soldiers marched on Rome to save the Republic from tyranny, as Sulla claimed his soldiers had done. They
marched instead because commanders to whom they were personally loyal had asked them to do so. And they were eager to fight on
their commanders' behalf. After fierce fighting between the Marian forces and the Sullan defenders outside of Rome, the Senate
agreed to remove the legal sanction against Marius and opened
Rome's gates to him and to Cinna.

Marius and Cinna entered the city and again followed the
path that Sulla had charted. They first pushed through a repeal of
all laws backed by their opponents. Then, like Sulla, they ordered
the execution of those Sullan loyalists who had opposed them.
They had, however, learned from Sulla that it was dangerous to
allow these men to flee. The condemned were instead rounded up
and their bodies were treated just as that of Sulpicius had been.
The heads of Octavius, Cinna's colleague as consul in 87 who remained loyal to Sulla, and Merula, the replacement consul the
Senate named after Cinna turned on Sulla, were soon mounted
on the Rostra alongside those of a host of other former consuls
and senators. After the bloodshed and looting abated, Marius and

Cinna had themselves appointed consuls for the year 86 BC. But Marius would not long survive this ignoble victory. He died less than a month after his seventh consulship began in January of 86 BC. The settlement of Italian affairs and the task of dealing with the specter of Sulla was then left to Cinna.[35]

Sulla was in no hurry to return to Italy and confront Cinna, in large part because he could not afford to leave the East without some sort of victory and some plunder for his soldiers. Indeed, the situation in the East had deteriorated dramatically by the time that Sulla had arrived. The turmoil in Rome in 88 BC allowed Mithridates to send a commander into Greece and stir up revolts in previously loyal cities like Athens. This forced Sulla to campaign in the East until 84 BC, eventually succeeding in pushing Mithridates out of Greece and, ultimately, back from Roman territory in Asia. These campaigns were both incredibly destructive and quite lucrative for the soldiers in Sulla's victorious army. Athens was sacked and its wealth distributed among Sulla's officers and soldiers. So too was the treasury at Delphi. Plutarch, who would serve as a priest in Delphi nearly two centuries after these events, wrote that Sulla did these things because he felt compelled to cater to the demands of his soldiers and thereby to "corrupt and win over to himself the soldiers of other generals."[36] If Plutarch is correct, it shows that Rome's political dysfunction now infected its foreign campaigns as well. There is no doubt, however, that Sulla remained keenly aware that his success in the impending civil war with Cinna's supporters would depend in large part on his ability to appeal to soldiers. His own soldiers needed to be happy with his leadership not just so that they would continue to fight for him but also so that armies led by other Romans might wish to defect to their cause. To Plutarch, this meant that Sulla "encouraged the evils of both treachery and debauchery at the same time."

Sulla's strategy sounds loathsome, but it worked. An army commanded by one of Cinna's associates was crippled by mass defections to Sulla's side when it arrived in Asia in 85. When Cinna tried to raise another army to confront Sulla in Greece in 84, a centurion unwilling to fight in a civil war that promised no plunder stoned Cinna to death. Then, after Sulla's army returned to Italy in the winter of 84–83 BC, Sulla secured the defection of an army that had been under the command of Cinna's ally, the consul Lucius Cornelius Scipio. As Sulla's forces moved toward Rome, his "army grew each day" as soldiers and civilians alike joined what seemed to be the successful campaign of a generous commander.[37]

One group of Sullan opponents remained steadfast. The Samnites, who had rejoined the Roman fold following their agreement with Cinna, fought on, alongside an army of new Roman citizens from Lucania and what remained of the army Cinna had raised. These soldiers knew full well what a Sullan victory would bring. Their resistance was motivated by fear of "destruction, death, confiscation, and wholesale extermination,"[38] but their numbers were too small to offset the continued desertions to Sulla and military setbacks elsewhere in Italy. Sulla ultimately won a decisive victory against them at the Battle of the Colline Gate in 82 BC, a battle that secured the city of Rome for Sulla and ended the resistance of his opponents.[39]

A bloodbath then ensued. Sulla ordered the massacre of six thousand Samnites, who were murdered in the circus at Rome, with the executions timed so that the cries of the condemned would echo through the Temple of Bellona right when Sulla rose to address a terrified Roman Senate. As the dying Samnites screamed outside, Sulla promised to repair the Republic by improving the lot of those who cooperated with him while severely punishing his enemies. Sulla was true to his words. He quickly published a list of forty senators and sixteen hundred Roman *equites* who were to be executed and whose property was to be confiscated, offering rewards to their assassins and to any informer who could help find them. More people across Italy were soon added to the list, as were people suspected of helping or being kind to the proscribed. In some cases, Sulla punished entire communities with heavy fines or the confiscation of tracts of land. The only crime of some of the proscribed seems to have been their possession of a large estate.[40]

The confiscation of such a large quantity of private property at a time of economic crisis gave Sulla immense power to remake the ranks of Rome's economic elites. Sulla used the land and property taken from the victims of the proscriptions to reward his most loyal supporters. Many men of humble backgrounds became spectacularly wealthy because of their connections to Sulla. Other Sullan veterans found themselves settled on land confiscated from Sullan enemies in Etruria, Campania, and elsewhere in Italy. The men who had stood with Sulla as he marched on Rome and fought against his countrymen would now serve as powerful civilian garrisons that could help maintain his control over Italy.[41]

The annihilation of Sulla's political opponents and the economic displacement of many of the Italian communities that had opposed him enabled Sulla to seize complete control of Roman political life. He took for himself the old Republican office of dictator. Previous dictators held that office for a maximum of six months in order to deal with a specific and immediate threat, and they sometimes stepped down early if the threat was neutralized before the term ended. Sulla, however, chose to hold the title indefinitely, for as long as it took him to remake the Republic into something that he deemed functional again. He also tightly controlled all aspects of political life. He allowed consular elections to proceed, but Sulla would not permit anyone he did not first approve to run. In one case, Sulla even ordered the murder of one of his allies in the Forum when the man tried to stand for consul without Sulla's permission.[42]

Sulla designed his new republic to prevent the rise of figures like Marius, Saturninus, and Sulpicius. Marius in particular had built a following by capitalizing on the frustrations that wealthy *equites* had with the seemingly closed and corrupt senatorial order. Many of Rome's most important businessmen were *equites* and, because *equites* sat on the juries that decided cases involving senatorial corruption, they represented an important constituency that, if sufficiently incited, could threaten the elite control of the Republic that Sulla sought to restore. Sulla undercut the ability of any future leaders like Marius to appeal to the *equites* by bringing the richest members of that group into an expanded Senate. These new senators would not really play an important role in senatorial policy deliberations. They would instead largely serve as jurors in cases that once had been judged by equestrian juries.

The most important Sullan reforms attacked the career path followed by Marius (and, probably, anticipated by Saturninus and Sulpicius). All three men had launched themselves into political prominence by advocating for popular causes as tribunes, with Marius using his actions as tribune to build a reputation that eventually brought him the consulship. Sulla shut off this route of political advancement. He decided to prevent any person who held the tribunate from ever holding any other office in the state, transforming the office of tribune from a platform for the ambitious to a final resting place for mediocrities. Tribunes also were forbidden from proposing new laws and even had their ability to veto laws restricted. Other people seeking magistracies were similarly constrained. All magistracies now had a minimum age of eligibility. They also could only be held in a specific order, with a minimum of ten years elapsing between tenures of the same office. In practice, this meant that a man could only become consul if he had not served as a tribune, if he had reached the age of forty, and if he had previously served as a quaestor, an aedile, and a praetor. The route for figures like Marius to take power had always been narrow. Sulla had effectively cut it off.

It is worth pausing to consider why Sulla inflicted such trauma on Romans and their Republic. Appian gives a plausible explanation. As Sulla prepared to move his army back to Italy in the winter of 84–83 BC, Appian reports that he received an embassy from the Senate seeking to negotiate a settlement that would ensure his security and prevent a renewed civil war. Sulla is said to have responded that as long as he had an army he could "provide per-petual security to himself and those exiles who had fled to him," but the Senate could not. "With this single sentence," Appian con-cludes, "he made it clear that he would not dissolve his army, but was instead contemplating seizing power."[43]

Appian is the only historian to report this exchange, but, even if Sulla did not speak these words, he certainly would have under-stood them to be true. Sulla marched on Rome both in 88 and in the winter of 84 because he had more trust in his abilities and his men than he did in the Republic. In 88, he marched because he had seen how the Republic had failed to protect the freedom and property of Metellus from Marius and Saturninus. In 84, he remembered the brutality inflicted on his supporters by Marius and Cinna. The system did not protect those men, and it would not protect him. Sulla, whose good luck was legendary, instead bet that his army would give him security that the Republic could not.

When Sulla made this bet, he reset the calculus of all other Romans. In the third century, political failure in Rome meant ig-nominy or anonymity. Now it meant death. In this new world, when political conflicts became too heated, leaders and followers alike needed to pick sides, raise arms, and fight one another. After Sulla's victory in 88, Marius and Cinna immediately realized that their political survival depended on raising armies more loyal to them than they were to the Republic. Both found Romans willing to join such forces, but they also identified large numbers of Etrus-cans and Samnites fearful of what Sulla would do to them now that the Social War had morphed into a Roman civil war. Sulla, by contrast, found ready followers among Rome's elite—both those who had been condemned by Marius and those who feared they might someday. And, when Sulla ultimately prevailed, the victors rewarded their supporters with the property of the vanquished.

The structures of the old Republic could not support this new social and economic order birthed by violence. For a time, Sulla could hold this new world in place with threats, but it would be sustainable only with a new governing structure that legalized Sulla's theft and normalized the powerful positions of his allies. This was the new Republic Sulla created and, in 80 BC, he resigned the dictatorship confident that his new Republic would protect him better than the old one could. He returned to private life, worked on his memoirs, and trusted that his reforms would endure. Unfortunately for any Roman who hoped that political stability might follow, he was wrong.

CHAPTER 7

REBUILDING AMID THE WRECKAGE

S ULLA'S DECISION TO RECONSTRUCT AN edited version of the Republic after the massive destruction and violence of the Social War and then the civil wars of the 80s prevented Rome from falling into a permanent autocracy. It did not, however, return Rome to the functional republic of the past. With its expanded Senate, neutered tribunate, and senatorial juries, Sulla's Republic was in fact a radical departure from the political system that preceded it—and it was one founded on widespread murder and theft. The historian Sallust, who was a young boy during Sulla's dictatorship, wrote that Sulla's success depended on "crime and treachery since he thinks that he cannot be safe unless he is worse and more detestable than your dread of him."[1] For this reason, Sulla created a climate in which men of "great family names" with "excellent examples among their ancestors"—men who, in different times, would have been comfortable competing for offices and honors within the rules of a functional republic—instead "gave their submission to Sulla in exchange for dominance" over other Romans.[2] Sulla deliberately co-opted these men so that they would share his guilt. He gave them public honors, sponsored them for public offices, and encouraged them to profit from the properties confiscated from the men Sulla proscribed. In some cases, Sulla even fronted these men the money that they used to purchase these confiscated properties. The guilt stained others as well. It was not just co-opted members of the Roman elite who profited from Sulla's proscriptions. He settled tens of thousands of his veterans on lands seized from the proscribed—one source counts 120,000 such men—and elevated many of his former soldiers into the reconstituted Roman Senate. Sallust called these minions who followed Sulla "satellites," a Latin word that meant morally suspect attendants. Sulla had ensured that the guilty were so numerous and powerful that the innocent feared confronting them.[3]

Sulla's powerful venom lingered in the Roman body politic as the 70s dawned, even after his retirement in 79 and his death in 78 removed the figure these "satellites" protected. Indeed, Sulla's departure from the scene only prompted more chaos. Some of those who embraced Sulla opportunistically quickly began to stray once he had no more to offer. Others had entered Sulla's orbit at the head of private armies whose soldiers were loyal primarily to their commanders, secondarily to Sulla, and not at all to Rome. These warlords lurked, some of them still commanding armies and others with enough new wealth that they could assemble another private army if needed. Their example inspired other Sullans to dream about circumstances in which they too might attract a large enough following to build an army of supporters.[4]

Sulla had created many opportunities for such mischief. Outside of Italy, forces loyal to Sulla's opponents in the recent civil war controlled Spain until 72 BC. In the Eastern Mediterranean, Sulla's hasty peace treaty with Mithridates of Pontus in 85 BC had left that king still strong enough to challenge Rome. Roman distraction had also opened the door for pirate raids at sea that could threaten both Rome's food supply and its security.

Sulla's heirs faced even more significant problems within Italy. Italy had yet to fully recover from the Social War, and Sulla had made its recovery much more difficult. While Sulla was in the

East, the regime of Cinna and Carbo held a census. Their work offered the first count of the many new Roman citizens created in Italy by the settlement of the Social War and constructed a basic municipal governing structure that could organize their cities.[5] Sulla's punitive measures undid much of this work. Sulla stripped citizenship from many of the newly enfranchised Romans who had opposed him in the civil wars. More prominent Italians suffered even more serious penalties as Sulla and his allies set about disrupting the historical power and economic orders in their cities. In Umbria, Sulla proscribed Sextus Roscius, a wealthy man who owned thirteen farms, and confiscated his land even though Roscius's son apparently murdered his father in an effort to avoid losing the family property. In the Southern Italian city of Larinum, Oppianicus, a local man acting in Sulla's name, replaced the local municipal board and proscribed many of its members. And an aspiring twenty-three-year-old warlord named Pompey—later to be known as Pompey the Great—did something similar in the towns of his home region of Picenum. These actions enriched Sulla's partisans and left large numbers of prominent and ordinary Italians furious. It was with good reason that Sallust could write that Sulla, "alone of all men of human memory, has devised punishments against later generations, so that they might be assured of injury before being born" by giving the fruits of generations of Italian labors to his supporters.[6]

Further instability grew out of the increasing use of slave labor on some of the large estates carved out of this confiscated property. It remains unclear exactly how much the slave population in Italy increased in the aftermath of Sulla's victory in the civil wars, but there is undeniable evidence that the political chaos of the late 90s and 80s led Roman senators to enslave some free Italians who, by the end of the Social War, should have been Roman citizens.[7] By the 70s, it seems that large populations of agricultural slaves (some of whom were formerly free Italians) worked some of the best land in Campania and other parts of Southern Italy, in many cases alongside some of the Italians whose families had been stripped of property and citizen rights by Sulla. Sulla had ripped up the basic social compacts that protected the life, freedom, and property rights of Italians and Romans in order to create a new Italy dominated by his supporters. Even the Italian farmers who kept their land struggled to compete economically with the larger and more efficient farming operations that some of their Sullan neighbors put together.

Tensions even simmered in Rome itself. Sulla had eliminated the financial supports for grain purchases that helped many urban residents pay for food, and he had lifted the price controls that kept grain from becoming too expensive. The lack of ambitious and capable tribunes who could make law or effectively advocate for the city's population prompted many urban residents to see rioting as the only option available for them to express their displeasure with rising food prices. The powers of tribunes and larger questions of political representation thus became increasingly contentious issues.[8]

Any one of these challenges had the potential to unravel the post-Sullan Republic and, during the years between 78 and 70, each of them posed a real threat to Roman stability. The problems began as soon as Sulla died. Catulus and Lepidus, the consuls elected for the year 78, immediately began arguing about whether Sulla should be given a state funeral. Sulla had opposed Lepidus's consular candidacy and, perhaps in response, Lepidus fought hard against giving Sulla the public commemoration, unprecedented in its lavishness, that he ultimately received with Catulus's support. A funeral procession composed of armed men, enthusiastic new senators, and people "afraid of his army" led Sulla's body to the Forum.[9]

After the funeral, Lepidus began agitating more aggressively against Catulus and the other Sullan supporters. He backed a measure to reinstate the distribution of subsidized grain in the city. He promised to restore to Italians the land that Sulla had taken from them. Despite strongly opposing a similar measure just a few months prior, he now advocated publicly for the restoration of the powers of the tribunes.[10]

This was an inopportune moment to have such divisions arise between the consuls. In Faesulae, a city located in the hills above the modern city of Florence, the people who had lost their land to the Sullan appropriations attacked those of his veterans who had been settled to colonize the area. Fearing a larger revolt in Etruria, the Senate directed Lepidus and Catulus to lead armies into the region and suppress the uprising, apparently ignoring rumors in Rome that "all Etruria was suspected of being inclined to revolt alongside Lepidus."[11] Things proceeded as one would expect. Although the Faesulae violence did not ultimately metastasize into a wider revolt, this seems to have happened more because Lepidus enlisted the rebels to support his own ambitions than because the two consuls worked together to suppress them.

Backed by these insurgents, Lepidus pushed his quarrel with Catulus even more aggressively. As the tensions between the consuls increased, the Senate intervened and compelled both consuls to swear an oath to keep the peace. It then attempted to further defuse the situation by sending Lepidus to govern Transalpine Gaul.[12] Lepidus set out to his province with no intention of returning to Rome before his term of office ended. Suspecting that Lepidus might be planning to build forces to eventually attack the city, the Senate soon summoned him back to Rome to superintend the consular elections for the year 78. Lepidus instead returned to Rome at the head of an army of Roman soldiers and insurgents from Etruria, demanding that he be awarded a second consulship. When he was prevented from bringing the army into the city, he ordered his men to take up arms. They were quickly defeated and Lepidus soon killed, but the survivors of his army fled Italy to join the anti-Sullan Roman commander Sertorius in Spain.[13]

Everyone in Rome recognized that Lepidus had attempted a rather clumsy, but still quite dangerous, imitation of Sulla. Although Lepidus had lacked the support, resources, and strategic intelligence to actually take control of Rome, he had come far closer than a man like him should have. His attempt underlined the inherent instability of the new political order that Sulla had created. And it escaped no one's notice that, even in defeat, Lepidus's supporters had still managed to reinforce the army of Sertorius in Spain.[14]

Things would not improve over the next few years. A grain shortage in 75 hit the city of Rome, Roman territory in Gaul, and even Rome's armies fighting in Spain. The Roman commanders battling Sertorius threatened to return to Italy if the Senate did not send additional supplies for the troops.[15] In Rome, the food shortage caused a different sort of problem. Stripped of a tribunate with the capacity to effectively address the problems of regular citizens and stuck with a political system designed to minimize their ability to influence policy, Romans reacted to the spike in food prices with the only weapon they still had. They took to the streets. The protests in 75 seem to have been spontaneous (and apparently leaderless) eruptions of popular frustration, but they were no less dangerous than the armed gangs mobilized by figures like Saturninus and Sulpicius in the 90s and 80s. At one point, hungry citizens attacked the consuls Gaius Cotta and Lucius Octavius when they were escorting a member of the Metellus family into the Forum. They overwhelmed the lictors (the civil servants who acted as bodyguards for the consuls and other magistrates who held imperium) and forced the consuls to flee to safety in Octavius's home.[16]

This protest had some important immediate effects on the Republic. Sallust describes Cotta changing into mourning clothes, addressing the crowd, telling them that war requires civilians to sacrifice, and then offering himself up for punishment if they felt that food prices had surged because of misconduct by the consuls. His dramatic display apparently calmed the situation for a time, as did a subsequent decision to send military forces against the pirates in the Eastern Mediterranean who had supposedly caused the grain shortage.[17] But the consuls and Senate recognized that this issue, or one like it, would erupt again if they did not tweak the Sullan system. Cotta took the first step by pushing forward a law, the *lex Aurelia*, that removed the restriction Sulla had placed on tribunes of the plebs ever holding another magistracy. In 73, the consuls sponsored a grain law that gave a limited number of citizens a small monthly grain allowance.[18] The Republic was slowly stumbling back toward the old order that Sulla had tried to replace.

These steps did not calm political life in the city of Rome or outside of it. Popular agitation for a more robust tribunate that was again able to propose legislation on which the people would vote grew as the 70s progressed. In 73, the tribune Macer argued vehemently for a full restoration of the traditional powers of the people and their tribunes. When Sallust dramatized this moment, he described a speech that contrasted "the rights left to you by your forefathers and the slavery imposed on you by Sulla" and exhorted Romans "not to change the names of things to suit your own cowardice" by "substituting the term 'tranquility' for 'slavery.'"[19] By 71, this call for a full restoration of the tribunate and the legislative powers it once possessed had become a centerpiece of successful consular campaigns. But no consul had yet been able to actually restore the pre-Sullan powers of the tribunes.

Outside of Rome, the Republic continued to be buffeted by the grinding war with Sertorius in Spain and then, in 73 BC, by a slave revolt led by the Thracian gladiator Spartacus. Both the Sertorian war and the Spartacus revolt found fuel in the anger of those left behind by the post-Sullan Republic. In Spain, Sertorius commanded an army made up both of Spaniards and of Romans who had fled from Sulla or his successors. In Italy, Spartacus mobilized tens of thousands of slaves from the gladiatorial training schools, farms, and plantations in the south of the peninsula. A not inconsiderable number of free Italians also fled their work in the fields to join his force, dramatically highlighting the desperation among those hit hardest by the Sullan land confiscations. Rome would ultimately put down both revolts. The Sertorian war ended after Perpenna, one of the followers of Lepidus who fled to Spain, turned on and assassinated Sertorius, and was then himself defeated in battle by Pompey. Spartacus defeated two armies commanded by praetors and, in 72 BC, a force jointly commanded by the two consuls, but his revolt was suppressed and most of his followers killed following a series of defeats in 71 BC inflicted on him by Crassus, another Sullan supporter from an elite family who, like Pompey, first came to prominence by recruiting a private army that served the dictator. After Crassus defeated Spartacus's army on the battlefield, Pompey then slaughtered the survivors as they fled toward Northern Italy.[20]

Sertorius and Spartacus both lost, but the conflicts they sparked emphasized to all that Sulla's Republic remained weak. Not only did significant resentment still course through Rome and its empire, but, more than a decade after Sulla's victory, the Republic still had not fully rebuilt the public monopoly on the use of violence that the dictator had destroyed. It could suppress revolts and stop riots eventually, but it had not shown the ability to prevent them from occurring in the first place. And, when violence erupted, Rome still had to depend on Pompey and Crassus, two of the warlords whose wealth and privately recruited armies had brought Sulla to power. It was not clear that the Republic could survive without such men. Even more alarming, as Pompey and Crassus led their victorious armies toward the city following the end of the Spartacus revolt in 71, many in Rome doubted that the Republic had the ability to stop them from bringing their armies into the field against one another, should the two rivals decide to do so. If Pompey or Crassus wanted one, the formal power of the state could likely do nothing to prevent another civil war.

Pompey seemed the more frightening of the two. He was the son of Gnaeus Pompeius Strabo, a cruel and calculating man who was the first in his immediate family to achieve senatorial

status and to win a consulship. Strabo had earned this office in
89 BC by combining undeniable military skill with a mastery of
Roman power politics. Strabo was committed to holding power
through the normal offices and military commands the Republic sanctioned, but he was not averse to securing these offices and
commands through the implicit threat of extraconstitutional
action. Strabo's background required him to play this outsider's
game—and he played it expertly. Thrust into command by the
emergencies of the Social War, Strabo rode military success in the
year 90 BC to the consulship in 89. He then retained command of
his army as proconsul in 88, sat out Sulla's initial attack on Rome,
and killed the man Sulla sent to take over his command in 88 BC.
Strabo retained command of his army through the year 86, fighting both for and against Cinna in the hope that he could prolong
the conflict, profit from the fighting, and use his army as a chip to
bargain for a second consulship. He died before any deal could be
struck, but his greed and disregard for the public good infuriated
those in Rome who nervously waited for public order to return.
His power had ensured that Strabo remained unassailable in life,
but nothing constrained people from expressing their anger after his death. As his funeral procession wound through the city, a
crowd pulled his body down from the bier and dragged it through
the filthy streets.[21]

Pompey was twenty years old when his father died, young
enough that he could have tried to sit out the civil war but intelligent enough to realize that he would be unlikely to survive un-
scathed if he did. His father had died a hated man, but he had left
his son some considerable advantages, including the money and
lands in the central Italian region of Picenum that he had used to
build a network of loyal clients. Pompey understood that Strabo
had used these reservoirs of wealth and supporters to consolidate a
particular sort of power in the tottering Republic of the early 80s.
Pompey knew too that they would be vital if he hoped to survive
and thrive during the looming civil war.[22]

Pompey also had learned how to play power politics from his father. Strabo never had the power that Sulla or Marius or Cinna did, and he knew that he would be soundly defeated if he had followed their lead and tried to seize Rome. He could not take power extraconstitutionally. But the threat that he might try to do so allowed Strabo to name the price for his continued cooperation with the Republic. He was savvy enough to realize that, if the price he set involved an office or a command that seemed consistent with normal Republican practices, it was likely to be met.

Pompey took these lessons to heart. Immediately after his father's death, the family home was ransacked and Pompey himself was put on trial for personally taking plunder during the capture of the city of Asculum that rightfully belonged to the Republic. But Pompey proved to be both too valuable and too charismatic to convict. The future consul Carbo was among the senators to defend Pompey, and Pompey so charmed the man presiding over the trial, P. Antistius, that he ended up engaged to his daughter Antistia. The wedding took place four days after Pompey's inevitable acquittal.[23]

Pompey remained allied with Cinna, Carbo, and the Sullan opposition until 84 BC, but, perhaps sensing the erosion in Cinna's position, Pompey left their camp just before the revolt that led to Cinna's death, later claiming that he had heard rumors of plots against his own life. He retreated to Picenum and waited to see how the civil conflict developed. When he heard of Sulla's landing in Italy, Pompey decided to side with Sulla. Many elites fled to Sulla alone or with their families, but Pompey had learned from his father's example. He knew that he could capitalize on changing sides in the civil war only if he approached Sulla with something substantial. Pompey thus marshaled his supporters in Picenum and urged them to revolt against the senatorial regime headed by Carbo. Pompey set himself at the head of a tribunal in the city of Auximum, ordered the city magistrates loyal to Carbo to leave, and then "proceeded to raise troops and appointed centurions and officers for them." Once he had collected troops in Auximum, he then did the same thing in all of the neighboring cities in the district. This legion would serve Sulla, but it was recruited and paid by Pompey. In due course, he would add to his army two more legions of soldiers drawn from the district.[24]

Pompey moved toward Sulla, fighting a number of engagements with enemy forces on his way to ensure that Sulla knew the quality of the support Pompey brought. When Pompey arrived at Sulla's camp, he offered Sulla the army he had recruited, the loyalty of the district from which it came, and the promise of additional troops should Sulla need them. In response, Sulla rose, uncovered his head, and greeted the twenty-three-year-old general as "imperator," a title that conveyed his respect for what Pompey had already achieved as a commander. Sulla then sent Pompey and his forces to Cisalpine Gaul to help Metellus Pius root out resistance there.[25]

When Sulla had nearly secured control of Italy, he tasked Pompey and his army with defeating those of his opponents who controlled Sicily and North Africa. The Senate voted Pompey some form of imperium over Sicily, a step that, for the first time, gave Pompey the official standing to command what remained of his private army. Pompey first defeated Carbo in 82, then took the province of Africa from Cn. Domitius Ahenobarbus, capturing and executing both men despite the fact that Carbo was still serving as consul. In Carbo's case, Pompey added even greater indignity by binding the consul in heavy chains and ensuring that he soiled himself just before the execution took place. Both were enemies of Sulla and certainly subject to death, but the brutal way in which they were executed shocked people to such a degree that Pompey earned the nickname *adulescentulus carnifex*, or "the teenaged butcher." Pompey, however, realized that harsh vengeance against a few leading men gave him the chance to show mercy to others and, potentially, transform those who survived into his own supporters. He used the victories in Sicily and North Africa to build relationships with people in those provinces who might later prove useful to him.[26]

Pompey's successes in battle and his skill in building a network of political allies outside of Italy seems to have disquieted Sulla. Pompey was not strong enough to directly threaten the dictator, but Sulla decided it was prudent to try to domesticate the young commander before he became capable of such a challenge. In 82, Sulla persuaded (or perhaps compelled) Pompey to divorce Antistia, the daughter of the judge at his trial, and instead marry Sulla's stepdaughter Aemilia, a match that Sulla had enabled by forcing Aemilia's husband to divorce her. Sulla hoped that this marriage would bind Pompey both to Sulla and to Aemilia's Metellan relatives, but Aemilia's death soon afterward while giving birth to a child fathered by her ex-husband thwarted this plan.[27]

After the defeat of Domitius in Africa, Sulla took an even stronger action. He ordered Pompey to send two of his legions back to Italy, with Pompey staying in Africa with his one remaining legion until another general came to replace him. Sulla evidently hoped that this would offer a way to integrate Pompey's private army back into the military structure of the Roman state by removing his soldiers from the commander to whom they were personally loyal. Perhaps just as importantly, this would diminish Pompey's power. Pompey had never held any Roman office and, though he had been given a command by the Senate, Pompey's authority over what remained a private army derived from the force of his personality and the power of his family, not the authority of Rome. Sulla knew that, if Pompey could be induced to relinquish command of his army, he would return to Italy extremely (and possibly fatally) diminished.

Pompey knew this too. He reacted to Sulla's orders much as his father would have, though with considerably more skill than Strabo ever managed. Pompey allowed news of the recall to spread among his army without publicly reacting to it. The soldiers quickly became alarmed, claiming that "they would never forsake their general" and telling Pompey "never to trust himself to the tyrant."[28] Pompey then called an assembly of the soldiers in which he asked his men to follow Sulla's orders, telling them that to do anything else would be treasonous. But it was likely clear to all that, despite what Pompey had said, he really hoped the army would refuse Sulla. And they did. When his words had no effect on the mood of the army, Pompey retired to his tent. As his legions continued to noisily demand that Pompey refuse Sulla's order, he reemerged in their midst and "swore solemnly that he would kill himself if they forced him to act as they hoped he would."[29]

Pompey had not revolted, but when word got back to Sulla about this display of loyalty by his men, it was enough to convince him that there was significant danger in compelling Pompey's army to leave their commander. He instead allowed Pompey and his private army to return to Italy together and, when the twenty-four-year-old commander arrived, Sulla greeted him as "Pompeius Magnus," Pompey the Great. Even this, though, was not enough to make up for the effort to take away Pompey's army, and Pompey responded to Sulla's welcome with a brazen request that Sulla grant him a triumph. Such a thing was unprecedented. Pompey was far younger than any commander who had ever celebrated a triumph, he had won his victory with an army that he commanded without holding any Roman office, and Pompey was not even a member of the Senate. Sulla pointed out to Pompey that granting him a triumph would be illegal, because Roman law reserved triumphs for consuls or praetors, and he told Pompey that he would personally oppose the request and prevent the triumph if Pompey persisted in asking for it.[30]

Pompey persisted. He told Sulla to remember that "more people worship the rising sun than the setting sun," implying that Pompey's star was on the rise while Sulla's was soon to be eclipsed.[31] Pompey was again playing his father's game, this time leveraging both his personal potential and the loyalty of his troops to secure for himself an honor the Republic had always reserved for a very different sort of commander. Sulla again relented. Pompey then staged a spectacular triumph that impressed Romans even though the narrowness of the city gate forced Pompey to abandon his plan to enter the city in a chariot drawn not by horses but by four African elephants.[32]

Pompey dismissed his army just before the triumph, and upon his return to Rome, he married his third wife Mucia (who like Aemilia had connections to both Sulla and the Metelli) in 79 BC. That year also saw Pompey make a strategic decision to break ranks with Sulla and back Lepidus in his campaign for the consulship of 78, a decision perhaps prompted by an expectation that Pompey would benefit from the political disorder Lepidus's victory would create.[33] Although Pompey did intervene against Lepidus's efforts to prevent Sulla's public funeral, his support for Lepidus so infuriated Sulla that, before the former dictator's death, he cut Pompey out of his will.[34]

The events of 79 and early 78 offered Pompey a chance to become something more than Sulla's *adulescentulus carnifex*. He had carefully managed to position himself in the middle between Lepidus, whom he had supported for consul, and the Sullans, whom he had supported in their push for a public funeral. Pompey's exclusion from Sulla's will emphasized that he truly belonged to neither camp but had instead carved out a place in the pragmatic middle between them. This made it natural that, when the Senate condemned Lepidus as a public enemy following his rebellion, it also granted imperium to Pompey to command an army that would help the consul Catulus suppress the rebellion.[35]

Although the Senate had given Pompey this command, he nevertheless refused the call of the consul Catulus to dismiss his army after the initial defeat of Lepidus. Instead, he pressed on to attack, defeat, and execute M. Junius Brutus, the Lepidan ally who governed Cisalpine Gaul. Then, after refusing again to dismiss his army, Pompey sought and received senatorial sanction to pursue those of Lepidus's forces that had joined Sertorius in Spain.

His military authority now shifted from the emergency imperium granted so that he might suppress Lepidus to a command akin to that exercised by a consul, with a status to match. The army he commanded was no longer a private force recruited by a private citizen. It was instead an army of the Republic that Pompey commanded legally with senatorial sanction. Pompey, however, cleverly hedged his position to ensure that this command would not be taken away easily. Until the food shortages of 75–74 made it untenable, Pompey elected to use his own money to pay the salaries of his troops and the expenses of the campaign, a situation that was both publicly known and undoubtedly an excellent way to build loyalty among the soldiers. He also continued the pattern he established in Sicily and North Africa of building relationships with influential people in Spain and, in some cases, even sponsoring grants of Roman citizenship to them. After Sertorius's death and the petering out of his rebellion, the consuls of the year 72 ratified Pompey's extensions of citizenship and thereby more closely joined these Spanish notables to their patron. Pompey also took the dramatic step of burning a set of papers given to him by Perpenna, the old ally of both Lepidus and Sertorius, that supposedly documented treasonous activities by a large number of senators. Though these alleged traitors were not bound to Pompey in the way that his Spanish clients were, they too undoubtedly owed him a debt of gratitude.[36]

When Pompey returned to Rome following his defeat of what remained of Spartacus's rebels in 71 BC, he did so as the most powerful man in the Republic. He led an experienced and loyal army, he possessed numerous supporters both within Italy and across Rome's western provinces, and he had even joined the growing calls for the full restoration of the tribunate as a way to build even greater popular support.[37] Pompey could have perhaps seized power at that moment, but he did not want or need to do so. Instead, he chose to stand for the consulship of the year 70, despite the fact that, under the terms set by Sulla's reforms, he was too young and had held none of the lower offices that legally qualified one to be consul. But this did not matter. Pompey was capable, popular, and likeable. He had worked to build ties with members of the traditional Roman elite and had also developed a profile that endeared him to the Roman masses. He was, Sallust memorably remarked, "moderate to all things except domination." As Pompey embarked on his campaign for the consulship, his moderation served to put a virtuous face on the "shameless heart" that had fueled his rise.[38]

Crassus, Pompey's most formidable competitor for the consulship in 70, brought different qualities to the campaign. The son of P. Licinius Crassus, a former consul and censor who had held a triumph in Rome, Crassus came from a well-established Roman family that had been deeply affected by the Marian and Cinnan capture of Italy in 87 BC. When the city of Rome fell, Crassus's father elected to commit suicide rather than be killed by the victors. Soldiers loyal to the new regime then killed Crassus's brother.[39] Crassus avoided death by fleeing to Spain and staying there until he heard about Sulla's imminent return to Italy. Like Pompey, Crassus decided to personally recruit an army that he could lead to Sulla and place in his service. He selected twenty-five hundred men out of a larger group of volunteers and sailed to North Africa to join up with the pro-Sullan forces Metellus Pius commanded there. Crassus soon left Africa and met up with Sulla in Italy.

Although Crassus and Pompey both came to Sulla leading armies, the reception the two men received from Sulla differed dramatically. Pompey was younger than Crassus, but he presented Sulla with twice as many men as Crassus and, unlike the troops Crassus commanded, Pompey's forces had already proved their worth in battles within Italy. Whereas Sulla greeted Pompey as an imperator, Sulla treated Crassus as a noticeably less influential figure. Crassus further diminished his standing in Sulla's eyes when he took for himself most of the plunder from the capture of an Umbrian city during the civil war. Even Crassus's heroic actions that secured

Sulla's victory at the Battle of Colline Gate did not fully make up for the damage to his reputation that his greed had caused.[40]

Crassus continued profiting from his association with Sulla after the latter's victory in the civil war. He was one of the most eager and strategic buyers of property taken from the proscribed. It was even said that he personally added people to the proscription lists in order to secure their property. Over time, he diversified his holdings to include mines, farmland, and even many of Rome's notorious tenements, which he renovated or rebuilt using a large team of slaves trained as architects and builders.[41]

Crassus saw his wealth as a tool to enhance his political power.[42] After his experience in the 80s, Crassus understood that money could buy military protection and often commented that one was not wealthy unless he could buy a legion.[43] But Crassus also appreciated that extreme wealth had other, more subtle applications in the post-Sullan Republic. Sulla's expansion of the Senate had made senators of men from families without any history of Roman officeholding. Even though Sulla surely expected these new senators to serve primarily as jurors, the fact that they now shared the same rank as scions of old Roman families like Metellus Pius inspired many of them to compete for public offices their ancestors could not have dreamed of reaching. Aspiration was costly, however, and Crassus set himself up as the lender of last resort to those who wished to chase high office. Crassus bankrolled the political campaigns of Sulla's new senators and their peers, offering interest-free loans as well as the strategic application of his political influence. Crassus argued cases for them, appointed them as officers during his campaign against Spartacus, and even allowed them to advertise his support for their legislation when Crassus's backing might conceivably aid a law's passage.[44] These men became Crassus's political allies, bound to him by a loyalty he either bought or earned.

Crassus understood that his wealth could also help him build a following among ordinary Roman voters. Plutarch wrote that "his home was open to all" and at his regular dinner parties, "the people he invited were ordinary people not members of great families." Crassus served inexpensive meals, but "they were good and there was a friendliness about them which made them more agreeable than the most lavish entertainments."[45]

It seems that Crassus chose to develop this sort of public profile in part because he realized that he would never be able to achieve the notoriety as a military commander that Pompey did. Whereas Pompey built his reputation through a series of military commands he secured without ever being elected to office, Crassus channeled his power and influence toward elected offices within the constitutional framework of the post-Sullan Republic. He made alliances with tribunes, secured election to a praetorship, and was given an enhanced command when he took over the war against Spartacus from the discredited former consul Cassius Longinus.[46] Pompey had expanded his influence by seizing command of armies without the formal constraints of an office; Crassus used his network of political supporters to climb the ladder of Republican offices until he gained a prestigious military command. Perhaps because Crassus had received his command through a regular political process, he ran the army he led against Spartacus differently from how Pompey commanded his forces. Pompey understood that his authority derived in large part from the enthusiasm that his soldiers had for serving under him. If this enthusiasm diminished, Pompey's soldiers would never go along when their commander sought to defy orders by holding on to command. Crassus, however, entered the war with six new legions and assumed command of the soldiers remaining in the two consular legions that Spartacus had defeated earlier in 72 BC. His authority over this army came from the office he held, not his personal popularity with the soldiers. This freed him to take dramatic steps to restore discipline.

Discipline would prove essential in defeating the slave rebellion. Much of Spartacus's success against earlier Roman commanders had been due to the terror that his troops inspired in

Roman soldiers. His followers had nothing to lose—they would either die fighting the Romans or be executed by the Romans if they surrendered—so they fought with a ferocity that the first Roman levies sent to confront them could not match. Crassus saw the danger this posed early in the campaign when two legions under the command of one of Crassus's deputies broke, dropped their arms, and fled. In response to the mass desertion, Crassus revived the old, draconian Roman punishment of decimation: he took five hundred of the survivors, divided them into fifty groups of ten men, and then executed one man chosen randomly from each group. The Roman levies understood that they now faced a difficult battle if they fought but brutal punishments if they fled.[47]

This tactic could not have made Crassus beloved by his soldiers, but they did fight hard and effectively for him during the campaigning season in 72 BC and into the winter of 72–71. Crassus first prevented Spartacus from crossing to Sicily and then pinned him in Southern Italy for most of the winter. By the spring of 71, Roman reinforcements were entering Italy from both the east and, as Pompey's Spanish army returned to Italy, from the north. Crassus decided to try to force a decisive battle with Spartacus before anyone arrived with whom he would need to share credit.[48]

Rash decisions like this one had backfired on many Roman commanders in the past, most notably the consuls who repeatedly stumbled into Hannibal's traps in the Second Punic War. In the troubled 70s, however, Crassus's decision was also, perversely, a hopeful sign for those who valued the norms the preceding decades had shredded. Crassus wanted sole credit for the victory over Spartacus because he hoped to pursue a conventional political career according to the traditional Republican pattern. Like Fabricius in the 280s, Crassus sought the honors and offices that only the Republic could provide, and he hoped to get them through the consent of the organs of the Roman state the Republic had empowered to award them. Crassus did not want to seize the consulship using force or the threat of force. He hoped to earn it through the connections he had built across Roman society and the prestige he had acquired by defeating Spartacus. Like Flaminius 150 years before, Crassus decided to risk a catastrophic military defeat because he trusted that the benefits of victory would be so significant.

Crassus's gamble only partially paid off. Crassus did force Spartacus into a decisive battle in which he defeated the slave forces and, apparently, killed Spartacus himself. And Crassus did receive public credit for "conquering the slaves in open battle." But Pompey had captured and killed the fugitives who escaped Crassus. This meant that Pompey was able to say that he alone had ended the war.[49]

Crassus and Pompey both returned to Rome with their armies by the middle of 71 to participate in public recognitions of their victories. Indeed, the last months of the year were filled with public commemorations of Roman military successes across the Mediterranean. Lucullus had returned from Greece with a massive cache of statues to display in a triumphal procession that celebrated a victory he had earned in Thrace. Metellus Pius was honored for his victories over Sertorius's armies in Spain. And Pompey celebrated a triumph for his Spanish victory, the second triumph he had celebrated despite not holding one of the requisite offices. Although Crassus's praetorship and the nature of his command both qualified him to celebrate a triumph, that honor was reserved only for commanders who had defeated foreign adversaries, and the slave Spartacus did not count as such an enemy. Crassus was instead voted an *ovatio,* a lesser celebratory procession during which the general marched in on foot rather than riding in a triumphal chariot. After lobbying from allies in the Senate, Crassus was permitted to wear the laurel wreath normally worn by one celebrating a triumph.[50]

Whereas Metellus and Lucullus both apparently had dismissed their armies before their triumphs, Crassus and Pompey did not. Pompey had already demonstrated a propensity for keeping his armies together even after they had accomplished the military objectives set for him, and it is possible that Crassus did not dismiss his forces so that they might serve as a check on possible mischief by Pompey. Within Rome, however, the presence of two armies commanded by two political rivals evoked uncomfortable memories of Sulla and Marius. Both Pompey and Crassus hoped to run for the consulship and, perhaps sensing the popular mood, the two men ultimately decided to dismiss their armies after the public celebrations of their victories had concluded.[51]

Crassus then decided on a remarkable course of action: he proposed an electoral alliance with Pompey. Because Pompey's military success and his recent strong support for a restoration of the tribunate virtually ensured his election, Crassus understood that he would be competing with other candidates for the second consular slot. Pompey's support would likely ensure that Crassus would enter office, but he would do so as Pompey's junior colleague. Pompey was receptive to the idea because he saw it as a way to get a "junior colleague devoted to him" while the two men were in office. He also assumed that this would put Crassus under an obligation to return Pompey's favor even after their consulships ended.[52] As expected, Pompey and Crassus both secured the consulship for 70.

The alliance that Pompey and Crassus struck did not last long past the election. Part of this had to do with the aggressive way in which Pompey pushed his reformist agenda. The first public speech Pompey gave following his election promised to undo many of the reforms Sulla had made to the Republic. Pompey called for the removal of the remaining limits Sulla had placed on the tribunate and a return to a system in which tribunes proposed laws that the *concilium plebis* voted to approve. Perhaps in response to complaints Pompey heard from his clients in Sicily, he proposed a reform of provincial government that would make it more difficult for senators to extort money from provincials. And, perhaps most controversially, Pompey pushed for a reform of the courts that judged senatorial misconduct so that their juries again included nonsenators. And as ambitious as this program was, Pompey hoped to do even more. Later in 70, a friendly tribune sponsored a law to award land to Pompey's and Metellus Pius's veterans from the Spanish war. Pompey clearly saw an opportunity both to create the same sort of geographically diffuse, intensely loyal following that Sulla's veterans settlements had provided him and to increase the personal loyalty that troops serving under him in the future might feel.[53]

Crassus may have always intended to break with Pompey once they were in office, but, after cooperating with Pompey on the restoration of the powers of the tribunes, Crassus seems to have become alarmed at the enthusiasm of Pompey's supporters both within Rome and in the provinces. Instead of serving as the loyal junior partner that Pompey expected, Crassus began mobilizing whatever resources he could to block his colleague. Crassus largely failed, however. Pompey succeeded in changing the composition of juries and even got a law passed that provided land to his veterans, though its implementation stalled when the Senate claimed that it lacked the funds to actually purchase the necessary land. By the middle of 70, frustrated at his inability to stop Pompey's proposals, it seems that Crassus busied himself with disparaging his colleague rather than trying to achieve anything on behalf of the public good.[54]

As the year progressed, people in Rome again became alarmed about where the rivalry between Pompey and Crassus might lead. The anxiety finally boiled over near the end of their term, at a public assembly at which both men presided. The details of the event vary slightly in the surviving accounts. Plutarch describes a man who jumped onto the platform where the consuls were seated and cried out that Jupiter had told him in a dream that Pompey and Crassus should not be allowed to step down from their office unless they reconciled with one another. Appian indicates that the call for reconciliation came instead from a college of soothsayers.

But both sources agree that this divinely inspired call gave the people attending the meeting the courage to voice their concerns about the two men's rivalry. They implored Pompey and Crassus to reconcile, reminding them of the horrors that grew out of the personal feud between Marius and Sulla and becoming louder and more frantic as neither man moved to resolve their differences.[55]

Crassus finally blinked. He stepped down from his consular chair, walked toward Pompey, and extended his hand. Pompey then rose to meet him. The two leading men in the Roman state then shook hands and agreed to put aside their rivalry for the good of Rome, its Republic, and their fellow citizens. In this way, Appian would write, "the conviction that another civil war would happen was happily dispelled." The two consuls may not have much liked each other, but they had agreed to place the good of the Republic above their own personal rivalry. Instead of mobilizing their considerable resources against one another as Sulla and Marius had done in the 80s and Lepidus and Catulus had done in 78, Rome's richest man and its most powerful general agreed to a truce. In years to come, both Crassus and Pompey would continue to chase the offices and honors the Republic offered, but they would do so only by using the tools that the political system permitted. For the first time in nearly two decades, the most powerful men in the Roman state clearly specified that they trusted the system to protect them from their rivals and to allow them to compete fairly within the rules it set. Romans could, for the moment, imagine that the Republic again set firm rules and enforced established norms that governed all ambitious Romans as they pursued offices and military glory. If it could, Rome might finally and fully emerge from both the horror of the civil war and the social, political, and economic distortions of its Sullan aftermath.

CHAPTER 8

THE REPUBLIC OF THE MEDIOCRE

THE RECONCILIATION OF POMPEY AND Crassus at the end of their joint consulship in 70 BC seemed to conclude the period of political experimentation birthed by Sulla's march on Rome. Pompey and Crassus had both supported Sulla, they had both used private armies to serve Sulla, and they had both spent much of the 70s becoming two of the most powerful figures in Rome. None could deny that their mutual decision to forgo conflict and to instead compete with one another within the Republic's political system clearly communicated that the rules of the Republic once again bound even the most influential Romans.

The result was a sudden and unexpected opening up of political competition. Crassus's wealth and Pompey's military reputation remained formidable, but they were now ex-consuls without any office. They still enjoyed a privileged status, but it was a status that they shared with others and one that many more could aspire to reach. Their willingness to step down from office when their terms ended allowed less capable and less well-resourced men to compete for the highest offices in the state. But the playing field remained tilted toward the powerful. Those who hoped to rival powerful figures like Crassus and Pompey could not do so by playing fairly. They needed to press any advantage they could find—and the past seventy-five years provided ambitious Romans with examples of how one might bend the rules to advance one's career or slow down the initiatives of others. Some perhaps saw no harm in bending the norms now that the Republic seemed to have returned to health; others cared less about the Republic than their own prospects. But, in the end, the moment of apparent stability Crassus and Pompey had created only cleared space for a new cast of characters willing to place their short-term ambitions above the long-term health of the Republic.

As the 60s dawned, a host of figures began jockeying for positions of influence. Some of these were members of old families such as the Metelli who saw the apparent return to a stable political order as an opportunity to reassert their family's traditional claims to high office. Thus Quintus Metellus served as consul and Marcus Metellus as praetor in 69, and Lucius Metellus followed them as consul for 68. Others were tribunes who chose to follow in the footsteps of Tiberius Gracchus and Saturninus by using the office to make divisive political gestures. In 67, the tribune Gabinius marshaled a mob of supporters willing to attack opponents and used the threat of removal to get a fellow tribune to rescind his veto. Like their predecessors in the later 110s, other tribunes built their reputations by claiming to root out senatorial corruption. In the same year as Gabinius's activities, the tribune Cornelius put forward a set of laws that stopped the Senate from exempting its members from laws and compelled praetors to follow their own edicts. He also tried unsuccessfully to bar the lending of money to foreign states and to curtail electoral bribery, both pursuits that advantaged senators in particular. Ambitious tribunes also sought to build support through manipulation of the electoral system. On the last day of 67, the tribune Manlius (who, like all tribunes, had started his term for the year 66 in the fall of 67) tried to take advantage of the fact that he was in office at the point when the terms of the consuls and other magistrates for 67 were about to end. Manlius used this moment of transition to slip through a vote to approve a law altering the composition of the voting tribes by distributing freedmen equally across them, a move that he presumably thought would improve his own chances of being elected to higher magistracies. Unfortunately for Manlius, this law was annulled when the new consuls took office on the first day of 66.[1]

Now that Pompey and Crassus had restored the ability of tribunes to stand for higher offices in the Republic, the most enterprising tribunes followed in the footsteps of Sulpicius and built their influence by inducing more powerful figures into alliances with them. One of the most consequential tribunal initiatives in 67 was the creation of a special, three-year-long command to fight piracy throughout the Mediterranean. Though Gabinius's law creating the command specified only that this extraordinary commander would be selected from among the living former consuls, there was no doubt that the position was designed for Pompey. Although it offered just the sort of chance for military glory without the confines of a traditional political office that Pompey had often seized, he held back from actively campaigning for the position. Pompey did, though, give a thoroughly unsubtle speech in which he listed his many military accomplishments for an audience that needed no reminding of them. Gabinius then proposed that Rome entrust the war against the pirates to Pompey.[2]

Gabinius's proposals for the creation of the command and the awarding of it to Pompey provoked strong resistance both in the Senate and among his fellow tribunes. In the Senate, an ambitious young senator named Julius Caesar stood out as the only vocal supporter of Gabinius's measures. The next most positive comment seems to have been the orator Hortensius's lukewarm statement that no one should have such power but, if someone were to receive it, Pompey would be his choice. The rest of the Senate vigorously opposed both the command and Pompey's selection to it. Among Gabinius's fellow tribunes, the proposals provoked additional resistance. L. Trebellius and L. Roscius Otho both were willing to use their veto to block its creation, though after Gabinius nearly had Trebellius deposed neither went through with the threat. After being shouted down by the pro-Pompey crowd, Roscius could do no more than hold up two fingers to register his view that more than one man should hold such power. Ultimately, the law was passed, the command was given to Pompey, and the size of the forces under his command was increased so that Pompey could now call on up to 500 ships, 5,000 cavalry, and 120,000 infantry. It is said that people felt so confident that Pompey would end piracy that the price of bread immediately dropped.[3]

When the historian Cassius Dio later wrote about this moment, he perceptively identified in it a set of tensions that lay beneath the seemingly stable Republic of the early 60s. One issue was the willingness of newly empowered tribunes to use Pompey's personal ambitions to advance their own careers in a rough political environment. Gabinius, it seems, conceived of the command either at Pompey's instigation or, perhaps more likely, as a lure to attract Pompey's patronage. A second issue was the way in which Pompey conceived of his place in the Republic of the 60s. Although he did not want to seize power as Sulla had, he clearly craved a special status that put him above others. As rumors of his appointment to the antipiracy command spread, Pompey came to see the commission not as an honor he might gain but rather as an entitlement he was owed. His "failure to hold it was a disgrace" that he could not bear. The reaction among senators also grew out of the particular conditions of the time. Although Pompey took care never to openly campaign for the command, the Senate responded to his name being floated with alarm. According to Dio, Catulus, the other consul when Lepidus rebelled in 78 BC, even delivered a speech in which he cautioned about the disasters that "lawless lust for power" had caused in Rome. His ominous words that "great honors ruin even great people" would loom over the rest of Dio's Republican narrative.[4]

Dio emphasized the destructive potential of a politics shaped by the aspirations of eager tribunes, the ambitions of already great men like Pompey, and the fears of senators at risk of being over-shadowed. But that potential was not immediately realized. Despite the Senate's concern about Pompey's new command, the effort he led against the pirates proved surprisingly successful. Pompey realized that the task of rooting out piracy was as much a social and economic problem as it was a military one. The biggest spike in pirate attacks had come after Mithridates's armies had devastated much of the farmland in Asia Minor, with the resulting poverty pushing the region's inhabitants into crime. Other people who attacked ships did so in part as a response to Roman territorial expansion into their regions. Late-second-century Roman attempts to dominate maritime trade in the Aegean had forced displaced merchants either to submit or to challenge Roman authority. Pompey understood that most of these pirates were not irredeemable villains, and accordingly he showed them mercy. In Asia Minor, he did not kill repentant pirates but instead settled them inland in order to repopulate areas devastated by Mithridates. Pompey's policies quickly integrated many of the erstwhile pirates back into the Roman imperial structure—while, crucially, making them his loyal political clients.[5]

The speed with which Pompey brought the piracy problem under control astonished Romans. His extraordinary command was to last for three years. Instead, Pompey needed about three months.[6] This led to a second effort in early 66 to give Pompey yet another extraordinary command, this time to prosecute another war against Mithridates that had thus far proved agonizingly inconclusive. Superficially, it might seem natural to have assigned this war to Pompey. He was already in the general area with the army he had led against the pirates, and Romans thought that Lucullus, the current commander, seemed to be making slow progress against the Pontic king.

The proposal actually had nothing to do with the military situation in Asia. The tribune Manlius proposed Pompey as a commander not because Lucullus had actually been unsuccessful but because Manlius needed to rebound politically. Manlius raised the issue of Pompey's command soon after the failure of his effort to redistribute freedmen across all tribes in January of 66. Feeling politically exposed, Manlius first tried to indicate that Crassus had backed the tribal reform measure, and when this failed to improve his position, he decided to pivot away from the unpopular proposal altogether. He turned toward Pompey in an attempt to court a new, more powerful backer. Manlius carefully crafted the Mithridates command so that it would appeal to the general. Pompey's authority would last indefinitely, it would supersede that of all other commanders (including Lucullus), and Pompey would also have the right to initiate wars elsewhere without consulting the Senate. Manlius appealed to Pompey's desire for popular approval by putting the command through the *concilium plebis* rather than the Senate.[7]

Pompey seems to have learned about the law while in Crete. His precise reaction to it is not known, but the response in Rome was electric. People looking to court Pompey rallied to build support for Manlius's motion. Julius Caesar again spoke in the Senate in support of Pompey, and the ambitious equestrian orator Cicero (who was then serving as praetor) lent his voice to the cause as well. Meanwhile, senators such as Catulus argued vigorously against the concentration of yet more power in the hands of one individual.

Dio again perceptively analyzes the debate, showing how neither the larger objectives of the military campaign nor the precedents set by the command's creation figured prominently in the positions that many of the principals took. Pompey wanted to retain an unmatched level of military authority. Manlius offered this to Pompey as a way to restore his own flagging political fortunes. Caesar supported the proposal because he thought that doing so would enhance his popularity in the short run and, in the long run, invite such envy of Pompey that Pompey's position might become weakened. Cicero, Dio asserts, backed the law because he sensed it would pass and he wanted to define himself as a leader in the Senate who could ensure that whatever side of a question he backed would succeed. And, though Dio does not claim this, Catulus and others in the Senate likely opposed the law out of fear that their influence would diminish as Pompey became even more powerful.[8]

In the end, Manlius's law passed and, when new legates were sent to Pompey for the campaign, the ex-tribune Gabinius was among them. This set in motion a series of conquests unlike anything the Roman world had ever seen. In a little more than three years, Pompey would defeat Mithridates, chase him through Armenia, conquer large swathes of Asia Minor and all of Syria, and reduce much of the rest of the Eastern Mediterranean to Roman client kingdoms that paid an annual tribute. This conquest was done with the same sort of political skill that Pompey had shown with the pirates. Pompey so capably regulated local affairs in the areas newly annexed to Rome that his local ordinances remained in effect for nearly three hundred years.[9] He did not hesitate to use his armies, but, when he was victorious, he offered favorable alliances to local kings and cities that left them particularly well disposed toward him. Pompey now enjoyed a network of friendly sovereigns that stretched from Armenia in the north to Judaea in the south.

While Pompey remade the Eastern Mediterranean, figures in Rome jostled to fill the vacuum his absence had created. Crassus continued to subtly expand the influential network of supporters that had brought him to the consulship. When Crassus served as censor in 65, he tried to push through a measure extending Roman citizenship to people on the northern side of the Po River, though this transparent attempt to create a large group of voters loyal to him was struck down by Catulus, the other censor of the year. Crassus pushed for a Roman annexation of the kingdom of Egypt, with Julius Caesar to supervise the handover. Catulus blocked this too. Crassus also developed an economic and patronage relationship with some of the people responsible for collecting taxes in the province of Asia.[10] This, at least, Catulus could not block.

New players with different sets of skills emerged as well. Two of them, Cicero and Julius Caesar, had already begun to influence

public life before Pompey departed. Each man had carefully cultivated a particular public persona. Cicero was an equestrian with a
gift for long-winded, self-congratulatory orations that nevertheless
often proved extremely persuasive. He had first risen to prominence when, as a twenty-six-year-old, he defended Sextus Roscius
against a charge of parricide in 80 BC. What defined his early
career, however, were the speeches he gave against Verres, the corrupt governor of Sicily, in 70 BC. In the Verrine orations, Cicero
showed himself to be both a sophisticated stylist and an extremely
effective advocate with the unique ability to playfully but powerfully shape a listener's perspective. These gifts propelled Cicero's
political career, allowing him to rise from the ranks of Italian *equites* to the Senate and, ultimately, to the consulship. But these
gifts imperfectly offset some significant character flaws. Cicero, as
Dio wrote, "was the greatest boaster alive and regarded no one as
equal to himself... he was wearisome and burdensome and consequently both disliked and hated even by those very persons whom
he otherwise pleased."[11] Often, Cicero could not manage to hold
his tongue, frequently seeming more enchanted by the rhetorical
jab he could throw than he was conscious of the enemy his words
might create.[12] Cicero could be a powerful ally, but his arrogance,
unpredictability, and general insufferability always threatened to
undercut the political gains he made.

Caesar was in many ways the opposite of Cicero. Cicero was
an equestrian from an Italian town whose family had never produced a consul. Caesar came from an old Roman patrician family
that claimed descent from Iulus, the son of Aeneas and thus the
grandson of the goddess Venus. Cicero was intolerable. Caesar was
affable and popular. Even their prose differed. Caesar was no less
accomplished a stylist, but his short, powerful sentences and precise words contrasted notably with the long, complicated construc-
tions Cicero preferred—stylistic differences as profound as those
that distinguish the prose of Hemingway from that of Faulk-
ner. Caesar also managed his personal relationships much more

skillfully than Cicero. Whereas Cicero had a unique capacity to anger even those who had once been friendly with him, Caesar's personality enabled him not only to build enduring friendships with his peers but even to bring together the bitterest rivals.

Caesar's greatest gift, however, lay in his remarkable ability to build and maintain popularity with the Roman public. Born in 100 BC, Caesar's efforts to develop a personal political brand began quite early in his life. His family had been strong supporters of Marius and Cinna. Caesar's aunt Julia was Marius's wife and, as a young man, Caesar married Cinna's daughter Cornelia. Caesar was not proscribed following Sulla's victory, but he still suffered under the dictator. His family property and his wife's dowry were both seized, Caesar was stripped of his position as priest of Jupiter, and he elected to leave Rome instead of obeying Sulla's order to divorce Cornelia. It took the intervention of his mother and the Vestal Virgins to get the threat against Caesar lifted.[13]

Caesar had the political genius to understand that misfortune under Sulla could be useful in crafting a political identity in the post-Sullan Republic. Aside from stepping in as priest of Jupiter when his father died in 85 BC, Caesar's age had prevented him from doing anything disreputable in support of the regimes of Marius and Cinna.[14] And yet he was still punished, a sympathetic victim of the loyalty that he continued to show to his family and the family of his wife. Indeed, Caesar's defiance of Sulla's divorce order also positioned him to later claim the positive legacies of Marius and Cinna, even as he denied any connection to the crimes the men had committed.

The massacre of so many of Marius's and Cinna's most prominent supporters had not eliminated the public support that the men once enjoyed. Indeed, as the horrors of Sulla's dictatorship and the disorder of the new Republic he crafted became clearer, memories of Marius became much fonder.[15] And yet Sulla had killed nearly everyone in Italy with a close enough connection to Marius to plausibly lay claim to his legacy. The position of Marius's political heir sat vacant and the power that could come from that title remained latent. Until Caesar.

Caesar carefully chose his moment. In 69 BC, soon after his election to the office of quaestor, Caesar's aunt Julia died. Caesar gave the funeral oration for her from the Rostra in the Forum. Then, in the funeral procession, he publicly displayed images of Marius and Marius's son, both seen on Rome's streets for the first time since Sulla had pronounced Marius a public enemy.[16]

Marius was a complicated figure with a complicated legacy that included both his brilliance in saving Rome from barbarians in the 100s and the horrible violence he inflicted on Rome in the 80s. Caesar believed it was possible to rehabilitate the public memory of Marius by emphasizing the former while ignoring the latter. In the immediate term, Caesar likely hoped that his display might provoke Sulla's partisans to respond with such irrational anger that they refused to even acknowledge the undoubtedly heroic achievements of Marius's first consulships. Caesar's choice of venue was also key. This was, after all, a funeral for Marius's wife. Vitriolic attacks against the family of the deceased would seem particularly tasteless in such a setting. An overreaction by Sullan supporters would then open the door to further commemorations of Marius, and for Caesar to both rehabilitate and claim the legacy of his uncle.

Caesar got the response he hoped for. The display outraged supporters of Sulla, but the enthusiastic applause of the Roman crowd drowned out their cries. Then, later in the same year, the death of his wife Cornelia gave Caesar another opportunity to publicly celebrate a woman connected to the anti-Sullan leadership. Women as young as Cornelia did not typically receive funeral orations. But as Caesar clearly understood, his departure from precedent when he nonetheless gave such an oration simultaneously humanized him and further refined the Marian legacy he aimed to embrace.[17]

After the funerals, Caesar set out to Spain for his service as quaestor, returning in 68 (before his term ended) to resume his career in Rome. The quaestorship qualified Caesar for the Senate, and it was as one of the Senate's most junior members that Caesar spoke in favor of giving Pompey the command against the pirates. Caesar also began to spend lavishly to cultivate the public, entertaining clients and potential supporters in a way that most of his contemporaries thought ruinously unsustainable.[18]

Caesar continued to refine his public profile when he was elected aedile for the year 65. In addition to the administrative responsibilities aediles assumed, they sponsored public games. Caesar saw great potential in these events. Although he shared the expenses and organizational responsibilities for the public games with his fellow aedile Marcus Bibulus, Caesar managed to get the bulk of the public credit for the success of these state-funded spectacles by paying personally for an additional set of 320 gladiatorial contests in honor of his late father.[19]

During his aedileship Caesar made another, more provocative claim on the legacy of Marius. He erected on the Capitoline Hill statues of Marius and "trophy-bearing Victories" that were decorated with gold and bore inscriptions commemorating Marius's defeat of the Cimbri. These monuments celebrated Marius as the Republic's savior, saying nothing about his tyranny in the 80s. Marius's monumental rehabilitation again stirred passions in precisely the way that Caesar had hoped. The statues' unveiling prompted a public display of anger by politicians opposed to Marius, but, as in 69 BC, the enthusiastic cheers of those who remembered Marius fondly drowned out the shrill calls that Caesar was plotting revolution. Plutarch describes a scene in which calls that Caesar had "shown himself worthy of his kinship with Marius" rang out amid tears of joy and raucous applause. When the Senate convened to discuss the controversy over the statues, Catulus, the old self-appointed champion of Republican values, supposedly told his colleagues that Caesar was now undermining the government. His harsh warning failed to convince. Many of the older supporters of Sulla in the Senate were dying out, and Caesar's defense of his actions combined with the enthusiasm of the crowd for Marius caused the Senate to let the matter drop.

A third figure who became increasingly prominent during Pompey's time in the East cultivated a very different sort of public image from that crafted by Crassus, Caesar, and Cicero. This was Marcus Porcius Cato, the great-grandson of the Marcus Porcius Cato who towered over Roman political life in the early and mid-second century BC. Cato the Younger, as he would come to be called, shared his ancestor's sternness and idiosyncratic commitment to vague (and sometimes inconsistently applied) principles of political propriety. And, like his ancestor, Cato the Younger carefully cultivated an image of unassailable virtue that caused later authors to gush that he was "most formidable, a man endowed with the greatest self-control, and inferior to no Roman in his commitment to the highest principles."[20]

Cato cultivated this political brand so well during his lifetime that his legacy would tower over Roman political life for centuries after his death. Cato the secular saint became such a fixture of Roman senatorial writings after the Republic's end that Cato the man has become an extremely difficult figure to reconstruct. Cato certainly became a vocal and active critic of any agenda that he saw as undermining the Republic and the freedom that elite men like him enjoyed under it, but these later activities have shaped the way that his earlier life is described. Plutarch describes him as a child who spoke eloquently while playing sports and who neither laughed nor became angry (though Plutarch does concede that, on some rare occasions, the boy did smile). Other stories of Cato's youth are equally absurd. Both Plutarch and Valerius Maximus recount how Cato, who was then a four-year-old orphan living in the home of Livius Drusus, was dangled out of a window after he refused to agree that citizenship should be extended to all Italians. Another equally implausible story told how Cato used to visit the home of Sulla because the dictator enjoyed conversations with the youth. One day, when Cato was fourteen, he came to Sulla's home and, entering the premises, witnessed the torture of many eminent men. Cato then supposedly asked his tutor, a man named Sarpedon, why no one had yet killed Sulla. When he was told that people feared Sulla even more than they hated him, Cato asked for a sword so that he "could free his homeland from slavery by killing" Sulla. This story is nonsense, of course, but it was retold in subsequent centuries because it reinforced the powerful idea that Cato would do anything to defend the Republic.[21]

The surviving tales of Cato's early adulthood are more plausible. When he became old enough to inherit his share of the family fortune, Cato received 720,000 denarii. This was a substantial sum that would permit Cato to live comfortably, but it paled in comparison to the fortunes of political rivals such as Crassus or even the amount of wealth that Cicero would come to possess. Cato thus made the decision to become a follower of the Stoic philosopher Antipater of Tyre. He resolved to live modestly, but, by doing things like walking the filthy streets of Rome in the morning without shoes or a tunic, he advertised his modesty ostentatiously.[22]

In these years Cato occasionally made speeches at meetings and in court cases, but his public career really began when, as a twenty-three-year-old, he enlisted to serve in the war against Sertorius. Again, Cato made sure that his displays of moderation and discipline stood out amid an army that had acquired a reputation for laxity. Then, when the campaign concluded, Cato continued the pattern of making ostentatious displays of his own righteousness. He campaigned for a military tribuneship (a midlevel military office that often represented the next step in an elite political career) without the customary help of an aide who could remind him of the names of the people with whom he spoke. Such aides were legally prohibited, but, in a city as large as Rome, their employment was tacitly accepted as a practical necessity. Cato was the only candidate to obey this law, and he made sure that everyone in the electorate knew it.[23]

Opportunistic displays of supposedly principled actions continued to define Cato's career as he moved from a military tribuneship through the quaestorship and, by the end of 64, into the Senate. As military tribune, Cato endeared himself to his soldiers by marching with them when other commanders rode horses and by dressing more like a common soldier than a commander. When his term of service ended, we are told, his soldiers wept uncontrollably and threw down their garments so he would not need to walk on the ground as he left the camp. As quaestor, he made a point of investigating the financial activities of treasury clerks and the accounts of previous quaestors to expose wrongdoing. Like Caesar, Pompey, and Crassus, Cato also butted heads with the old ex-consul Catulus by unsuccessfully prosecuting one of his associates for corruption. And, in an attempt to further demonstrate his independence, Cato also initiated legal proceedings to take back some of the public property that Sulla had awarded to people who had killed men that Sulla had proscribed.[24]

When Cato entered the Senate, he had very effectively cultivated a public identity as an incorruptible, philosophically pure principal defender of Republican liberty. He came from a family whose name had become synonymous with the protection of traditional Roman virtues, he made sure to offer regular demonstrations of his moderation, and he had carefully chosen public occasions in which to pose as the morally upright voice of probity in a depraved world. He was not a populist like Caesar nor a spectacular orator like Cicero, but the moral authority he asserted gave Cato a potency that the gifts, talents, and achievements of figures like Cicero, Caesar, Pompey, and Crassus would struggle to neutralize.

Caesar and Cato joined the Senate in the mid-60s amid a seemingly endless series of political crises. The arguments about Pompey's commands in 67 and 66 gave way to a new controversy about a bribery law that, when it took effect in late 66, led to the disqualification of both of the candidates elected to serve as consul in 65 BC. Then, the consular election in 64 laid the foundations for another political crisis. That election pitted Cicero against two other candidates, Lucius Sergius Catilina (often called Catiline by

people today) and Gaius Antonius Hybrida, both of whom came
from senatorial families. Campaigns for consulships were extremely
costly affairs, and successful candidates often formed alliances to
pool their support. Catiline and Antonius made such an alliance
during the campaign and based their appeals around the idea that
Cicero's low birth should disqualify him from so high an office.

Despite their attacks, Cicero came first in the voting, making
him the first "new man" to be chosen consul since the election of
Pompey's father in 89 BC.[25] Cicero's victory owed a great deal to
both the skill with which he campaigned and the opportunities
for rhetorical attack that the checkered careers of his opponents
provided him. Cicero particularly targeted Catiline, who had benefited financially from Sulla's proscriptions in the 80s and then,
following a governorship in Africa in 67–66, was prosecuted for
extortion.[26] The most dramatic encounter between Cicero and his
opponents occurred in a Senate meeting devoted to questions of
electoral bribery in which Cicero savaged Catiline with allegations
of corruption and secret, murderous plots against political opponents.[27] Catiline and Antonius could only respond with a tired
attack on Cicero's family.

Cicero seems to have quickly found a way to work effectively
with Antonius during their joint consulship, but reconciliation
with Catiline was both unnecessary and not particularly advisable.
Catiline was prosecuted for murder in the autumn of 64. Although
a number of senators spoke in his defense, Cicero was not one of
them. Catiline also seems to have been growing increasingly desperate. As the year 63 progressed, he was rumored to be deeply in
debt. He stood again for the consulship, but this time the field was
much more crowded than it had been in 64. In an effort to distinguish himself, Catiline elected to pose as a champion of the op-
pressed and downtrodden, a group with which he perhaps identified
more than the average observer understood. He sensed that many
Romans were coming to believe that an unfair economic structure
had created two tiers of Romans, and he tried to position himself as

the candidate who could best address this divide. It was not a bad electoral strategy. Early in 63, Cicero had blocked a tribunician law pushing land redistribution and, later in the year, it became clear that many of the Sullan supporters who had received property from the proscriptions also faced financial problems. The patrician Catiline proved a poor messenger, however, and when Cato threatened to prosecute him for bribery a couple of weeks before the election, Catiline's chances took a further hit. He failed to win election in a crowded field and his political career seemed over.[28]

In the months after his electoral defeat, Catiline began planning a revolt, the centerpiece of which was an army that ultimately grew to perhaps ten thousand. Cataline saw this army as the focal point of a complicated (and rather impractical) plan that also involved a Gallic tribe called the Allobroges, a series of assassinations of leading officials (including Cicero), and a wave of arson attacks in Rome. It is unclear how the plot could have succeeded by itself, but Catiline possibly saw it as part of a bigger game. Catiline may have anticipated that Pompey, who was concluding his campaigns in the East, would return to Italy just as Sulla had. If Pompey did intend to seize power, Catiline's ramshackle army could serve as an advance force that might make Pompey's task easier.[29] If this happened, Catiline and his followers could reasonably expect the same sort of financial and political windfall that they had received from Sulla two decades before.

There were two significant problems with Catiline's plan. First, as subsequent events would make clear, Pompey had no intention of using his army to seize power. Catiline had appointed himself the vanguard of a revolution that would never happen. Second, and more importantly, Catiline's plot was discovered rather quickly. On October 20 of 63, Crassus and some other senators handed over to Cicero a set of letters warning of a massacre that was planned in Rome. Cicero informed the Senate, the Senate voted to empower the consuls to take any measure necessary to protect the state, and Catiline's general Manlius then decided to prematurely raise the flag of rebellion. On October 29, news of the revolt reached Rome. Catiline was indicted on October 30. After a failed attempt to assassinate Cicero on November 7, Cicero gave an oration attacking Catiline and urging him to leave Rome. Catiline fled on the night of November 8. Then, on the night of December 2, envoys from the Allobroges met with and received letters from conspirators in Rome. Cicero knew about the meeting and had the envoys and one of the conspirators arrested as they left the city.[30]

The Senate met on each of the next three days to decide how to handle the situation. Cato, Caesar, and Cicero would all play prominent roles in the discussions. On December 3, Cicero presided over a senate meeting in the Temple of Concordia to which the implicated conspirators were summoned. They were compelled to confirm that the unopened letters seized the night before bore their seals. The letters were then read aloud, revealing to all that the conspiracy reached into the capital itself. The five conspirators were placed under arrest and each was entrusted to the care of an individual senator. The Senate voted Cicero an official commendation. He then delivered a public oration to the people in which he described the conspirators' plan to burn the city and recounted their arrest. The crowd erupted in joyful cheers.[31]

Cicero had expertly staged the events on December 3, but he was less successful in controlling developments on the following day. On December 4, the Senate heard from Lucius Tarquinius, another conspirator who had been captured while he was making his way to Catiline. Tarquinius too described a conspiracy that involved arson, assassination, and an attack by Catiline's rebel army, but he also implicated Crassus in the plot. Crassus's clients and friends immediately raised an outcry that these charges were completely false and, after discussing them, the Senate agreed. Tarquinius was then placed back under arrest while speculation began to swirl about why he had lied. Crassus, however, became convinced that Cicero had persuaded Tarquinius to implicate him in the plot.[32] On the same day, Catulus and Gaius Piso first attempted to bribe Cicero to lodge a false accusation against Julius Caesar and, when that failed, began circulating their own rumor that Caesar too had been involved in the conspiracy. As the meeting adjourned, some of the men guarding the Temple of Concordia even drew their swords on Caesar after hearing about his possible involvement.[33]

On December 5, the Senate convened to discuss what to do with the five men under arrest. The consul-elect for the year 62 began by recommending that they be put to death. Then Julius Caesar rose and gave a speech in which he reminded senators of the many times in Roman history in which Romans put their dignity ahead of their desire for revenge. Caesar acknowledged that the crimes the conspirators planned were horrific, but he also emphasized that the punishment of execution had no precedent in Roman history, because Roman citizens found guilty of a crime were instead given the option of exile. He also emphasized that "all bad precedents originated in cases that were good" and warned that execution would provide grounds for future incompetent or malicious officials to kill citizens who did not deserve such punishment. Caesar proposed that a better response would be to confiscate the property of those implicated in the conspiracy and imprison them for the rest of their lives in towns outside of Rome.[34]

After some more discussion, Cato rose to speak. He reminded his fellow senators that, though they might think of their possessions, houses, paintings, and statues as things that might fall victim to Catiline's revolution, they needed instead to be mindful that what Catiline truly threatened was their liberty. Their belongings, their luxuries, even their power meant nothing if the Republic did not survive. The fundamental duty of the Senate was to preserve Rome's republic and, if senators would stop looking to their private interests and pleasures, they would understand that this matter was too serious to allow for any error. The conspirators, Cato concluded, should be punished as if they were caught committing the crimes they intended. They should, Cato implied, be treated as violent enemies of the state, and executed.[35]

When Cato finished speaking, it was clear that his motion had carried the day—so much so that there were even rumblings about the Senate punishing Caesar himself for advocating a more moderate punishment for the conspirators. With the Senate resolved to execute the conspirators, Cicero ordered the magistrates responsible for the prisoners to lead them into a dungeon below the Capitoline Hill, where they were strangled. That evening Cicero was given a triumphal escort by torchlight as he headed home. In the afterglow of his greatest triumph, Cicero seemed very much to have earned the title that would soon be voted to him: "father of his country."[36]

Unfortunately for Cicero, the Catilinarian conspiracy did not end on December 5. Cataline himself remained with his army in Etruria and, as Caesar predicted, Cicero's decision to execute Roman citizens without trial quickly proved to be a horrible miscalculation. Some of the new tribunes who took office on December 10 immediately exploited the complicated feelings of fear, unease, and remorse provoked by the Catilinarian crisis and Cicero's response to it. On December 29 of 63, as Cicero prepared to address the Roman people for the final time as consul, Metellus Nepos, one of the new tribunes elected for 62 who had already taken office, used his veto to prevent Cicero from giving the speech because he had killed Roman citizens without a trial. Cicero elected instead to swear a public oath that he had saved the Republic.[37]

With Cicero out of office, Nepos continued his efforts to exploit the Catilinarian situation. On January 3, he introduced a motion to recall Pompey so that he might lead his army against Catiline's forces. The desertion of 70 percent of Catiline's army after the executions on December 5 meant that Nepos's proposal was completely unnecessary. It was, however, alarming to those who suspected that it would serve as a pretext to allow Pompey to return to Italy without dismissing his army. The alarm increased when Nepos also joined to it another measure that would allow

Pompey to stand for the consulship in absentia. Cato, who had stood for the tribunate expressly for the purpose of vetoing measures proposed by Nepos, physically blocked the public reading of the proposed law, first by preventing the herald from reading its text and then by placing his hand over Nepos's mouth when the tribune tried to recite it from memory. He did this before an assembly presided over by Caesar (who was serving as praetor and was supportive of the measure) and in front of a crowd composed of large numbers of Pompey's supporters, who were flanked by armed men. The armed men charged Cato, scattering most of the crowd, and he fled to the Temple of Castor and Pollux. The Senate ultimately instructed the consuls to do whatever was necessary to restore order and suspended both Nepos and Caesar from office. Sensing that this was a lost cause, Caesar quickly backed down and was reinstated. Nepos, however, fled Rome to join Pompey.[38]

These five days spanning the end of 63 and the beginning of 62 show how the gifted but flawed men who had gained prominence while Pompey campaigned abroad tried to capitalize on the chaos Catiline had generated. For Cicero, the suppression of the Catilinarian conspiracy brought him the greatest political triumph of his career. It generated some of his most powerful speeches and earned him one of Rome's most prestigious titles. But his decision to permit the execution of five Roman citizens without trial, an act that Cicero hoped would show his great competence as a leader, instead backfired quickly. Less than a month later, the true significance of what Cicero had done dawned on Romans—and they were horrified by it. Actions praised at the beginning of December had, by month's end, become serious political liabilities. Cicero's eloquence ensured that he would remain a useful political ally, but his actions against Catiline undermined the central claim that he had made about his great competence as consul and created a political vulnerability that would forever limit his future influence.

Cato had come out of the Catilinarian conspiracy with a different set of opportunities and limitations. He had argued publicly for the execution of the conspirators, but, unlike Cicero, he had not been directly responsible for their deaths. He had also articulated his position in a way that was consistent with his larger idea that the overriding goal of all political actions should be the preservation of the liberty that the Republic represented. Cato's entire public profile grew out of his complete and unwavering commitment to this ideal. As his efforts to silence Nepos showed, the Catilinarian conspiracy had only empowered Cato to make more public stands of this sort. By January of 62, he had defined himself as Rome's leading voice of principled opposition to any policies that he claimed could undermine the Republic. Indeed, the very act of Cato opposing a policy could be interpreted as a criticism that the policy threatened the integrity of Rome. Cato's criticisms could be extremely potent, but, in a world in which Roman citizens had real problems they expected the state to address, Cato's unbending commitment to abstract principles also had its limitations.

Caesar responded to the Catilinarian chaos quite differently from how Cicero and Cato did. Whereas both Cicero and Cato hoped to reap immediate political benefits from the incident, Caesar continued to play the long game. The actions Caesar took in December and January of 63–62 BC fit a larger pattern of careful attention to his public perception. Caesar's position was much more nuanced than Cicero's claim to competence or Cato's commitment to the principle of freedom, but it was no less carefully developed. Caesar was the heir to the popular legacy of Marius, but he was a much more capable populist than the man whose inheritance he sought to claim. Caesar's response to the Catilinarian conspiracy, which might seem rather scattered at first glance, actually reveals an astute sense of where popular sentiments were likely to end up. Indeed, in the speech to the Senate that Sallust reconstructs, one sees why Caesar had such concerns about the illegal killing of Roman citizens. Sulla, he reminds his audience, used the same argument to justify his initial round of executions when he took Rome. But, Caesar continues, the killing did not stop there.

Instead, those who rejoiced in the earliest executions "were themselves dragged away not long afterwards and there was no end to the killing until Sulla filled all of his followers with riches."[39] Some of those riches came from the property Caesar's family had once owned. Others came from property once held by the people to whom Caesar was appealing.

By early 62, the care Caesar had taken for building his popularity with voters and cultivating friendships with powerful allies had led him to a string of electoral victories that shocked observers. In 63 alone, Caesar had won election to the office of *pontifex maximus* and praetor. These victories were expensive and they left Caesar effectively bankrupt, but the political return had been immense. Caesar had also developed a keen sense of how to use the popularity of the distant Pompey as a tool to advance his own interests. Caesar supported all of the tribunal initiatives to grant Pompey extraordinary commands, but he never personally proposed them. This made him appear supportive of the popular general, but not obsequious. It also gave him the ability to easily walk away from failed measures, such as Nepos's proposal to invite Pompey's army to Italy and to let him run for consul in absentia. Caesar was building a much subtler but potentially more enduring sort of influence. And, unlike Cato and Cicero, Caesar had built it without alienating large segments of the population.

This was the world to which Pompey prepared to return in 62 BC. Though Pompey had certainly been kept abreast of events in the capital, he had no way to truly appreciate how the political dynamics in the city had changed. Not only did he now have to contend with three forceful and distinctive new rivals, but Pompey also had to deal with a Republic in which he himself had become a vessel in which supporters placed their hopes and opponents placed their fears. Pompey would return a man, but Romans expected either a hero or a monster. It is unsurprising, then, that Pompey's arrival did not go as he planned.

CHAPTER 9

STUMBLING TOWARD DICTATORSHIP

POMPEY RECEIVED NEWS OF MITHRIDATES's death while in Jericho, settling affairs in Judaea.[1] The old king, who had encouraged the genocide of tens of thousands of Romans, crashed the Roman economy, and defeated or evaded two generations of Rome's best commanders (including both Sulla and Pompey), ended up dying as the result of an assassination plot hatched by his own son Pharnaces. Romans, however, did not care how Mithridates had died—only that he was in fact dead. And when word of Mithridates's death reached Rome, the city rejoiced with a ten-day-long festival of thanksgiving.

For some Romans, joy turned to worry as Pompey slowly made his way back to Italy. Pompey's unparalleled military and political authority was tied specifically to the task of defeating Mithridates. With this enemy dead, and with Nepos's attempt to extend Pompey's command by empowering him to march against Catiline having failed, Pompey controlled a massive army without any clear legal authority to do so. It was impractical to expect any commander to dismiss an army while abroad, but some of Pompey's activities in the winter and spring of 62 looked suspicious. As he made his way home, for instance, Pompey stopped in

Mytilene, Ephesus, Rhodes, and Athens. Each city greeted him with well-choreographed celebrations of his achievements. These included a poetry competition in his honor in Mytilene and public performances by orators in Rhodes and philosophers in Athens. Pompey reciprocated with gifts to the cities and the performers— including a grant of 300,000 denarii to the city of Athens.[2]

Observers in Rome knew that this victory tour was a way to simultaneously celebrate what Pompey had accomplished and reinforce the ties that Pompey had built with his clients in the East. But they did not know what these steps meant for people in the capital. Were these celebrations of Pompey by provincials who were genuinely grateful for the peace he now brought and the benefactions he had given in the past? Or was Pompey instead reinforcing his support outside Rome as part of his preparations for an imminent civil war? Cicero, for one, had his suspicions. In a letter he composed in June of 62, Cicero indicated that people in Rome held out hope that, when Pompey landed in Italy, he would march on the city. Cicero then suggests, in typically Ciceronian fashion, that the appropriate thing for Pompey to do in the circumstances would be to extend congratulations to Cicero for saving the Republic. But, as Pompey drew nearer to Italy, Plutarch reports that rumors that Pompey "would straightway lead his army to the city" caused Crassus to flee with his children and his money "because he was truly afraid or rather, so it seems, because he wished to make the rumor seem trustworthy and make the ill-will [toward Pompey] harsher."[3]

Pompey likely was aware of these rumors and the effect they were having on his popularity. Before he even arrived in Italy, he sent a letter to the Senate indicating he would return in peace. Then, when he arrived in the Italian port of Brundisium near the end of 62, Pompey dismissed his army without even waiting for a triumph. No author explains the extraordinary nature of Pompey's decision better than Cassius Dio. Pompey, Dio writes, enjoyed "tremendous power both on sea and on land; he had supplied himself with vast wealth...he had made numerous rulers and kings his friends and he had kept practically all of the communities he governed happy...with these things he could have taken Italy and gained for himself all that Rome controlled...and yet he did not do this." Instead, he called his army together when they disembarked, thanked them sincerely for all that they had been able to accomplish together, and gave them liberty to return to the towns from which they had come.[4]

Many in Rome reacted in the same way that Dio did more than two centuries later. Surprise that Pompey had decided not to follow Sulla's example in marching on Rome gave way to elation as Pompey moved unarmed through Italy.[5] Most ancient authors do not comment on the fact that Pompey's decision, which earned such immediate praise, ended up being a horrible miscalculation. There were, after all, very good reasons that prominent commanders did not usually dismiss their armies immediately upon their return from fighting overseas. Even when a commander was too weak to imagine marching on Rome, his army offered leverage that ensured that both he and his soldiers would be treated fairly even by political opponents. And they needed to be treated fairly. Generals who had made arrangements for the dispensation of provinces or cities needed senatorial endorsement of those decisions. And very successful military leaders like Pompey also hoped to be able to reward their veterans' service with gifts of land, something that the messy politics of land distribution made exceedingly difficult to manage. And yet, as Dio noted with great surprise, Pompey dismissed his army "without waiting for any vote to be passed by the Senate or the people and without concerning himself at all even about the use of these men in the triumph."[6] He understood, Dio continued, that Romans "held the careers of Marius and Sulla in abomination and he did not wish to cause them any fear, even for a few days, that they might undergo a similar experience."

Whereas Sulla had marched on Rome because he did not trust the Republic to protect him or his interests, Pompey had unilaterally disarmed before the political debates over his triumph, his eastern settlements, the nature of his conquests, and the rewards for his veterans had even begun. Some of Pompey's other actions in 62 suggest why he took this dramatic step. Although Pompey trusted the procedures of the Republic more than Sulla, he did not imagine that Rome had become the sort of system in which successful generals waited patiently for honors and recognition. But he also seems to have assumed that, given the magnitude of his accomplishments, no one would dare deny him the recognition and rewards he had earned. Indeed, although Pompey's recent commands had derived from a combination of alliances with populist tribunes and the use of a sort of military blackmail, he apparently believed that his influence had become so overwhelming that he would be welcomed into the very center of the Roman social and political establishment. Even before he returned to Rome, Pompey had decided to divorce his wife Mucia, who was a member of the Caecilius Metellus family and the sister of the tribune Nepos. Ostensibly, Pompey had done this because he suspected she had committed adultery, but this had always been a political marriage. When Mucia had married Pompey in 79 BC, he was an ambitious young man looking to forge an alliance with one of the Republic's most powerful families. In 62, however, Pompey was no longer a parvenu. He felt that he had outgrown the Metelli and saw the need in particular to distinguish himself from his brother-in-law Nepos. He was now Rome's most influential figure and he wanted a marriage that would better match his status as Rome's leading citizen.[7]

Pompey decided to replace the marriage alliance with the Metelli with one that would bind Cato to him. Cato had two nieces and Pompey proposed that he would marry one of them and Pompey's son could marry the other. Pompey here may have been inspired by Sulla's marriage alliance with the Metelli in the 80s, but Cato was not a Metellus. Instead of a mutually beneficial alliance, Cato "detected that this was a plot to corrupt him."[8] Cato had already built a coalition of senators opposed to Pompey,[9] and Pompey had now unwittingly solidified Cato's status as his most committed and principled opponent by offering the young senator the opportunity to ostentatiously reject a marriage alliance with Rome's most powerful man.[10]

This was one of many rebuffs that Cato would deliver to Pompey in the coming months, but Cato was not Pompey's only problem as he returned to the capital. Political life in the city ground to a halt from January of 61 until May because of a peculiar scandal that erupted when Publius Clodius, the son of the ex-consul Appius Claudius, was discovered at Julius Caesar's house wearing women's clothing and attending the religious rites of the Bona Dea, a religious ceremony from which all men were barred. This incident, which took place at the home of Rome's chief priest, combined a serious act of sacrilege with the salacious suggestion of an adulterous affair between Caesar's wife and Clodius. Both ordinary Romans and senators could not stop talking about Clodius and the particular developments of his trial, a series of distractions that prevented the Senate from taking up any of the measures Pompey needed it to address. And, without his army around him, Pompey lacked the leverage to redirect the Senate's attention.[11]

In the meantime, Pompey's influence eroded. Pompey declined to play a role in the prosecution of Clodius. When asked for his views, he muttered bromides about supporting the Senate and all of its decrees. No progress was made on finding land for Pompey's veterans or on securing senatorial approval of his recent conquests and the other political arrangements he had made to settle the East. Pompey was accorded a triumph, which was held in September of 61 and which was the most spectacular celebration of its kind that Rome had ever seen.[12] Pompey made sure that the event illustrated the sheer enormity of his achievements by listing all of the nations and regions he had conquered. In subsequent commemorations, Pompey even mentioned the revenue streams his conquests had opened for the Republic. But, as the

Senate continued to delay action, Pompey decided that his other concerns would best wait until the new magistrates for the year 60 took office.[13]

Pompey had reasons to be optimistic. The two new consuls taking office in 60 were both men who had served under Pompey and had been friendly with him in the past. One, Pompey's former legate, Afranius, owed his election to Pompey's financial support. The other, Metellus Celer, was the older brother of Nepos and Pompey's ex-wife Mucia. Although the Clodius trial had distracted the consuls and Senate for most of the first part of 61, Pompey's spectacular triumph (and the subsequent commemorations of it) reminded Romans of his unparalleled successes—and, subtly, of the unresolved business from his expedition. With consuls who Pompey imagined would be friendly to him soon taking office, he clearly expected these outstanding issues to be quickly addressed.

Pompey again had miscalculated. Afranius quickly showed himself to be incompetent, and, following Pompey's divorce from his sister Mucia, Celer had come to loathe the arrogant general.[14] Celer found powerful allies in Cato and Lucullus (who remained angry that Pompey had replaced him as commander in the war with Mithridates). When Pompey began working with the tribune Flavius to advance a law giving land to his veterans, Celer blocked it. An even more significant confrontation occurred over Pompey's eastern settlement. When these issues finally came under discussion in the Senate, Lucullus took the lead in blocking them, arguing that some of Pompey's arrangements had undone agreements that Lucullus had previously made and that, therefore, every component of Pompey's settlement of Asia Minor, Syria, and Judaea needed to be investigated and voted upon individually. Cato and Celer quickly voiced their approval for this approach as well.

Flavius then grouped the land distribution and eastern settlement together to try to force a vote on all of the measures at once, hoping that the consul might relent rather than antagonize

Pompey's tens of thousands of veterans. But Pompey's veterans had long since scattered to their hometowns and posed no immediate threat. Celer called Flavius's bluff and then attacked the tribune so aggressively that Flavius invoked tribunal sacrosanctity and had Celer put in prison. The situation soon became farcical. Refusing to back down, Celer ordered the Senate to assemble outside his cell. Flavius then put his tribune's bench in front of the door of the prison to prevent anyone from entering. Celer responded by commanding workers to cut a hole in the wall of his cell so that he could preside over the Senate when it gathered outside. Pompey finally asked Flavius to back down. Pompey was reduced to petulantly proclaiming that Celer, Cato, and Lucullus were merely jealous while privately "repenting of having let his legions go so soon and placing himself under the power of his enemies."[15] All the while, the political fate of tens of millions in the Eastern Mediterranean and the economic futures of perhaps a hundred thousand Roman veterans remained in a limbo created by Pompey's overconfidence, Celer's and Lucullus's personal grudges, and Cato's desire to stymie anyone he decided deserved it.

Pompey was only the most prominent of a host of figures whose interests were stymied by Cato and his allies as the end of the 60s neared. In late 61, the *equites* who had won contracts to collect the first round of taxes after the establishment of peace in Asia Minor began complaining that the war damage in the region had depressed revenues so much that they would not be able to recover their costs. Crassus, who had likely loaned some of the money these businessmen had paid up front, encouraged his equestrian associates to ask that their contracts be canceled and their money refunded.[16] Crassus then strongly backed their proposal. Cicero found the request "disgraceful" and "a confession of foolhardiness," but he felt compelled to back it as well because, as the self-appointed champion of the equestrian order in the Senate, his own position would be compromised if he opposed it. Celer, who was consul-elect at the time of the Senate's first meeting to discuss the issue, came out against the measure and Cato made it clear that he too opposed it, though there was not time for Cato to give the speech he had planned.

Once Celer took office, the measure to rework these contracts stalled, with Cato's obstruction in particular drawing the ire of its backers. Cicero continued to acknowledge that the legislation was shameless, but he argued that it should nonetheless be endorsed so that the Senate could keep the good will of Roman *equites*. Though Cato had "the best of intentions and unimpeachable honesty," Cicero wrote in June of 60, "he does harm to the Republic because the opinions he delivers belong in the *Republic* of Plato rather than amidst the filth [of the Republic] of Romulus."[17] Cato's insistence on abstract principles of propriety, Cicero complained, had led the *equites* to essentially boycott the Senate. For Cicero, the breakdown in cooperation between the Senate and *equites* dented his personal prestige. For Crassus, who probably lost money and appeared politically impotent to his clients, Cato's obstruction had both political and financial implications. Whereas Cicero was embarrassed, Crassus was angry.

Even as he and his allies blocked Cicero and Crassus on the tax contracts, Cato also started a fight with Caesar in 60. After his praetorship in 62, Caesar was assigned the governorship of Lusitania in Spain, a position that he clearly hoped to use as a stepping-stone to the consulship. Soon after Caesar arrived in his province, he provoked a conflict with Spanish tribes so that he might win a significant enough military victory to gain a triumph. Then, after he had defeated the tribes on the battlefield, Caesar left his province before his successor arrived so that he might first celebrate a triumph and then campaign for the consulship of the year 59 BC. Caesar returned to Italy in the spring of 60 to begin his campaign, but his haste had caused a problem. A triumphant general was not allowed to enter the city until the time of his triumph, but a candidate for the consulship had to declare his candidacy within the sacred limits of the city of Rome at the beginning of July. Caesar's triumph could not be scheduled so quickly and he thus petitioned for an exception that would allow him to remain outside the city and declare his candidacy in absentia.[18]

Although most senators had no objection to Caesar's proposal, Cato was resolutely opposed. Not only did Cato dislike Caesar, but his brother-in-law Bibulus also planned to run for consul. After Caesar had received most of the credit for the games the two men had jointly sponsored as aediles, Bibulus likely feared being outshone or outpolled by Caesar again. On the day that the Senate was to consider Caesar's request, Cato began a filibuster that lasted for the entire senate meeting so that no vote could be taken. Caesar recognized that Cato's obstruction would not end and elected to forgo the triumph so that he could campaign for consul. But, in a move that Cato surely backed, the consuls for 59 BC were given the "woods and pastures" of Italy as their province instead of a heavily garrisoned province like Gaul. This was a clear sign that some in the city wanted to prevent Caesar from getting control of an army in the event of his victory in the consular election. Then, when the electoral campaign began and Caesar forged an alliance with Lucius Lucceius, Suetonius reports, "even Cato did not deny that [electoral] bribery under such circumstances was for the good of the commonwealth." Discarding his long-standing, principled opposition to such practices, Cato began spending money to try to buy votes for Bibulus.[19]

Caesar understood that Cato's obstruction and hypocrisy had victimized so many people—Pompey, Crassus, Cicero, and more—that it offered Caesar the opportunity to build an exceptionally broad and powerful coalition of supporters. Cicero ultimately rebuffed Caesar's invitation to join an alliance, so Pompey and Crassus became the two key figures in this coalition. The two men hated each other nearly as much as they hated Cato, but Caesar had strong relationships with both of them dating back many years. In the Senate, Caesar had been the most vocal supporter of Pompey's commands against the pirates and against Mithridates.

He had even been suspended from office because of the backing he had given to Nepos's motion to recall Pompey to confront Catiline in 62 BC. Caesar also enjoyed such a strong relationship with Crassus that Crassus had loaned Caesar money so that he could pay off enough of his creditors to be allowed to depart Rome to assume his governorship in Spain in 61.[20]

Crassus and Pompey both brought their political partisans out to vote for Caesar. Caesar won election, but Bibulus polled second and became his colleague as consul. Caesar then understood that, if he wanted to accomplish anything as consul, he needed his alliance with Pompey and Crassus to endure for longer than the election campaign. If their bonds could be further solidified, the three men had the chance to sideline the obstructionists who had gridlocked the Senate for most of the past two years. Caesar therefore set out to end the feud between Crassus and Pompey. He knew that "without the aid of both...he could never come to any great power. If he made a friend of either of them alone, he would by that very fact have the other as his opponent and would meet with more failures through him than successes through the other." According to Dio, Caesar's great insight was that men like Pompey and Crassus would fight much harder to block their enemies than they would to help their friends. The only way to truly benefit from an alliance with the great general and the wealthy businessman was to reconcile them with one another and work together as a group.[21] Caesar also understood how to explain to Pompey and Crassus that their rivalry had caused their individual political fortunes to stagnate because it only "increased the power of such men as Cicero, Catulus, and Cato, men whose influence would be nothing if Crassus and Pompey would only unite."[22]

This process of reconciliation likely began before Caesar took office, continued in the first weeks he was in power, and was effectively concluded when Pompey married Caesar's daughter Julia in the spring of 59. This wedding ended a remarkable process that had taken Pompey from a possible marriage alliance with Cato to a pact that bound him to Crassus and Caesar. What emerged out of the three men's conversations was a working agreement that scholars have come to call the First Triumvirate.[23] Though Romans just a few decades later would see in this agreement the beginning of the end of the Republic, this was an outcome that no one imagined at the time. Pompey, Caesar, and Crassus had not decided to overthrow the state. They had instead agreed simply that "they would do things in common on behalf of each other."[24] Each man would pursue his own objectives, asking the others for help when needed and providing it when asked. Each man also agreed not to actively take any steps that might impede the ambitions of the other two. That was it. But that was enough. Cato and the obstructionists could now be overpowered by the combination of Caesar's political skills, Pompey's devoted clients and veterans, and Crassus's wealth whenever they tried to block initiatives that were important to a member of the alliance. These three individuals now could overcome the checks the Republic could place on their activities.

Part of the reason that the alliance succeeded was that Cato's tactics in 61 and 60 had engendered tremendous frustration in nearly every segment of Roman society. *Equites* and their senatorial backers hoped to renegotiate Asian tax contracts, Pompey's veterans looked for land to reward their service, and the most powerful men in Rome were tired of being rendered impotent by a high-minded but hypocritical philosopher-senator and his allies. Caesar understood this frustration. He recognized the longing Romans felt for someone to break the political gridlock and, perhaps more importantly, a growing willingness to tolerate unconventional political methods if they ensured that the Republic functioned. And now, with the alliance of Pompey and Crassus, Caesar had the resources to finally make things happen again in Rome.

The first major piece of legislation that Caesar sponsored as consul was a land law designed to move some population from the crowded capital, settle some of Pompey's veterans, and return certain parts of Italy to cultivation. The new farms would be on land that belonged to the Roman state, but the fertile public lands in Campania would be exempt from distribution. Any additional land that was needed would be purchased from private property owners using funds from Pompey's campaigns. Caesar also proposed the creation of a land commission. Unlike the small Gracchan land commissions headed by men who proposed the land law, Caesar's commission would have twenty commissioners (including Crassus and Pompey), but, to avoid suspicion of corruption, Caesar would not take part in it.

The law offered a reasonable solution to what had seemed an intractable political problem. Caesar understood that he had the influence to force it through should that prove necessary, but he designed the law so perfectly that no one could raise a reasonable objection against it. Caesar also put the law up for discussion in the Senate in the most transparent way possible. He had the text read aloud and then called on each senator by name and asked him whether he had any criticism of the law or any clauses to which he had particular objections. Much to the chagrin of Cato and his associates, no one could find anything wrong with the text of the law. "They were particularly upset," Dio writes, "that Caesar had crafted such a measure as would admit of no censure even while it weighed heavily" upon their personal interests.[25]

The senators did not yet understand it, but Caesar had baited the perfect trap. No senator spoke against the text of the law, but as had become customary, they began the process of delaying action on it. Cato again took the lead: "Even though he could find no fault with the measure, Cato nevertheless urged them generally to continue with the present system and to take no steps outside of it."[26] Cato had gone too far. Caesar threatened to haul him to prison, but, when Cato offered to go willingly, Caesar changed course. He let the conflict with Cato drop. Stealing a page from the playbook of rabble-rousing tribunes like Tiberius Gracchus, Caesar bypassed the Senate and had the measure put before the people for a vote. When the Senate complained that such things were not done, Caesar replied simply that he had given the Senate the opportunity to comment on the law and strike any provisions it found objectionable. Because no one found any such provisions, the people should now be free to decide on the matter themselves.

Caesar had learned from the frustrations of the past two groups of consuls. Cato and his associates could indeed shut down the Senate, but they had no direct power to stop a vote of the people. Caesar, as consul, had adopted the tactics that recent tribunes had used to get around senatorial obstruction: simply ignore the Senate and proceed.[27] Ordinarily, such a maneuver might invite hostility, but Caesar had orchestrated the situation so well that any reasonable observer would agree that he had no choice but to take his measure directly to the people. Caesar had forced senators to show that they had no real objections to his law other than the facts that Caesar had proposed it and Pompey would benefit from it. Whatever Cato and his minions might say, the true intentions of the hostile senators were clear to all.

Caesar wisely used Pompey and Crassus to build support for his land reform among the people. Both men spoke in favor of it. Then, when it became clear that Caesar's opponents might resort to violence to block a vote in the popular assembly, Pompey went so far as to indicate that, if force was used to stop passage of the law, he would be compelled to use force himself to secure its passage. Caesar's strategic appeal to the two men not only honored them but also frightened opponents who saw that Caesar had the backing of two of Rome's most influential figures.[28]

The senatorial obstruction of the past few years had made Romans unusually tolerant of forceful actions that brought results, but Caesar also understood the danger in appearing too heavy-handed. This led him to publicly appeal for Bibulus to either support the measure (an outcome that even Caesar would have known to be unlikely) or at least decline to obstruct the vote. But Bibulus

was loyal to Cato and used three allied tribunes to delay the vote
for as long as he could. When he ran out of reasons to delay it,
Bibulus then declared the remainder of the year a sacred period in
which no assemblies could be held or votes taken. Caesar simply
ignored this absurd pronouncement and scheduled a vote. When
the day came, Bibulus forced his way through the crowds and began speaking against the law. He was swarmed, the ceremonial
axes carried by his consular bodyguard were broken, and the tribunes allied with him were beaten. Bibulus then fled and Caesar's
law was approved.

Caesar's opponents could do no more than make symbolic acts
of protest. On the following day, Bibulus appealed to the Senate
to annul the law, but, intimidated by the popular enthusiasm for
Caesar's proposal, no one took up the motion. Bibulus then retreated to his house and did not leave again until the final day of
his consular term. His only official actions for the rest of the year
consisted of sending notices to Caesar before every subsequent
vote he called indicating that the day was sacred and Caesar was
committing a sacrilege by taking action on it. The tribunes allied
with him followed Bibulus's lead and refused to take part in any
public business for the rest of the year.

Cato's response was only slightly less pathetic. Caesar's law
contained a provision that required all members of the Senate to
swear to uphold the law. This stipulation had, of course, been part
of the land law that Saturninus had passed in 100 BC, and Metellus Numidicus's failure to swear such an oath had led to his exile.
Cato and Metellus Celer evoked this earlier incident of popular
overreach and claimed that, like Metellus Numidicus, they would
refuse to swear to uphold an objectionable law whose passage was
clouded by violence. When the last day to take the oath without
penalty arrived, however, both Cato and Celer broke down, perhaps, as Dio explains, "because it is human nature to utter promises and threats more easily than to actually carry them out...or

because they were going to be punished for no purpose without helping the Republic at all with their obstinacy."[29]

Caesar's genius in crafting the land reform law allowed him to repay Pompey by rewarding the general's veterans and provide benefits to a large number of Roman citizens not loyal to Pompey who would now look to Caesar as their primary benefactor. Caesar did the same thing with another measure that sought to offer some relief to the equestrian businessmen who were losing money on the contracts they had purchased for Asian taxes. This law, which lowered by one-third the obligations these men owed the Republic, passed a few weeks after the land law, probably in mid-April of 59. This gratified Crassus, but it also positioned Caesar as an advocate for the *equites,* a stance that partially undercut Cicero. Again, Cato was reduced to petulant passive aggressiveness. Although he did not object to the law itself, when he enforced it as praetor, Cato refused to mention that the law bore Caesar's name.[30]

In May, Caesar advanced a third major law that ratified Pompey's eastern settlements.[31] This measure provided for a substantial reorganization of Roman provincial rule in much of Asia Minor, the establishment of the Roman province of Syria, and the confirmation of a number of pro-Roman sovereigns in command of territories in Asia Minor and Judaea. By ratifying the complicated relationships that Pompey had established with these clients, Caesar's law solidified Pompey's status as the most influential man in the Republic. It also validated the immense personal wealth that Pompey had built up through his eastern campaigns.

The law opened up substantial streams of revenue for the Republic, and Caesar decided to take advantage of these to settle more Romans on public land in Italy. The fertile Campanian public land exempted from Caesar's earlier land reform was distributed to Roman families with three or more children at roughly the same time as the approval of the eastern settlement, a savvy move that enabled Caesar to substitute the revenue coming in from the East for the revenue lost from rents paid to the state on the Campanian land.[32] And, of course, Caesar got the full credit for this law from those Romans who now settled on their new farms in Campania.

By May or early June, Caesar moved to take advantage of the popularity his laws had generated. Vatianus, the tribune with whom Caesar had most closely aligned, sponsored a law that gave Caesar a military command in the provinces of Cisalpine Gaul and Illyricum after his term as consul ended. This included control of three legions and the right to name all of his own military legates.[33] This law represented the final tear in the web of obstruction that Cato and his allies had woven to thwart the ambitions of Pompey, Crassus, and Caesar. Instead of a meaningless command over the woodlands and trails of Italy, Caesar now had charge over two of the provinces to Italy's north. Then, later in the year, Pompey sponsored a motion in the Senate to add the frontier province of Transalpine Gaul to Caesar's command and give him an additional legion with which to campaign. Perhaps prompted by news that the Gallic tribe of the Helvetii were moving toward Roman territory, Pompey's measure gave Caesar a unified command over both Gallic provinces. These moves clearly anticipated a campaign beyond the Roman frontiers. No one, however, could have imagined the scale and scope of what Caesar would actually do when he set out for Gaul in early 58.

In just a few months, Caesar succeeded in breaking through the senatorial gridlock that had slowed Roman political life in the later 60s. This enabled him to accomplish a great deal. He had distributed land to Pompey's veterans and other landless Romans. He had legalized Pompey's annexation of territory in Asia Minor and Syria as well as his political reorganization of Roman client kingdoms across the East. He had renegotiated the Asian tax contracts for Crassus's equestrian associates. Most importantly, Caesar had set up the next spectacular stage in his career by securing a command in Gaul that gave him a large army and considerable latitude to use it as he wished. Caesar had done this by expertly deploying a blend of potent personal relationships, skillful political maneuvering, and the threat that obstruction or disruption might be met with violence. Other ambitious Romans quickly absorbed these lessons. By the time Caesar departed for Gaul, Rome was again facing the onset of political chaos. This time it was caused both by the example Caesar had set and by one of the few miscalculations that he made during his consulship.

Publius Clodius Pulcher stood at the center of the gathering storm. Clodius had already become a notorious figure after he was found wearing women's clothes in Caesar's house during the all-female rituals of the Bona Dea. Whereas Caesar had elected to divorce his wife on suspicions of adultery, he forgave Clodius for his role in the incident. Other senators, however, had denounced Clodius both during and after his trial. No one took greater pleasure in this than Cicero. Cicero not only attacked Clodius with great vigor but even delighted in telling friends about how totally his words had decimated Clodius in the Senate. Unfortunately for Cicero, this was another occasion when the orator had dramatically overestimated his own importance and the actual power of his words. Clodius was far from destroyed. Instead, he was invigorated and filled with a passion for vengeance.[34]

Although Clodius was the son of a consul and a member of a prominent patrician family, he recognized that the infamy he earned in the Bona Dea affair made it unlikely that he could build the sort of political career that his father and grandfather had enjoyed.[35] But Clodius had other options. His ties to Crassus were close enough that Crassus decided to bribe jurors to secure Clodius's acquittal. Caesar bore him no lasting animosity. Clodius also possessed both personal charisma and a rapidly growing crowd of supporters willing to use violence in support of his objectives. Instead of the scion of one of the most prominent patrician families, Clodius would remake himself into a rabble-rousing tribune of the plebs.

The only problem was that, as a patrician, Clodius was ineligible to run for this office. So, in 59, Clodius arranged to be adopted by the plebeian P. Fonteius. The move was as utterly transparent as it was absurd. Fonteius, Clodius's new father, was actually younger than Clodius. Clodius also chose to violate the Roman custom of taking on the name of his new family. He instead merely changed his patrician clan name Claudius to the plebeian-sounding Clodius. Clodius then began looking for priestly endorsement of the adoption, as was required by Roman law.[36]

Caesar here made the most significant political mistake of his consulship. In March of 59, amid the extremely active first months of Caesar's consulship, Cicero's old consular colleague Antonius was put on trial. Cicero took up Antonius's defense out of a sense of obligation for his help in the Catilinarian crisis. In his statements at the trial, Cicero got carried away and attacked the violence and intimidation with which Caesar and his allies now seemed to be dominating Roman politics.[37] Caesar acted with uncharacteristic rashness. Usually, when someone behaved in a way that displeased him, Caesar avoided direct action. He often pardoned people for their offense, or, if he felt the need to retaliate, he did so by empowering intermediaries who could limit the offending party's ability to do further damage. But in this case, perhaps frazzled by the challenges of the first months of his consulship and rumors of a plot to assassinate Pompey that also supposedly involved Cicero, Caesar and Pompey both overreacted.[38] Cicero spoke against the consul in the morning. That afternoon, Caesar, acting in his position as *pontifex maximus,* presided over Clodius's adoption and Pompey, who was an augur, officiated at the ceremony. Although the matter had not been presented to the *comitia centuriata* as it properly should have been, Caesar's pontifical endorsement of it effectively cleared Clodius to stand for the tribunate.

Caesar and Pompey knew that Clodius had wanted revenge against Cicero ever since the orator aggressively attacked him during the Bona Dea scandal, and they suspected that the prospect of Clodius as a tribune would terrorize Cicero into silence. It did, but Pompey and Caesar soon realized that they had paid an enormous price to shut up the arrogant orator. Clodius was extremely charismatic, unpredictable, and loyal only to his own ambition. This made him both an unreliable partner and a potential source of trouble for the men who had recently pushed through laws that remade significant parts of Roman life. Pompey and Caesar tried to find ways to divert Clodius from his electoral campaign by offering to send him on embassies abroad. They also offered Cicero ways to get out of Rome. Caesar suggested that Cicero take a position as a legate in his army, and Pompey proposed that Cicero go on an embassy to Alexandria. None of it worked. Cicero refused to leave and Clodius merely became irritated. As the summer began, Clodius even intimated that he might make the power of Caesar and Pompey an issue in his campaign for tribune.

Clodius won election that summer and began his time in office with a spurt of legislation designed to boost his popularity. On January 4, 58, he introduced a package of laws designed to appeal to both the people and the Senate. It appealed to the people by creating a free grain dole for the urban population of Rome and attracted senators by limiting the power of censors, the magistrates who set senatorial membership as part of each Roman census. With both groups happy, the measure passed without any veto.[39] Clodius then moved against Cicero. He proposed a measure that would exile any Roman who had put citizens to death without trial and tried to win the acquiescence of the consuls by pairing it with a provision shifting the commands allotted to them to more favorable provinces. Facing exile, Cicero withdrew from Rome. Clodius followed his departure with a law requiring that Cicero remain more than four hundred miles from the city. When a mob then attacked Cicero's house on the Palatine, Clodius had the damaged building replaced with a shrine to Libertas (the divine personification of Freedom). This act simultaneously mocked Cicero's claim of having saved the Republic from tyranny and prevented Cicero from rebuilding his home by making the plot of land sacred space.

Both ruthless and shrewd, Clodius understood how to keep Caesar, Pompey, and even Cato off balance while he pushed forward his agenda. Caesar, who was now campaigning in Gaul, could be held in check by the idea that all of his legislation as well as the law giving him his Gallic command could be voided if Clodius moved to recognize Bibulus's prohibition on votes being taken. Pompey could be cowed both by rumors of assassination plots and by fears of unpopularity. And Clodius exploited Cato's commitment to public service and his ambition by offering him a command to annex Cyprus. Behind all of this lurked Clodius's remarkable ability to build and organize a powerful and violent network of supporters that could intimidate people at public assemblies and in the streets of the city.

Clodius's emergence as the leader of an organized political mob would come to paralyze Roman political life for much of the rest of the decade. Clodius's supporters were soon met by mobs organized by his rivals. The most notable of these was led by Milo, a figure whose violent supporters proved an effective match for those of Clodius. But Milo was far from the only person to imitate Clodius's methods. These competing mobs and their leaders rapidly created a far deadlier culture of obstruction in the 50s than anything found in the 60s. Whereas Cato had used legislative tools to block the policy initiatives of his rivals in the Senate, Clodius and Milo used violence on the streets to effectively shut down large segments of the Republic.

The first signs of this troubling dynamic appeared in 57 when clashes involving partisans of Clodius and Milo effectively prevented the *concilium plebis* and Senate from meeting to decide on the possible return of Cicero. The measure only passed that August when it was put instead before the centuriate assembly, a body that did not usually vote on laws because its structure strongly privileged the votes of Rome's wealthiest citizens. The situation became even worse as the year progressed. Opponents of Clodius used violence to delay the election for aedile, an office for which Clodius stood, because they hoped to put Clodius on trial before ascension to that office gave him immunity from prosecution. The situation became so tense that supporters of Milo physically occupied the Campus Martius for a number of days in mid-November to block allies of Clodius from announcing unfavorable omens that might prevent public business. Supporters of Clodius then broke up senate meetings in which Clodius's violence was to be discussed.[40]

Things deteriorated further in 56. Clodius was elected aedile in January. He then put Milo on trial and began verbally attacking Pompey. Pompey became concerned enough that he first summoned supporters from the countryside in February and then, as spring approached, decided that he would run for consul for the year 55. In April, Pompey met with Caesar in the Tuscan city of Luca and, following on a separate agreement that Caesar had made with Crassus, the three men renewed their political alliance. They agreed that Pompey and Crassus would stand for the consulship of 55 and that Caesar, who had in the past several years conquered much of the territory that is now France, Belgium, Switzerland, and the Netherlands, would have his command extended for a further five years so that he could consolidate the lands he had taken.

This was easier said than done. The consular election pitted Pompey and Crassus against L. Domitius Ahenobarbus, the brother-in-law of Cato, and such violence marred the campaign that the vote was delayed until after the start of the year 55. Pompey and Crassus won the long-delayed election only when Caesar's troops returned to spend the winter in Italy. Although Caesar never threatened to use his forces to intervene in the campaign, the presence of an army commanded by an ally of Pompey and Crassus convinced their opponents that further disruptions would be unwise. The new consuls then extended Caesar's command for an additional five years, again thwarting Cato's attempts to block the measure. When their consular terms concluded at the end of 55, Crassus set off for Syria. He hoped to surpass both Pompey and Caesar by using this province as a platform to conquer the Parthian Empire, a massive kingdom that stretched from modern Pakistan to Iraq. Pompey was awarded a command in Spain, but he elected to delegate control of his army to deputies. He would instead stay just outside of the city of Rome in order to monitor the situation in the city.

Subsequent events proved the wisdom of Pompey's decision. The election campaign to choose the consuls of 53 was so delayed by violence and bickering that voting did not occur until the summer of 53, leaving the state without consuls for most of that year. Their election came so late that the campaigns for the consuls seeking to serve in 52 had already begun at the time of the vote. Making matters worse, in May of 53, Crassus stumbled into an ambush outside of the city of Carrhae in northwest Mesopotamia, a site that now sits astride the modern border separating Turkey and Syria. Crassus was killed, along with perhaps thirty thousand of his soldiers. This not only destabilized Rome's eastern frontier but, coming a few months after the death of Caesar's daughter and Pompey's wife Julia, it also dissolved the triumvirate. The alliance of Caesar, Pompey, and Crassus had worked so well because none of them was powerful enough to prevail over the combined resources of the other two. With Crassus gone and the marriage alliance binding Caesar and Pompey now finished, there was nothing to prevent the two surviving partners from becoming rivals.

This did not happen immediately, however. Caesar initially remained in Gaul, consolidating his conquests and embarking on campaigns into Britain and across the Rhine into Germany in the later part of the 50s. As he did so, he sent to Rome annual commentaries that celebrated his achievements (or, in the case of his German campaign, concealed his failures), generated public recognition for the scope of his conquests, and generally enhanced the reputation he already had earned as a powerful and inspirational commander. To the Roman public, Caesar seemed a larger and more accomplished version of the character he had always been.[41]

Pompey, meanwhile, found himself thrust into a new role as a stabilizing force in Rome. He had already taken small steps in this direction in 57, when he calmed Rome after Cicero had pushed through a measure giving Pompey imperium to control a rapid increase in the price of grain in the capital. But the real catalyst for Pompey's transformation into a pillar of the Republican establishment came in 52. In mid-53, the populist rivals Clodius and Milo both began campaigns for offices with terms to begin in 52. Violence between their followers prevented the elections from being held in 53 as custom dictated, and, as 52 began, they threatened to postpone the votes indefinitely. When the terms of the consuls for 53 ended, an interrex stepped in to perform their duties until consuls for 52 could be elected. Then, on January 18, supporters of Milo chanced upon Clodius while he was traveling the Appian Way outside of Rome. In the ensuing scuffle, they ended up killing Clodius as well as a number of his followers. Clodius's funeral the following day degenerated into severe rioting. The crowd of mourners burned the senate house and began to publicly call for the immediate appointment of Milo's rivals to the consulship or, failing this, the selection of Pompey as dictator.[42]

After the riot, the interrex moved quickly to have Pompey selected as sole consul for the year 52, a remarkable break with the Republican notion that all regular magistrates should have colleagues. Pompey had already been empowered by the Senate to raise troops to calm the violence following Clodius's death, and the Senate consequently backed Pompey's appointment as sole consul as well, though the historian Asconius suggests that many did so only because it was preferable to having Pompey taking power as dictator.[43]

During the remainder of 52, Pompey did what many must have regarded as impossible. Backed by the army he had raised, he stabilized the city and initiated a series of reforms designed to destroy the power of gang violence as a political tool. The centerpiece of this effort, a law that made prosecutions of those engaged in violence easier, led to the conviction of a number of people involved in the Appian Way battle that led to Clodius's death. Pompey then presided over the election of a consular colleague for the rest of 52, saw to the extension of his own command in Spain, and oversaw the orderly election of magistrates for the year 51 with time enough to spare that they were able to take office when their terms began on January 1.

Pompey's successes, however, only partially obscured the dangerous reality that 52 had revealed. The Republic now could only function when superintended by Rome's most powerful man—and then only when he had military backing. Pompey did not govern like a dictator, of course, but the Republican system now effectively required the visible hand of a strongman to keep it from descending into repeated crises. Pompey was the pillar on which the Republic rested, even if no one at the time was willing to admit it.

This reality had another important implication. Pompey's stabilizing of the Republic had transformed both his perception within Rome and his relationship with Caesar. Conservative figures such as Cato still did not exactly trust Pompey, but they understood the vital role that Pompey now played in ensuring regular elections and the orderly cycling of magistracies. A Republic protected by Pompey remained a Republic in which consuls, praetors, aediles, and quaestors could be elected, senators could enjoy honors, and leading men could use the same markers their ancestors had to measure their achievements.

Caesar offered Romans no such assurances. At some point in the winter of 53–52, Caesar made the first exploratory move for the next act in his political career. Although he still had two years remaining in his Gallic command, Caesar received legal sanction to stand for the consulship in absentia.[44] Whatever Caesar initially planned to do with this authorization, events in Gaul interceded.

A major Gallic revolt erupted in 52 and, though the capture of the stronghold of Alesia ended most of the danger, mop-up operations lasted into the campaigning season of 51. Caesar, who had by then conquered more territory than any Roman commander except Pompey, certainly wanted to get full credit for his achievements by seeing his Gallic wars through to a definitive conclusion.

This meant that Caesar wanted to stay in Gaul until the end of 51 and, perhaps, even try to remain on campaign into the year 50. The problem, however, was that the consuls of the year 51 were overtly hostile to Caesar and even suggested during that year that Caesar's command should end in March of 50. Pompey argued against setting a firm date, but discussion of how and when to end Caesar's Gallic command persisted until after the consular elections for the year 50, a fact that virtually ensured that Caesar would have to return to Rome holding no office.

By late September of 51, the question had become more pressing. The Senate began a series of debates about Caesar's command, considering proposals that included the discharge of some of his soldiers and the designation of Transalpine Gaul as a province to be allotted to one of the consuls who served in 50. At this meeting, Pompey supported the idea that a discussion of who would take over Caesar's provinces should begin after March 1 of 50. When he was questioned about whether Caesar should be permitted to be consul while commanding his Gallic army, Pompey indicated that such a thing was unthinkable by replying: "What if my son wishes to beat me with a stick?" This comment resonated loudly because it suggested that Caesar was Pompey's inferior, that he would not dare to contravene the wishes of Rome's leading citizen, and that, if he did, Pompey could easily beat his challenge back. Pompey was, yet again, implicitly reassuring senators that he would act to preserve the stability of the Republic in the unlikely event that Caesar chose to defy him.[45]

Pompey's personalization of the collective problem of Caesar's command offered the most striking evidence of how Roman

politics had changed in the preceding years. Pompey was not alone
in recognizing that, where once Rome's republic had been governed by a collection of elites who collaborated to build broad
political consensuses, now two powerful individuals shaped its political dynamics. Others also understood this, and they saw potential benefits that could come from exploiting the growing tensions
between the two men. None did this more than the tribune Gaius
Curio. Curio apparently had won election as a candidate who
pledged to resist Caesar, but, after a measure to roll back some of
Caesar's land reforms in Campania failed to generate the attention
he desired, Curio "began to speak for Caesar" and started advocating for positions that would help Caesar's political position. Much
like the tribunes in the 60s who tried to proactively build relationships with Pompey by proposing measures that favored him, Caesar likely had very little to do personally with Curio's shift. This
was instead an opportunistic act by a politically ambitious man
who understood that one now made his mark in Rome by carving
out a space beside one of the Republic's titans.[46]

By the middle of 50, Curio had begun calling for both Caesar
and Pompey to dismiss their armies at the same time. This was
thoroughly impractical, because Pompey's command still had
years to run. But many in Rome nevertheless cheered the idea of a
mutual disarmament that might spare the Republic an armed conflict. And Caesar, of course, particularly welcomed a measure that
put him and Pompey on a sort of equal footing. Pompey, however, refused to yield. He instead proposed a sort of compromise
through which Caesar's command would end in November of 50,
a date that made it possible for Caesar to run for consul in absentia
during the summer and retain control of his army until just before
he took office. This seemed reasonable on the surface, but, with
elections now regularly postponed, no one could guarantee that
the consular elections would actually take place in the summer of
50. Caesar, therefore, neither accepted this date nor placed himself forward as a candidate for consul, fearing, with some reason,

that the election might be delayed until after he had dismissed his army. This would leave him open to prosecution if he did not hold an office or a command and, potentially, at risk of assassination if he lacked the protection of his army.[47]

The last senate meeting of 50 showed that the Republic lacked the capacity to stop the personal conflict between Caesar and Pompey. The Senate voted on three resolutions. One motion, which called on Pompey alone to dismiss his army, was defeated. Another motion, which ordered only Caesar to give up his command, was approved. But a third motion, which echoed Curio's calls from earlier in the year that both men dismiss their forces, was endorsed by a 370–22 vote.[48] The Senate and the people of Rome alike wanted both men to step back from conflict. Pompey refused to do so and ended any hope for a compromise by taking control of the forces in Italy.

The Senate and people of Rome were dragged along as Pompey prepared for a war they did not want. The incoming consuls for 49 pressed the Senate to appoint a successor for Caesar in Gaul and Illyricum and, when tribunes loyal to Caesar tried to veto the act in order to keep Caesar in command of the army there, the Senate passed an emergency decree. Fearing for their safety, the tribunes fled to Caesar. In this way, a decade that began with Caesar's shattering of the Catonian political gridlock that had paralyzed the Republic ended with a Republic too weak to resist as two leaders marched it into civil war. The republican system no longer constrained the individual. Roman political life now consisted of a struggle among individuals seeking honor and power through the complete control of the city and the resources of its empire. And, for the first time since Sulla, it was clear that this was a fight to the death. No institutions existed that could protect the life or property of the loser. The final march from the Republic to the Empire had begun.

CHAPTER 10

THE BIRTH AND DEATH OF CAESAR'S REPUBLIC

T HE CONFLICT THAT ENDED THE Roman Republic began with
a politically momentous crossing of a physically insignificant
river. On or around January 10 of 49 BC, Caesar led his army
across the Rubicon. It was not an extraordinary logistical achievement. The Rubicon now is so narrow that, even near its mouth, a
man can practically jump from one bank to the other. But leading
an army across the Rubicon had immense political significance.
The river represented the political boundary between Italy and the
province of Cisalpine Gaul, and, when Caesar crossed it, he would
be in open revolt against the Republic. This effectively foreclosed
the chance for a peaceful resolution to his conflict with Pompey.

This should not obscure the fact that Caesar had meticulously
laid the military and political groundwork for such a move for
much of the previous year. When Caesar's war commentaries cov-
ering the events of 50 BC appeared a few years later, they ended
with a section bridging the conclusion of his Gallic campaigns and
the beginning of the civil war. In it, one sees how Caesar's final
actions in the Gallic war blended together with his preparations
for the clash to come. During the first months of 50, when most
of Rome still hoped for a peaceful resolution of Caesar's conflict

with the Senate and Caesar was still based in Belgium, the general attempted to secure his conquests by giving generous gifts to the Gallic chieftains in charge of the territories he had recently conquered. With the support of these Gallic figures now solidified, Caesar left most of his troops and officers behind as he traveled south to the towns and colonies of Cisalpine Gaul with which he had built a relationship. Ostensibly, Caesar did so in order to campaign for his quaestor, Marcus Antonius (commonly known to English speakers as Mare Antony). Antony was standing in an upcoming election for a vacant priesthood. This feeble pretext evaporated when Antony was elected before Caesar even arrived in the region. Caesar then reframed the trip as either a tour thanking the voters for supporting Antony or, alternatively, a way to build support for his own plan to run for consul for the year 48. In practice, though, Caesar's visits were carefully orchestrated to remind residents of his achievements in uniting Gaul. Entire towns turned out to greet Caesar, sacrifices were made to mark his arrival, and communities laid out couches in marketplaces and temples as if they were setting up feasts for a festival.[1]

Caesar then returned to his army, which was encamped not far from the modern city of Lille. He reinforced it with troops based in what is now western Germany and steadily led his forces south just as, in Rome, Caesar's ally, the tribune Curio, began making motions that both Caesar and Pompey disarm. Caesar's supporters framed Curio's measures as actions to ensure "a state at liberty and under its own laws" because "the armed domination (*dominatio*) of Pompey created no small terror in the Forum."[2] This contrast between the liberty that Curio claimed to protect and the armed dominance over Rome exercised by Pompey and the senatorial faction supporting him drew upon deeply felt notions of Roman republicanism. Caesar's opponent Cicero once wrote, "We are all slaves of the laws so that we might be free," a concise statement of the general principle that the Republic depended on all Romans being governed by rules set collectively that served the interests of all.[3]

Pompey, Curio implied, now headed a faction willing to use force to compel all other Romans to serve only his interests and those of his allies.[4] According to this line of thinking, Pompey's continued command of forces based in Spain threatened Roman liberty.

Much of what transpired between the middle of 50 and Caesar's crossing of the Rubicon in January of 49 lent additional credence to the claim that Pompey headed an armed faction aiming for the elimination of Caesar's power. From Caesar's perspective, a breaking point occurred in the summer when the Senate recalled one legion of Caesar's from Gaul and a legion that was supposed to belong to Pompey for service in a planned campaign against Parthia. Caesar sent a legion as directed, but Pompey, instead of sending forces loyal to himself, designated a legion that he had lent to Caesar for his Gallic campaigns. So, in practice, Caesar lost two legions that served under him and Pompey lost none. Then, when the legions arrived in Italy, they were not sent to the East. They were instead held in Italy and, in December of 50, they were placed under the command of Pompey. This step gave Pompey control of armies based in both Spain and Italy.[5]

Pompey and his allies gave Caesar additional cause for concern in the first days of January 49 when Cato, the new consul Lentulus, and other long-standing enemies of Caesar prevented tribunes loyal to Caesar from using their vetoes to stop a debate about removing Caesar from command. Cato and his allies had again shown their particular talent for political cynicism as they claimed to protect the Republic even as they refused to respect the checks on power required for its proper functioning. Frightened by this breach of republican precedent, the tribunes fled to Caesar. The Senate then decreed that "the consuls, praetors, tribunes, and all the proconsuls who are near the city will ensure that the Republic comes to no harm," the formula used to declare a state of emergency that, since the murder of Gaius Gracchus, had been used to sanction the use of lethal violence against Romans deemed to be threats to the Republic.[6] Caesar was now effectively a public enemy.

The Senate and consuls had run off the tribunes loyal to Caesar and then placed Pompey in command of the military forces that would oppose him, steps that seemed to support Caesar's claim that Pompey and a faction of senators had been conspiring against him. All of them, Caesar could now convincingly state, had prevented the tribunes from imposing their vetoes (acts contrary to both Roman law and the popular will) just so that they could prevent Caesar from "being on the same level of dignity" as Pompey. Caesar's army, his Gallic clients, and his supporters within Italy all understood the stark choice that Caesar now faced. He could march on Rome or he could wait for Pompey to build so large an army that it would guarantee Caesar's death in Gaul. And, if they believed his version of events, Roman liberty would live or die with him.[7]

The struggle between Caesar and Pompey had both personal and political components. Pompey's condescension and unwillingness to recognize that Caesar's achievements in Gaul were similar in scope to his own conquests in the East irritated the proud commander. Caesar also saw that the political steps Pompey's allies had taken to deprive him of armies, to prevent him from running for office, and, ultimately, to force tribunes to flee before Caesar was declared a public enemy represented profound violations of all of the Republican norms they claimed to be defending. But, to Pompey and his supporters, Caesar represented an overly ambitious figure willing to do whatever was necessary to rise to prominence in the state. Pompey saw this as a threat to his personal position in Rome, but he and his allies also feared that, whatever they did, Caesar would never pursue a normal political career and respect the constraints of the Republic's institutions.

Though both sides had compelling reasons to want to fight, it is important to understand that, at the civil war's outset, Caesar seemed extremely unlikely to prevail. Not only did Pompey have armies under his command in both Spain and Italy but he had also spent the better part of the past three decades building networks of clients and supporters across the Mediterranean. These included the client kings whose rule he had affirmed in Asia Minor and the Near East in the late 60s, the former pirates he had settled in coastal Asia Minor in the mid-60s, the Spaniards with whom he had been building and maintaining relationships since the Sertorian war in the 70s, and the Italians from around his home region of Picenum who had formed the first army he led into battle in support of Sulla in the 80s. And now Pompey was also fighting with the official backing of the Senate and the active support of most of Rome's leading senators. Seeing these advantages, the Senate tasked Pompey with assembling a new massive force of 130,000 troops that could confront Caesar in Italy. He was to call up his veterans, use his ties to Italian communities to recruit as many other troops as possible, and build an army large enough to crush Caesar when the general finally made his move.

No one anticipated that Caesar would make his move into Italy during the same week when the Senate voted. Caesar recognized the great strategic disadvantages he faced, but he also understood that he had two advantages that Pompey and the Senate could not immediately counter. The first of these grew out of the nature of Caesar's command. He had only ten legions, but they were very experienced, well-trained veterans who were intensely loyal and deeply inspired by the leadership Caesar provided.[8] Caesar also had the ability to move quickly. Pompey's forces far outnumbered him, but the 130,000 men the Senate had tasked him with raising in Italy had not yet been assembled. The only forces Pompey had in Italy on January 10 were the two legions that Caesar had sent to him at the Senate's orders in 50 BC. If Caesar moved into Italy quickly, Pompey had nothing else on the peninsula with which to counter him.

This is why Caesar led only three of his ten legions across the Rubicon on January 10. The other seven stayed in reserve in Gaul, protecting it in case Pompey's forces in Spain attempted to attack his rear. Before he crossed the river, Caesar actually sent a small force ahead of his main army to take the town of Arminium, the first community on the Italian side of the provincial border. Caesar himself entered Arminium just after dawn on the tenth and then quickly dispatched troops to occupy other Northern Italian towns.[9] As Caesar's forces continued moving south, panic spread in Rome. Pompey fled the city and stopped all levies of new troops around it. He moved first to Capua, then to the Southern Italian region of Apulia, and finally crossed to Greece with the consuls of 49 and most of the Senate. The army of 130,000 troops he was supposed to raise never materialized.[10]

Pompey's decision to move closer to his friends and clients in the East made strategic sense, but it had obvious drawbacks. By abandoning Rome so quickly, Pompey left Caesar both the world's largest city and the public treasury, without putting up a fight. Caesar responded by reassuring the terrified city that he would not treat his enemies as Marius and Sulla had. Instead of killing them, he would pardon them and allow them to either stay in Italy or go unharmed wherever they wished without fear or loss of property. For evidence of his leniency, Caesar's supporters cited his treatment of Lucius Domitius Ahenobarbus, the governor who had been sent by the Senate to take over Caesar's Gallic command. Ahenobarbus had mounted some of the only significant resistance to Caesar's advance in Italy, but, when Pompey failed to reinforce him, Caesar captured Ahenobarbus and then released him without punishment.[11] This act further reinforced Caesar's claim that he was not a tyrant but a benevolent figure who had been wronged by Pompey, Cato, and their power-hungry senatorial faction.

Pompey not only handed Caesar a political victory by fleeing Italy but also ceded to Caesar much of the military initiative in the Central Mediterranean. Caesar quickly sent out legates to take charge of Sardinia, Corsica, and Sicily in an attempt to secure some of the sources of the capital's food. Cato, who had been sent to hold Sicily, bowed to the inevitable, gave the island up without a fight, and retreated to join Pompey. Sardinia and Corsica, too, quickly fell into Caesar's hands. Pompey's allies did hold North Africa, but, by the spring of 49, Caesar had secured Italy and the surrounding islands.[12]

Caesar still faced the problem of Pompeian forces arrayed to the south, east, and west of Italy. Instead of immediately pursuing Pompey in Greece, Caesar decided to attack Pompey's army in Spain. In less than a month, he marched his forces north through Italy, arrived in Spain, defeated Pompey's legates there, and again pardoned those of his enemies he captured. After they were released unharmed, Caesar told the soldiers and their officers to communicate news of their fates to Pompey and the forces he was assembling in the East.[13] When he returned to Rome in December of 49, Caesar was the master of all of the Roman territory in Europe west of the Adriatic. Even more importantly, his very public acts of clemency now made it impossible for Pompey and his supporters to credibly claim that Caesar was a new Sulla.

This gave Caesar political cover for his next move. Upon his return to Rome, Caesar was appointed dictator by the praetor Lepidus because the consuls had fled to Pompey. Caesar held the office for eleven days so that he could preside over his own election to the consulship for the year 48 BC, an office he held alongside a loyal colleague. Caesar left Rome before the New Year and led his army south to the port of Brundisium where they could cross the Adriatic to Greece. Pompey had been meticulously gathering forces in the winter of 49–48, assuming that Caesar's lack of ships would prevent his rival from landing an army in Greece. But Caesar again surprised. Pompey had placed Bibulus, Caesar's fellow consul in 59 BC, in charge of using the six hundred ships under Pompey's command to prevent Caesar from bringing an army across the sea. On January 4 of 48, however, Caesar used small crafts to ferry part of his army from Brundisium to what is now southern Albania. Bibulus only managed to intercept some of the ships when they tried to make a second trip carrying the rest of Caesar's forces.

Caesar had caught up to Pompey, but his army remained severely outnumbered. Not only did Pompey have more men but he also had at least two hundred Roman senators with him as well as a host of other commanders who held some sort of imperium over Roman forces.[14] But Pompey's massive coalition of troops, senators, and notables was united primarily by hatred of Caesar. And, after Pompey handed Caesar a significant defeat outside the city of Dyrrachium on July 7, he developed a plan to finally finish off his rival. Pompey understood that, though Caesar had been forced to retreat south into Thessaly in central Greece, his forces were not yet finished. But their morale was declining. Some of Caesar's troops had mutinied at the end of the battle at Dyrrachium, and Pompey believed that the army would eventually turn on Caesar and surrender as hunger and lack of supplies set upon it.

This strategy might have worked. In the imperial period, most Roman civil wars would end in just this way, with an army turning on its commander when his cause looked lost. Caesar, however, had a gift for managing the emotions of his soldiers that many of these later imperial commanders lacked. Roman generals often punished mutinous troops with random executions, but Caesar, like Sulla, understood that, in a civil war that could be approaching its end, mercy better rebuilt morale than fear. He publicly shamed some of the mutineers but otherwise refused to consider any other punishment, a strategy that made both the mutineers and the rest of the army even more dedicated to him.[15]

On the other side, the motley crew of senators, commanders, and other notables campaigning with Pompey assumed that the war had already effectively been won. Eager to return to Rome, they pushed Pompey to move aggressively to finish Caesar. Pompey apparently thought this unwise and preferred to wait for Caesar's forces to surrender, but, under the circumstances, an aggressive move seemed politically expedient. Therefore, Pompey linked his forces up with those commanded by Metellus Scipio, and the combined army set upon Caesar outside of the Thessalian town of Pharsalus. Pompey and Scipio commanded twice as many infantry and seven times as many cavalry as Caesar, but Caesar's tactical brilliance and the experience of his forces outweighed Pompey's numerical advantages. Caesar neutralized Pompey's cavalry, overwhelmed his infantry, and then ultimately captured his camp. Pompey fled the battlefield on horseback. He went first to the port of Larisa and then, ultimately, sailed to Egypt.[16]

The reverse at Pharsalus had been so sudden and complete that Pompey chose to sail to the kingdom of the Ptolemies to regroup. He had worked closely to enroll Ptolemy XII, the father of Egypt's current king, among the ranks of Rome's officially recognized allies and was hopeful that Ptolemy XIII would reciprocate the favor done to his father by offering Pompey refuge in Alexandria. The war could perhaps still be won, somehow, if Pompey could receive Egyptian help. But the young Egyptian king and his advisers had apparently already decided that Pompey had lost. They were already embroiled in their own civil war with Cleopatra, the queen who was both the wife and the sister of Ptolemy, and they had no interest in becoming involved in Rome's civil war too. Although Ptolemy's messengers had indicated that Pompey would indeed find shelter in Alexandria, the king instead had Pompey beheaded as soon as he arrived in the city.[17]

The death of Pompey did not end the Roman civil war. Caesar had pursued Pompey to Alexandria to prevent him from continuing the war from there. When he landed in the city after Pompey's murder, Caesar was met by an angry mob incensed that his presence and that of his armed troops infringed upon the sovereignty of the king. Caesar soon found himself drawn into the Egyptian civil war, wasting the rest of 48 and much of 47 sorting out affairs in Egypt before securing the kingdom's throne for Cleopatra. While Caesar tarried in Egypt, other problems erupted. Pharnaces, the son of Mithridates, invaded Pontus, forcing Caesar to return to Rome via Syria and Asia Minor. The war against Pharnaces ultimately ended with such a swift victory in August of 47 that it prompted Caesar's famous line "Veni, Vidi, Vici" (I came, I saw, I conquered).[18] But the travel and logistical preparation required before Caesar could utter this short phrase had real consequences while Rome's civil war still raged.

Not everyone who had once sided with Pompey continued fighting after Pharsalus. Many Romans simply switched sides and took advantage of Caesar's offers of amnesty, Cicero among them. But a core group of senators pressed on and whatever men remained of the forces Pompey commanded regrouped while Caesar was in the East. Cato emerged as the inspirational leader of this group. Pompey had placed him in charge of three hundred ships and, after Pharsalus, Cato led this fleet and the remnants of the army to North Africa where they combined forces with troops provided by the Numidian king Juba. Caesar pursued them there, and after an initial reverse, he again emerged victorious, defeating the combined forces outside of the city of Thapsus in April 46. Cato, Juba, and Lucius Scipio all committed suicide following the battle. Pompey's two sons, Gnaeus and Sextus, escaped from Africa to Spain to continue the resistance, but Caesar defeated them too at Munda in March of 45. Gnaeus was killed following the battle, but Sextus Pompey evaded capture and continued to mount naval raids against Italy for most of the next decade.

Caesar's dramatic military campaigns offer only limited insight into the ways that he changed Roman political life during the early part of the 40s. Caesar understood intuitively that his long-term survival demanded that he become utterly indispensable to the smooth operation of Rome and its empire. This dynamic already had become clear in 48, before the victory at Pharsalus. After Caesar chased Pompey and his senatorial supporters out of Italy, the credit market collapsed as people anticipated that Caesar would institute proscriptions and asset seizures like those undertaken by Sulla. Not only did this threat to private property depress the prices of Italian real estate but it also encouraged lenders to call in loans before all of the value of the collateral disappeared. This, in turn, prompted calls throughout Rome for a cancelation of all debts, a move that would have caused even more damage to the Roman financial system than Mithridates's killing of Roman tax farmers had done in 88 BC. More ominously, panic about Caesar's intentions prompted hoarding of gold, silver, and coined money in Italy as people sought to keep as much of their wealth as possible in easily movable precious metals in case they needed to flee.[19]

Caesar recognized the narrow space in which he could act. Debts could not be abolished without inflicting massive economic damage, but Caesar also appreciated that he needed to somehow stabilize the tumbling prices of assets against which loans had been made. Caesar's clemency for those who opposed him in the civil war formed one part of the solution, helping to reassure Romans that the proscriptions and confiscations of Sulla would not be repeated. But it could not completely calm the city. Even if Romans trusted that Caesar would not repeat Sulla's proscriptions, the war remained unresolved and no one could predict what his opponents might do if Caesar eventually lost, or what property might be destroyed should fighting resume in Italy.

These persistent fears prompted Caesar to act to further stabilize the value of property and, by extension, to calm the credit market. He created an arbitration process through which people could appeal the value set on the property that served as collateral for a loan. The arbitrator would presumably set this value not by looking at the current price the property might fetch but instead by considering its higher, pre-crisis value. Setting an artificially high value for property would discourage people from seizing land or goods that could only be sold for a much lower price. Caesar's measure thereby ensured that it made more financial sense to renegotiate a loan than to seize the collateral and attempt to sell it. It worked so well that no one apparently felt the need to bring a case before its arbitrators.[20]

The calm did not last long. Once Caesar left Rome and headed to Greece to fight Pompey, his political enemies in Rome began working to undermine support for the arbitration process. At first, the praetor Marcus Caelius Rufus proposed stopping interest collection on loans for six years. When this did not generate any popular enthusiasm, he then backed legislation that would cancel all debts and all rents paid to landlords. Caelius and his followers then attacked the urban praetor (the praetor responsible for managing legal affairs in the city) after he failed to back the measure, prompting Caesar's consular colleague to suspend Caelius from office. Caelius's next move involved linking up with Clodius's old adversary Milo to foment a pro-Pompey rebellion in Italy. Both men were killed in skirmishes before their rebellion could develop into a significant threat, but Caelius had shown that concerns about debts and rents could be exploited politically while Caesar was away.[21]

The violence did not end with the deaths of Caelius and Milo. Another round of demagogic exploitation of the issues of debt and rents prompted such unrest that Caesar's deputy Marc Antony felt compelled to lead troops into the city, occupy the Forum, and kill the riotous citizens. The city settled down only when Caesar returned briefly in September of 47 while on his way from the East to campaign against Cato in Africa.[22]

Caesar's presence calmed the civil disturbances in the capital, but he now confronted a new problem. Groups of his best soldiers, some of whom had been fighting for more than a decade, demanded their discharge and the payment of the bonuses that Caesar had promised them. The soldiers became so angry that they declined an additional 1,000-denarii bonus that Caesar offered in the hope of inducing them to serve on his African campaign. Then they almost killed the historian Sallust when he arrived to try to negotiate with them.[23]

Caesar's response to this dangerous situation established the template for how an individual could use money and charisma to control the loyalties of armies in the Roman world in the decades to come. Caesar first ordered the legion that Antony had used to control the civil disturbances in Rome to come to serve him as a bodyguard. Then, Caesar went to the rioting soldiers personally and shamed them into repentance. Specifically, he agreed to discharge the rioters, telling them that he would fight in Africa with other soldiers. He would still pay all bonuses he had promised the rioters, but he would do so only when the African campaign was over and those other units marched in his triumph instead of his disloyal veterans. The ashamed soldiers then begged to be returned to service. Caesar accepted them all back except for the members of the tenth legion, the most accomplished group of his soldiers, because their disloyalty stung him the most. Caesar then made an extraordinary promise. He told the assembled soldiers that, when the wars concluded, he would give lands to all of them. Caesar would not, however, do as Sulla had and reward his soldiers by stealing from other Roman citizens. Instead, the soldiers would receive property from the stocks of public land and, if there was insufficient public land, they would receive land and agricultural implements purchased by Caesar out of his own private fortune.[24]

Caesar had made himself utterly indispensable to his soldiers. To be certain, commanders in the past had relied on the Republic to reward their soldiers using public property. Even the confiscated property distributed by Sulla had passed through public control before his followers received it. Caesar, however, promised to make his land distributions using both public resources and his own private funds. Because the program could not work without both sources of support, Caesar's army now needed him to be both alive and empowered to receive its promised compensation. They had become simultaneously servants of the Republic and of the individual who led it. Caesar had found a way to ensure that Rome would be stable only if he remained in charge of it.

Between 46 and 44 BC, Caesar expanded this system of buttressing the public activities of the Republic with his own private resources. Following his successful war in Africa, he celebrated a massive quadruple triumph that included distributions of gold and silver to his soldiers and to other Roman citizens. The triumph also involved musical performances, gladiatorial games, mock battles and naval engagements, and even an event where two teams of twenty elephants fought each other. He also began construction of a new forum anchored by a temple to Venus Genetrix, the goddess from whom Caesar claimed ultimate descent. The funds for all of these came from a mixture of public and private resources, both of which Caesar now controlled.[25]

Caesar also inserted himself into the political processes of the Republic in carefully crafted ways. At the end of 48, he was again

10.1. Forum of Julius Caesar and the Temple of Venus. Photo by Manasi Watts.

appointed dictator with a term that extended across 47. From January of 46 onward, he held the office of dictator and was made one of the two consuls who took office at the start of every year. After his Spanish victory in 45, Caesar also took complete control of both public expenditures and all Roman armies. Caesar's annual consulship then became a tool that he could use to reward supporters to whom he passed the honor. Perhaps nothing shows Caesar's control over the consulship better than the situation in 45 BC. Caesar began the year as consul but soon resigned the position and appointed Quintus Fabius to serve the remainder of the year. Fabius, however, died on the last day of his consular term. Caesar then appointed Gaius Caninius Rebilus to serve the last few hours that remained, a stint as consul that Cicero jokingly remarked revealed such bravery and prudence that Rebilus never slept for even a moment of his term.[26] The consulship had once been among the most prestigious honors the Republic made available. It remained incredibly prestigious, but the consulship had now become a sort of private benefaction that Caesar could bestow upon whomever he wished.

By 44, Caesar's control over the offices through which the Republic had once rewarded service and conferred honor had become nearly complete. Not only did he appoint consuls but he also effectively appointed the candidates for lower office by reserving the right to accept or reject the results of elections. Then, as Caesar prepared for what he imagined would be a lengthy military campaign against Parthia, he created a list of magistrates who should hold office in subsequent years. For 43, he prepared a list that covered all magistrates, and for 42 he chose the consuls and the tribunes. Caesar would, of course, continue as dictator, though, in a move that puzzled many Romans, his deputy (the man who held the office Romans called master of the horse) would now be neither Marc Antony, who had served in this capacity in the early 40s, nor Lepidus, the man filling the role in 43 and early 44 BC. Instead, as soon as Lepidus went off to govern the provinces of

Gallia Narbonensis and Hispania Citerior, the new master of the horse would be a boy of eighteen named Gaius Octavius. No one at the time could imagine that this boy (better known to modern historians as Octavian) would grow up to become the emperor Augustus.[27]

Caesar nonetheless struggled to define the power that he now exercised, and to articulate the authority he now claimed, in ways that did not offend Roman sensibilities. Many in Rome understood the particular challenge he faced. During his quadruple triumph in 46, his own soldiers are said to have shouted to Caesar in unison: "If you do right, you will be punished. If you do wrong, you will be king."[28] Everyone, including Caesar himself, understood that the army was correct. If Caesar ever did what was right and voluntarily surrendered power, he would be prosecuted or executed. If he held on to power, however, Caesar would have no choice but to effectively become like the kings whose rule the Republic had replaced more than four centuries before.

Between 48 and 44, Caesar repeatedly teased the possibility that he might ultimately move toward openly having himself declared king. Rumors of Caesar taking this step evidently began circulating in 45, talk that, at one point in early 44 BC, prompted some in Rome to greet Caesar as king. When people groaned at this action, Caesar blamed opponents in the Senate for conspiring to make him look like a tyrant. But, when the consul Marc Antony placed a crown on Caesar's head during the Lupercalia festival in February of 44, none could deny that Caesar was testing the popular mood to find a moment when he might officially assume the title.[29]

In many ways, the title Caesar held would have made no difference in how he ran Rome and its empire. Kingship had not existed in Rome for almost five hundred years, and any effort to formally reinstitute it would have required reenvisioning the office and its powers in light of the dramatically different context of the first-century Republic. But, in practice, Caesar already exercised whatever powers he might have given to himself had he declared himself king. Caesar had served as *pontifex maximus* since 63, a position that already made him the chief religious figure in Rome. His legal authority over the Republic ultimately derived from the dictatorship, which he assumed on a permanent basis in 44 BC after being named dictator three times before, in 48, 47, and 46. In addition to the formal powers of dictator, by 44 Caesar also enjoyed power over the treasury, complete command authority over all Roman armies, the freedom to use a publicly owned residence, the effective ability to appoint or approve magistrates, and, as time passed, a free hand to remake the Senate through selection of the magistrates who would qualify for membership.[30] He was, in effect, already an absolute monarch regardless of the title he held.

But the title mattered greatly. Though most Romans bitterly hated the idea of a king, kingship offered a potential avenue through which Caesar could distinguish himself from the other Romans with whom he had once been equal or to whom he had once been subordinate. Roman kings of the pre-Republican period did not inherit the throne but were instead elevated to the position by their peers after showing they merited selection. If Caesar did want the title (and one cannot know for sure whether he really did), kingship was a status that might acknowledge both his current authority and the support he enjoyed from the other members of the Roman Senate.[31]

But the efforts to create a sense of majestic superiority around Caesar went far beyond just experimenting with a royal title. Later sources are full of lists of the honors that the Senate voted to Caesar in 45 and 44 BC. Among the most notable of these are the decrees that Caesar's body was to be inviolable and holy, that he should wear the special clothing normally reserved for men celebrating a triumph when he sacrificed to the gods, that he should transact all public business from a gold and ivory throne, and that Rome should create a cult in his honor with quadrennial festivals "as to a hero" and with statues of Caesar erected in cities controlled by Rome as well as in all temples within the city.[32]

The evolution of Caesar's claims to distinctiveness can perhaps be seen most clearly in the coins that he issued between 49 and 44 BC. The first notable issue, a denarius minted as Caesar's army moved through Italy in 49, shows an elephant trampling a dragon above the legend CAESAR on the obverse and pontifical elements on the reverse, a combination that references Caesar's status as *pontifex maximus* and the onset of the civil war.[33] By 47, the iconography shifted to one that more clearly alluded to Caesar's claims of descent from the goddess Venus and from Aeneas, the legendary Trojan hero whose descendants founded the city of Rome. In that year, a mint traveling with his army in Africa issued a coin with Venus on the obverse and an image of Aeneas on the reverse above the legend CAESAR.[34] The coin issues of 44 BC, however, reflect a later stage in the struggle to define in acceptable ways Caesar's superiority to all other Romans. Unlike the military mint issues of 49 and 47, the coins of 44 were issued by moneyers, and these magistrates affixed their names to the issues. Although the coins were issued by men holding a normal Republican office, they broke a significant Roman taboo against depicting living figures on coins by featuring the face of Caesar himself. The coins also bore evolving legends as Caesar's titles changed in the first two months of 44 BC. They began by showing Caesar's face and the words CAESAR DICT QUART, a reference to Caesar's fourth term as dictator. Then, when the Senate voted Caesar the honorific title Imperator, CAESAR IMP or CAEASAR IM appeared alongside his portrait on the obverse of the coin. Finally, when Caesar's dictatorship became permanent, the legends again shifted to CAESAR DICT PERPETUO or CAESAR DICT IN PERPETUO.[35]

10.2. A denarius of Julius Caesar depicting Venus on the obverse and Aeneas carrying his father on the reverse, two images that allude to the dictator's claims of descent from the goddess and the line of Rome's founding family (Crawford 458/1). Private collection. Photos by Zoe Watts.

By early 44, it had become clear that Caesar's experiments in autocracy had alarmed some elements in the city of Rome. Graffiti began appearing on statues of Brutus, the man Romans credited with expelling the kings and founding the Republic, bemoaning the fact that he was no longer alive. Some even called on his descendants to show that they were worthy of his name.[36] They had one particular person in mind: Marcus Junius Brutus. Excluding perhaps only Cato, no Roman had linked his public profile more closely to the principled defense of the Republic and the liberty it supposedly represented than this Brutus had. When he served as moneyer in 54 BC, Brutus affixed his name to two silver coin types. The first featured the portrait and name of the goddess Libertas on the obverse, and a reverse showing the Brutus who founded the Republic walking with lictors above the legend BRUTUS. The second showed a portrait of that same Brutus with an identifying legend on the obverse and, on the reverse, a portrait of Servilius Ahala, a Roman politician who murdered Spurius Maelius in the fifth century BC so that Maelius would not become king.[37]

10.3. A denarius of Brutus showing Libertas on the obverse and the Republic's legendary founder Brutus on the reverse (Crawford 433/1). Private collection. Photos by Zoe Watts.

These two coins fit the narrative of the early Republic that Romans liked to believe. The Republic, in this telling, came about because Romans could not bear to be under the political domination of one man. Liberty, in this conception, meant life under a constitutional and legal framework that ensured the participation of citizens and protected them from political domination.[38] Ahala's murder of Maelius was a heroic action undertaken to ensure that Romans remained free from Maelius's illegal and unconstitutional seizure of power. The images of the founder of Rome's Republic and of the tyrannicide who saved it advertised a conviction that murder was justified (and even admirable) if it upheld Rome's legal order.

In the 50s, Brutus's invocations of the Republic's founder and one of its saviors offered a powerful statement that he stood for liberty under the law, to be defended by violence if necessary, despite the violent political climate cultivated by men like Clodius and Milo. By 44 BC, however, ideas of liberty, legality, and even republicanism had all become much more complicated. Though Caesar effectively controlled Rome, the Republic still operated in a legal sense. Elections for offices continued, Roman law continued to govern commercial and personal transactions, juries continued to hear trials, and Romans continued to enjoy the right of appeal. Even amid the talk of his seizing the kingship, Caesar in fact exercised power as a dictator, a formally defined Republican office whose term he had extended. The extensions defied true Republican precedents, but they had been done using legal means and with apparent popular support. Caesar also exercised power as a consul (at least until his latest planned resignation of the office before heading to fight Parthia). If Caesar ruled through the offices integral to Rome's legal and constitutional order, and if his rule had popular support, could his murder still be justified as a defense of liberty?[39]

A politician named Gaius Cassius Longinus seems to have forced Brutus to confront this question early in 44 BC.[40] Both Brutus and Cassius had served with Pompey in the initial stages of the civil war before accepting Caesar's clemency and finding themselves reincorporated into the administrative fabric of Caesar's Republic. But both had become disenchanted with Caesar's growing autocracy. They seem to have easily found a group of people who felt similarly, including some of Caesar's longtime supporters as well as some of his most implacable opponents. The group decided that Caesar must be killed before he departed for his Parthian expedition on March 19 and determined that the Senate meeting on March 15 would offer the last, best opportunity to do this.

On that day, the Ides of March, the Senate assembled in a building near the expansive theater and garden complex that Pompey had dedicated in 55 BC on the site of the modern Campo de' Fiori. As Caesar entered the building, one of the conspirators stopped the dictator to ask a favor. When Caesar answered, the conspirator grabbed Caesar's robe, pulled it from his neck, and urged his fellow plotters to attack. They exposed concealed daggers, set upon Caesar beneath a statue of Pompey, and stabbed him twenty-three times. An autopsy would later reveal that only one of the twenty-three wounds inflicted by the senators proved fatal.[41] Even Caesar's assassins seem to have been uneasy with the deed they had committed.

The apprehension many of the conspirators apparently felt about killing Caesar extended to Rome as a whole. Brutus had chosen a meeting of the Senate as the moment for the assassination because he imagined that even those senators who did not know about the plot would immediately applaud its success. He even had composed a speech celebrating the reestablishment of Roman liberty that he believed had been achieved by Caesar's murder. But Brutus never got to give his speech. The senators fled in terror, fearing both the possibility of more violence in the Senate and the unrest that they worried would descend on a city now suddenly deprived of the man who ensured its stability. As news spread, panic followed. Gladiators bolted from the theater before they could perform, with the audiences running just behind them. Some crowds spilled out into the marketplaces, plundering shops even as shopkeepers escaped. People who reached their homes dared not go out again. They barred the windows, shut their doors, and prepared to defend their houses from the tiled roofs that, in an emergency, could be broken up and made into the sort of lethal missiles that once killed Pyrrhus.[42]

On March 15, 44 BC, no one knew how to respond to a murder that was committed in the seductive name of liberty, even as it threatened to reignite the horrible chaos of civil war. Caesar was dead, and the threat many felt he posed to the Republic was over. But it remained to be seen whether the Republic could survive without him at its center.

CHAPTER 11

THE REPUBLIC OF OCTAVIAN

THE EVENTS OF MARCH 15, 44 BC, went completely according to the plan hatched by Brutus, Cassius, and their fellow
conspirators—until the moment Caesar died. Shockingly, they
had no idea what to do next. The Senate had emptied in panic
rather than erupting in applause. The one surviving consul, Caesar's ally Marc Antony, fled to his house, fearing that he might be
the next one killed. As the conspirators emerged into the city carrying a cap on a spear, a symbol of the liberty they felt they had restored, they were disconcerted to see Rome descending into chaos
rather than celebrating them as liberators.[1] At that moment, Brutus, Cassius, and their fellow conspirators realized that they truly
understood neither what Caesar had accomplished by restoring
stability to the capital nor what their fellow citizens thought about
him. It now dawned upon them that the tyrant they thought they
had killed had also served as the dam that held back the chaos of
an empire yet to emerge from civil war. Perhaps for the first time,
Brutus realized that liberty cannot exist without security.

The city of Rome at that moment contained a legion of armed
Caesarian soldiers commanded by Lepidus, who had been, as
the dictator's master of the horse, Caesar's deputy. Antony, one
of the consuls of 44, was also in the city and, with Caesar eliminated, he alone had the power to bring legal motions against the

conspirators in the popular assembly. And the people of the city of Rome presented a no less daunting obstacle. The city was full of Caesar's veterans who now had been deprived of both their patron and the resources he had promised them. Much of the rest of the city was unsure what to make of the murder, but the rioting it had provoked did little to inspire confidence that the conspirators' liberty would be preferable to the order of Caesar's dictatorship. Seeing all of this, the conspirators did what was perhaps natural. They rushed to the Capitoline Hill, fortified positions on it using their own hired gladiators, and, if later sources are to be believed, began using bribes to draw people to their side.[2]

Both the conspirators and Caesar's supporters spent the afternoon and evening of March 15 in a frenzy. Senatorial opportunists who had not been involved in the plot began positioning themselves to benefit from its aftermath. Cicero climbed the Capitoline Hill to advise Brutus to summon the Senate, condemn Caesar as a tyrant, and, if necessary, have Antony killed as well. In the Forum below, the praetor Cinna made a show of throwing off the garb of his office as the foul fruits of a tyranny, and Dolabella, the charismatic young man scheduled to take over the consulship from Caesar when the dictator left the city on March 18, appeared in consular robes and denounced Caesar, his erstwhile patron. Lepidus, for his part, understood that he commanded an army angrily seething about Caesar's murder. He saw that he could use the soldiers' demands for vengeance to position himself as a credible heir to the dictator. By the morning of the sixteenth, Lepidus had used some of these troops to seize the Forum. They now stood there looking up at the hill on which Brutus and Cassius were encamped.[3]

Three crucial figures had not yet decided how to respond. Brutus and Cassius remained on the Capitol on the fifteenth. Although Brutus did have the authority to summon the Senate, he chose not to follow Cicero's advice to do so. Instead, Brutus asked Cicero to go to Antony and to try to convince him to use his authority as consul to defend the Republic from the chaos now descending upon it. Cicero refused, but other messengers did go to both Antony and Lepidus to try to negotiate a resolution to the tensions. His courage fortified by his army, however, Lepidus had already decided to defend Caesar's legacy. Hiding in his house, meanwhile, Antony had yet to recover from the shock of Caesar's murder, a condition that Cicero believed would cause Antony to agree to anything the conspirators offered.[4]

Each of these men resolved on a course of action during the night. By the morning of the sixteenth, it seems that Brutus had decided to address the crowd in the Forum with a speech that defended his actions while also affirming that Caesar's veterans would receive the rewards the dictator had promised them. This was, of course, a bow to the reality that troops recruited by Caesar now controlled the Forum, and that his angry veterans roamed the streets of the city. But it also offered an explicit endorsement of some of the untraditional measures taken by a man Brutus held to be a tyrant. This was an important concession that Antony would soon exploit.[5]

Antony's house was near the Temple of Tellus, located on the Esquiline Hill across the Forum from the Capitoline Hill where the self-styled "liberators" now hid. After he recovered his nerve, Antony held a meeting of some of the leading Caesarian supporters on the afternoon of the sixteenth. Arguing from a position of momentary strength, Lepidus pushed for the Caesarians to take immediate vengeance on the conspirators using the military forces that he commanded. Like his father, the rebellious consul of 78 BC, Lepidus lacked the subtlety to disguise this attempt to seize power in the city for himself, and no one seems to have been inclined to support him in this ambition.[6] Hirtius, one of the men who had been designated by Caesar to assume the consulship in 43 BC, instead proposed that Antony facilitate some sort of reconciliation with the assassins. Antony realized that this was both an apparently reasonable course and the way forward most likely to enhance his own position. Antony needed time to assemble the popular and military resources necessary to frame an effective response to the murder. He understood that Lepidus's position grew weaker the longer he could be forced to restrain his army from violence. He also knew that Brutus's tactical error in acknowledging the validity of some of Caesar's actions had opened up the possibility that more of the dictator's legislative legacy could be salvaged. And Antony understood the powerful support he could secure for himself if he came to be seen as the one who had salvaged these things for Caesar's followers.

The meeting adjourned with the participants having decided to call the Senate to convene at the Temple of Tellus on the seventeenth. Antony had already secured Caesar's papers from his widow Calpurnia and possibly some of his money as well, steps that made Antony confident that he could claim the mantle of Caesar's political heir. He also developed an approach to the upcoming senate meeting that would allow him to stabilize the situation long enough that he might be able to use his connection to Caesar to improve his own position in the city. The senate meeting showed how fluid the situation remained two days after the murder. The senators turned up to the temple to find it surrounded by both Lepidus's troops and groups of Caesar's veterans. Brutus and Cassius understandably refused to come to the meeting. The praetor Cinna, who had made a public display of shedding his praetorian robes two days before, showed up wearing them again. Dolabella also lost some of his militancy, and Cicero, speaking publicly, now advocated reconciliation. No one wanted to take too extreme a position, and the various speakers instead tried to sniff out where the senatorial consensus might settle. Antony waited patiently to weigh in. As the discussion moved toward a motion to condemn Caesar as a tyrant, Antony then made the day's most powerful point, a point that Brutus's conciliatory words toward Caesar's veterans had made possible. If Caesar were declared a tyrant, Antony explained, this would require the Senate to invalidate the acts that he had taken while in power. That would include all the honors and offices Caesar had bestowed on many of the very men there gathered and all the offices he had set aside for them in the future.[7]

The senators wanted no part of this. The meeting descended into chaos as senators began clamoring against the previous proposal once they realized that it meant that many of them might be deprived of offices they expected to hold in coming years. While the senators bickered, Antony and Lepidus left the meeting to address the crowd gathered outside. When Antony heard a call from the crowd that he should take care so that he did not end up like Caesar, he loosened his tunic to reveal that he was wearing armor underneath—a precaution that a consul would never before have thought to take when attending a meeting of the Senate. This incited the crowd, many of whom began to call for Caesar to be avenged. Antony told them that, as an individual, he wished to avenge Caesar, but, as consul, he had to defer to the common good. Caesar's partisans then called on Lepidus to exact vengeance, but he too said it was impossible without any allies willing to join him.[8]

Antony returned to the Senate to find that Dolabella had been droning on about his consulship to an increasingly irritated and uneasy senatorial audience. Antony decided to seize the initiative. He proposed that the Senate ratify all of Caesar's acts as dictator while also extending an amnesty to his murderers. This compromise could maintain the peace by offering safety to the conspirators and by mollifying senators, soldiers, and veterans alike. After agreeing that Caesar's will would be read aloud and that he would be given a public funeral, the grateful Senate approved this compromise. On the evening of March 17, Antony and Lepidus dined with Brutus and Cassius to mark the amnesty.

Few of the senators could have understood that their decision to grant Caesar a public funeral and allow the public reading of his will would shape the next fifteen hundred years of Roman history. Antony had now been given a text, written in Caesar's own words, around which to construct a public ceremony that would define the dictator's legacy for the people of Rome. And a few days later he embraced this opportunity. When the will was read out, the Roman people learned that the man they had been told was a tyrant had left money to every Roman living in the city and had even turned his private gardens along the Tiber River over to them as a public park. The money was appreciated, but the park was perhaps just as significant in a crowded, filthy city of a million. Two other provisions of the will were equally important. First, the will provided for Caesar's adoption of Octavian, the eighteen-year-old grandson of Caesar's sister, and named him the primary heir to Caesar's estate. Second, the will named one of Caesar's assassins, Decimus Brutus (a distant relative of the more famous Marcus Brutus), as another of the will's main beneficiaries. Other assassins were also named in the will, a fact that underlined for all the personal nature of their betrayal of Caesar.[9] Appian, probably relying on the contemporary account of Asinius Pollio, describes the widespread feeling among the mourners that Decimus Brutus and the other conspirators had committed a horrible sacrilege that violated both the public vows they had taken to protect Caesar and the private ties they had maintained with him.[10]

The dramatic reading of Caesar's will set the stage for the masterful display of public emotional manipulation that Antony planned for Caesar's upcoming funeral. When the time for the funeral arrived, Caesar's body was brought to the Forum and quickly surrounded by mourning crowds. It had not been cleaned. Caesar's "gaping wounds" remained visible beneath the dried blood that had pooled around them.[11] Antony then rose to give a funeral oration even more powerful than the famous speech Shakespeare would later put in his mouth. Antony spoke few words of his own. His speech instead largely repeated text included in the honors that the conspirators and the rest of the Senate had voted to Caesar over the past several years, with Antony simply adding small pieces of commentary. The crowd heard how Caesar alone had avenged the Gallic sack of Rome in 390 BC, a trauma whose scars had been seared into the historical memory of all Romans for the past three and a half centuries. They were reminded that he had been voted an exemplar of clemency, that he had given refuge to all enemies who sought it, and that all had sworn that he was to be sacred and inviolable. And yet his brutalized body now lay in front of them, destroyed by some of the very men who had said and sworn these things months before.[12] As the anger of the people neared its boiling point, Antony lifted Caesar's bloodstained robe high above his head so that the crowd could see it. Someone else raised a wax image of Caesar's murdered body up on a mechanical device, so that it spun slowly around and showed the crowd all twenty-three places where Caesar had been stabbed.

"The people," Appian writes, "could no longer bear the most pitiful sight displayed for them."[13] They erupted into the streets, fired by an uncontrollable cocktail of anger and grief. Crowds immolated Caesar's body in the Forum, with soldiers and ordinary people throwing armor, clothes, and jewels into the fire, making offerings to the dead dictator as if he were a god. Other angry Romans burned the senate chamber and then searched the city for Caesar's murderers so that they too might suffer some punishment for their faithlessness. One mob murdered the tribune Cinna simply because he had the same name as the praetor who had so ostentatiously thrown away his robes on the fifteenth. Others attacked the houses of members of the conspiracy, with household slaves and neighbors only barely able to prevent the incineration of entire city blocks. A group of Caesar's supporters soon set up an altar to the deceased dictator on the site where his remains had burned. Led by Amatius, a man claiming to be the grandson of Marius and, therefore, a relative of Caesar, some of them even began stalking Brutus and Cassius in the hope that they might find an opportunity to avenge the dictator.[14] Amatius was an extremist, but, as he and his followers showed, Antony's display had convinced a significant number of Romans that Brutus was wrong. Caesar was not a tyrant whose removal meant liberation but a Roman hero whose death portended disorder and tragedy.

No one knew what would happen over the coming days and weeks. Many of the conspirators fled the city. Those to whom Caesar had assigned provinces to govern hurried off to them. Decimus Brutus headed to Cisalpine Gaul and Trebonius set off for Asia

Minor.[15] Marcus Brutus and Cassius still held offices in Rome and, though Caesar had assigned Marcus Brutus the province of Macedonia and Cassius that of Syria when their terms in those offices ended, the threats from Amatius persuaded them to leave the city early to begin building armies with which they might protect themselves. Elsewhere in the Mediterranean, Sextus Pompey, the son of Pompey the Great, continued to wage his father's war, though an objective observer would rightly see him as more of a pirate than a Republican at that point. Within the city, Cicero assumed a leading role in the Senate, working to direct Rome's political course back toward something that looked like the Republic. But he was fighting an extremely difficult battle. Caesar's funeral had shown that the Roman crowds no longer instinctively hated autocracy, as long as the autocrat was benevolent and capable of maintaining order. They could certainly be persuaded to accept another Roman who took ultimate control of the state—and a number of figures aspired to follow Caesar's path by staking a claim to the late dictator's legacy.

Some of them, like Amatius, represented nothing more than annoying demagogues. Others seemed far more menacing to men such as Cicero. Lepidus had an army and a desire for supreme power, but he lacked the political talent of Caesar. Marc Antony was more dangerous. He lacked an army, but, as his performance at Caesar's funeral showed, his political skills surpassed those of anyone else in Rome at the moment. He quickly bought off Lepidus with a marriage alliance and an appointment to the office of *pontifex maximus* that Caesar's death had left vacant. This was enough to get Lepidus to leave for his designated command in Spain and southern Gaul. In the meantime, Antony decided to build power for himself by simultaneously appealing to Caesarians and by offering reassurances to the Senate that he would not act in ways contrary to senatorial consensus. Not only had Antony arranged the amnesty for Caesar's assassins, but, in mid-April, Antony arrested and ultimately executed Amatius and some of his followers without trial. In response, the Senate voted him

permission to enroll bodyguards to protect himself against popular anger. They were, of course, shocked when Antony recruited
not a few dozen gladiators but instead six thousand former centurions to serve in this capacity.[16] In a little more than a month, Antony had very skillfully acquired a bodyguard of trained soldiers
and positioned himself as the political lynchpin of what seemed to
be emerging as a post-Caesarian Roman political order.

But one player was only now entering the field. Octavian, the
adopted son and legal heir of Caesar, had been waiting for the dictator in the city of Apollonia (in what is now Albania) so that he
might accompany Caesar and his armies on his planned Parthian
campaign. There were many reasons not to take Octavian seriously. He was a sickly eighteen-year-old boy who was unknown
to the wider public in Rome and too young to hold any significant office in the Republic. His prospects seemed so dim that his
mother Atia and his stepfather, the ex-consul Marcius Philippus,
urged the boy to remain safe by renouncing the adoption and inheritance that Caesar had provided him.[17]

Octavian decided not to take their advice. The time that he
had spent with Caesar's soldiers in Apollonia had allowed him to
build strong enough bonds with some of his adoptive father's officers that they pledged to protect him if he came to Italy. When he
landed in Brundisium, the soldiers he met there also received him
as Caesar's son. And, when he changed his name to Julius Caesar
in accordance with a provision in Caesar's will, "multitudes of men
from all sides flocked to him as Caesar's son, some from friendship
to Caesar...and with them soldiers who were either conveying
supplies and money to the army in Macedonia or bringing money
and tribute from other places to Brundisium."[18] As he journeyed
toward Rome, groups of Caesar's veterans joined his instant army
of supporters, an army that grew larger as it became clearer that he
sought to avenge the murder of his now namesake.

When Octavian arrived in Rome around April 11, he did so following a cold calculation about how to best position himself amid

the swirl of competing claims for authority within the city.[19] His trip through Southern Italy had shown Octavian the power of Caesar's name and the resonance that could accompany his unwavering devotion to the deceased dictator's legacy. Unlike Antony or Lepidus, Octavian was untainted by any compromise with the assassins. And, unlike the radical Amatius, Octavian had a legitimate claim to Caesar's legacy. Considerable political space sat open for him to occupy.

Octavian understood, however, that he needed to be extremely careful in how he filled that space. He could be neither too radical in pursuing Caesar's murderers nor too compromising in forgiving them. Octavian also appreciated the distinct advantages that came from being underestimated by older and more experienced Roman politicians, none of whom seemed to have imagined that Caesar might have named the boy his heir because he possessed an uncommonly precocious political mind. Everyone from Antony to Cicero expected the young Octavian to be easy to manipulate, and all of them thought that they could use their own savvy to exploit and then dispose of the boy. But Octavian knew to expect this approach. He grasped that politeness and deference to those who wanted to use and discard him could be extremely useful political tools. Older political hands would read these symbolic steps as signs of weakness, but they cost Octavian nothing. He might appear guileless, but he would retain the ability to act independently. The men who thought they controlled the youth would then be the easiest targets should Octavian eventually choose to strike.

This moment was still a long way off in April, but Octavian's arrival catalyzed a dramatic reshuffling of affairs in the capital. He entered Rome while Amatius still occupied the Forum and Brutus still remained in the city. By the time Octavian left several days later, around April 15, both of these things were no longer true. Between April 12 and April 14, Antony had arrested and executed Amatius and Brutus had fled, both events precipitated in part by Octavian's assertion of his prerogatives as Caesar's heir. Three actions by Octavian stand out during those few days in April. First, Octavian publicly claimed his inheritance by appearing before the *praetor urbanus,* an office then held by Marc Antony's brother. Second, Octavian sought legal recognition of his adoption by Caesar and his assumption of Caesar's name. And, finally, Octavian sought to use the occasion of the upcoming games dedicated to the goddess Ceres to display the throne and crown that Caesar had been permitted to use at all games.[20] If he had his way on all points, Octavian would have succeeded in asserting both his legitimacy as Caesar's heir and his role in ensuring the continued public celebration of Caesar's unique status.

Antony understood this as well as Octavian. He did nothing to prevent Octavian from accepting his inheritance, but Antony had no intention of allowing the youth to assume Caesar's name or take custody of Caesar's public legacy. Antony used procedural delays to block the adoption, an easy enough thing to do because it required both the endorsement of Roman priests and the presentation of the matter to the *comitia centuriata* assembly by the *pontifex maximus.*[21] Antony had to be more explicit in denying Octavian's request to display Caesar's throne and crown at the games, but he did so nonetheless. (Later in the year, Antony would again reject a request by Octavian to display the crown and throne at games celebrating Venus that Octavian himself would put on.) Antony's obstruction had consequences, however. Octavian had forced Antony to go on the record opposing Caesar's explicit wishes. In these few days, Octavian had publicly, powerfully, and nonviolently affirmed the purity of his own devotion to Caesar in a way that diminished Antony's claim to the dictator's legacy while doing nothing to alarm Republicans like Cicero. For those who loved Caesar, Octavian represented his clear champion. For those who wanted the Republic restored, Octavian remained useful as a potential ally. For Antony, he looked like a much more formidable potential rival.

Octavian retreated from Rome by April 18 with his inheritance secure but his other objectives largely unrealized as a result of Antony's obstruction. This obstruction would prove convenient for Octavian as the year progressed. Octavian would largely fail to deliver on the promises to avenge Caesar, to honor his legacy, and, for a time, even to pay the money that Caesar's will had promised to Romans. But Octavian could now argue that these failures were not his fault. He was a pious young man blocked at all turns by the cynical and duplicitous Antony. Octavian did not hesitate to let people know of his supposed victimization by Antony. When Antony withheld some of the property that Octavian claimed belonged to Caesar, the young man made a show of selling his own personal possessions so that he could secure enough money to pay the legacy Caesar had promised to each Roman. When a raft of lawsuits arose contesting Octavian's rights to certain pieces of Caesar's estate, Octavian again blamed Antony for initiating them. When Antony preemptively prohibited Octavian from running for the tribune position vacated by Cinna's murder, Octavian could highlight the injustice of explicitly barring him from something that he never intended to do. And, after each confrontation, Octavian took care to arrange meetings with Antony to try to smooth things over. The neophyte now appeared more statesmanlike than the consul.[22]

As the year 44 progressed, Octavian was helped by good fortune and by the erosion of the positions of both Antony and Caesar's assassins. In late July, a comet passed over Rome while Octavian presided over games celebrating Caesar's victory at Pharsalus. Octavian claimed that the comet was Caesar's soul ascending to heaven and dedicated a statue of Caesar with a star above its head in the temple to Venus in the new Forum that Caesar had been constructing adjacent to the existing Roman Forum. He now seemed even more like Caesar's true heir. Antony overreached in the meantime. In June, Antony pushed a measure through that changed his provincial assignment for 43 BC from Macedonia to Cisalpine and Transalpine Gaul, the provincial base from which Caesar had begun his Gallic campaigns. Then, later in the summer, Marcus Brutus and Cassius were reassigned the tiny provinces of Crete and Cyrene. This was both an insult and a step designed to rob them of any possibility of commanding a significant army. Both Brutus and Cassius left Rome by the end of the summer. Neither went to the provinces assigned to them. Instead, Brutus went to Athens and Cassius traveled east, ultimately ending up in Syria. A backlash then emerged against Antony. In August, Caesar's father-in-law Piso attacked Antony in the Senate. Then, in September, Cicero took on Antony as well. Their feud became even more serious when, in October, Cicero penned his brutal Second Philippic, a vicious and potent attack against Antony's character.[23]

The growing hostility from both Caesarians and senators such as Cicero left Antony reeling. He spent the early part of October trying to rebuild public support. On October 2, he repudiated the amnesty that he had negotiated in March by proclaiming that there was no place in the Republic for Caesar's killers. Then, one week later, he left Rome for Brundisium to meet up with the experienced legions Caesar had intended to lead into Parthia. These were, Antony trusted, going to form the backbone of the force that would support his claim to Cisalpine Gaul. Perhaps hoping to solidify their support while discrediting his rival, Antony also charged Octavian with trying to assassinate him.[24]

These efforts all backfired. Many people in Rome and in the army thought that Antony had manufactured the assassination charge against Octavian. Antony's efforts against Caesar's heir also prompted Octavian to recruit a force of Caesar's veterans from Campania with the promise of a 500-denarii bonus. Octavian then sent agents to the troops that Antony would meet in Brundisium, who told those soldiers about the bonus that Octavian was paying. This meant that harsh laughter erupted when Antony met the Macedonian legions and offered them a bonus of just 100 denarii per person. Antony responded by rounding up and killing some members of these legions. The laughter ended, but the legions silently seethed under his command.

By November, it had become clear that Antony and Octavian both were ready to battle one another. It is important to understand the significance of this fact for the Republic. Octavian had no position in the state and held no office. Even his adoption by Caesar, the primary claim he had to any sort of authority in Rome, was not yet legally valid. But he was ready to lead a few thousand men into battle against a consul. Antony's position was only slightly less dubious. He did have imperium as a consul, and he did have command of the Roman troops he intended to lead into battle, but he had no legal grounds to use those armies to fight what remained a private quarrel. If we expand our gaze beyond Italy, we see Sextus Pompey, who had never held an official position in the Republic, commanding a fleet and army made up of former soldiers of his father as well as freed slaves and other recruits. In the fall and winter of 44–43 BC, Brutus and Cassius also busied themselves with recruiting armies and extorting money from places as diverse as Judaea and Greece. They too had no legitimate authority to build or command the immense forces they soon would head. Rome had seen civil strife before, but at least then there was a patina of legitimacy to it, with leaders possessing plausible claims to authority. Personalized, dynastic civil conflict of this sort was new.

These principal figures may have been ready for war, but their soldiers were not—yet. Many of the veterans Octavian had summoned asked to be dismissed when they learned that they would be fighting Antony rather than protecting Octavian and helping him to chase down Caesar's assassins. Octavian retained some of them only by paying more bonus money. Antony had even less luck. When he returned to Rome from Southern Italy, Antony summoned the Senate to convene on November 24, hoping to coerce it into voting to declare Octavian an enemy of the state. But Antony failed to show up to this meeting after one of his legions switched its allegiance to Octavian, diminishing Antony's perceived military advantage over Caesar's heir. Then, at a second meeting that Antony scheduled for November 29, Antony again decided not to propose the motion condemning Octavian when another legion flipped to his rival. The best that Antony could do in the last month of his consulship was to get the assassins Trebonius,

Marcus Brutus, and Cassius stripped of their provinces. This, of course, meant nothing to Marcus Brutus or Cassius because they had never gone to the places assigned to them.[25]

In mid-December of 44, Antony entered Cisalpine Gaul and began operations against Decimus Brutus. Both the Senate and Octavian reacted quickly. Octavian pledged to deploy the legions loyal to him against Antony if the Senate should need them. Because Octavian now was using his private forces to help the Senate rather than himself, his troops proved more willing to embrace his leadership. They provided him with lictors, the bodyguards that typically accompanied someone with imperium, and they urged him to assume the title of propraetor. Octavian accepted the lictors but told the soldiers that the Senate should award him the title. He then dissuaded his soldiers from going to Rome to demand the title for him with the ominous warning that the Senate would surely approve it anyway, "particularly if they know your eagerness and my hesitation." Armies could now try to claim for their commanders the offices and honors that the Republic once awarded through the votes of its assemblies. And Octavian had the political astuteness to understand that the Senate would feel compelled to retroactively validate whatever powers and honors his soldiers had arrogated to him.[26]

Octavian had judged the cynicism of the Senate quite well. Many of the men who had once fought alongside Cato and applauded the principles of the Republic were now perfectly content to make use of Octavian and the troops loyal to him if it meant defeating Antony. In a senate meeting on December 20, Cicero praised Octavian for agreeing to serve the Senate. Then, when the new consuls Hirtius and Pansa took office on January 1 of 43, the Senate voted to grant Octavian the imperium of a propraetor and agreed to pay the bonuses he had promised his soldiers from public funds. Each of these moves retroactively regularized the military authority Octavian had claimed, on the terms that he had already set. The Senate also instructed Hirtius and Pansa to recruit legions of their own that they could lead against Antony. After an embassy to Antony failed to come to any agreement in February, the Senate then voted that the consuls and Octavian were to use their armies to ensure that Antony did no harm to the Republic. Rome had again fallen into civil war.[27]

The armies would not come to blows until April 14, when Antony attacked four legions of raw recruits commanded by Pansa about eight miles outside of Mutina in Northern Italy. Hirtius, however, had sent one of Caesar's old legions, the fearsome *legio Martia*, to meet Pansa. By the time they arrived, Antony's forces had nearly beaten Pansa's recruits and had wounded Pansa in the fighting. When the *Martia* legion took the field, however, the battle quickly turned into a rout. Antony's legionary standards were captured amid his chaotic retreat. Then, a week later, Antony decided to risk attacking the armies of Octavian and Hirtius. His forces again were defeated, with Antony forced to flee north to the provinces controlled by Lepidus, leading the remnants of his army and trusting that Lepidus would continue to support him. But Hirtius died in the course of the second battle and Pansa died of his wounds not long after Antony fled. The consuls were dead, and Octavian commanded the victorious armies alone.[28]

Cicero and his fellow senators received news of Antony's defeat with elation, followed by a truly remarkable display of arrogance. Rather than acknowledging the real victory that Octavian had won, they instead voted awards and honors to a range of other men, as if Antony's defeat had been some grand Republican triumph in which a host of noble defenders of liberty had all played a role. The Senate awarded a triumph to Decimus Brutus even though he and his army had sat behind the city walls for much of the fighting and had refused to pursue Antony as he fled north. It recognized Cassius's position in Syria, although Cassius had made no contribution at all to the victory; he had instead been busy extorting money from client kings to assemble an army in the East. And Sextus Pompey, who had also done nothing in either battle, was made prefect of the Roman fleet.[29]

The young Octavian, meanwhile, received no offices and not even an *ovatio*. His troops saw their bonuses cut, and they were ordered to leave Octavian's command and serve under Decimus Brutus. But Octavian had no desire to be rendered a historical footnote, and his soldiers, the best of whom had all served under Caesar, had even less reason to listen to a senatorial command that they now serve under one of Caesar's murderers. They were loyal to their commander, Caesar's heir, not to the Senate. And they were so enraged that both they and Octavian ignored the Senate's commands. In its arrogance, the Senate had alienated its own most powerful military commander and his troops.[30]

In late May, it became clear to the senators how badly they had miscalculated. On May 30, a letter arrived from Lepidus declaring that he and Antony had joined forces in order to avoid further bloodshed. The Senate immediately voted him a public enemy, a relatively meaningless gesture since the only army of any consequence standing between Lepidus and Rome belonged to Octavian—and it no longer obeyed senatorial commands. Belatedly, a commission was sent in late June to try to make amends by offering rewards to Octavian's soldiers. But the Senate had again completely bungled the situation. They deliberately left Octavian out of the negotiations with the soldiers, instead separately offering him the chance to stand for election as praetor. Octavian and the soldiers both responded with outrage. The soldiers sent their own embassy to the Senate and demanded the Senate make Octavian consul. When the Senate rejected this demand, Octavian held an assembly of the soldiers in which they charged him to lead them to Rome so that they might seize for him the consulship the Senate had denied.[31]

Octavian and his armies entered Rome in August of 43. His forces grew when one legion stationed in the city and two legions summoned from Africa to fight for the Senate all defected to him. On August 19, with his forces encamped nearby, Octavian and his relative Quintus Pedius, another of Caesar's heirs, were elected to fill the consulships vacated by the deaths of Hirtius and Pansa.

Octavian arranged for his soldiers to be paid 2,500 denarii each from public funds. He then had his adoption by Caesar legally recognized. His colleague pushed through a law rescinding the amnesty given in March of 44 to Caesar's killers and, following a short public trial, those who had perpetrated the murder and their ally Sextus Pompey were all convicted in absentia.[32] With Brutus, Cassius, and Sextus Pompey all commanding forces that could oppose him and now formally designated as outlaws, Octavian left Rome and marched north again to meet Lepidus and Antony. This time, however, Octavian would arrive as a friend.

The three men met on an island in a river near Bononia (modern Bologna). Over the course of two days, they agreed that Octavian should resign the consulship he had just secured and join with Antony and Lepidus to form a board of three men, a triumvirate for the organization of the Republic, that would hold consular imperium and appoint magistrates for the next five years. They then agreed to divide the western provinces among them. Lepidus would remain in Rome while Antony and Octavian headed east to fight Brutus and Cassius. They also agreed to confiscate and allot to their soldiers the land of eighteen Italian cities and to establish a list of rivals who would be proscribed, with their property confiscated after their executions.[33] When the agreement was set, Octavian communicated all of its terms except the proscription list to the soldiers of all three commanders. The soldiers responded with cheers and embraced one another in celebration of their reconciliation. No one at Bononia seems to have cared that the Senate and popular assemblies had no involvement in this conference that would rearrange the Roman polity and redistribute vast quantities of Italian land and wealth.[34]

The triumvirs marched to Rome and had the powers they had set for themselves approved at a public meeting on November 27 of 43. A list of 130 proscribed men, including an explanation of why each was proscribed, appeared on November 28. The triumvirs offered rewards of 25,000 denarii to any free man who brought them the head of one of the proscribed. Cicero, the most prominent name on the list, was captured and killed on December 7, with Antony paying his murderer ten times the promised bounty and then ordering the orator's head and hands hung from the Rostra in the Forum. But the initial wave of killings and asset seizures did not yield enough money—so more people were added until the list came to include 300 senators and 2,000 *equites*. When even this failed to bring in enough revenue, the triumvirs instituted a special tax on 1,400 rich Roman women. It is telling that this tax provoked more of a public outcry than the proscriptions, largely because the triumvirs hesitated to silence their female critics by inflicting on women the same lethal violence they used against men.[35]

Brutus and Cassius acted nearly as autocratically in the East as the triumvirs did in Italy. The victims of their rapacity were Roman subjects and Roman clients instead of Roman citizens, but the theft and destruction perpetrated by the "liberators" was no less severe than that of the triumvirs. For instance, Cassius extorted 700 talents of silver from Judaea (enough silver to mint 6,000,000 denarii), sold entire towns into slavery when they refused to pay the amounts he demanded, and assessed fines as large as 1,500 talents to cities he perceived had undermined him. He later attacked and plundered the independent island of Rhodes, forcing its residents to turn over their property and executing those who failed to do so. Brutus, for his part, seized money and property from communities in western Asia Minor, sacking places like Xanthus and Patara when they resisted him. And, with the massive amounts of bullion they seized, the "liberators" minted large quantities of gold and silver coins, some of which proclaimed *libertas* and others of which featured the portrait of Brutus. In their hands, liberty had come to look nearly indistinguishable from autocracy.[36]

The armies of the liberators and those of the triumvirs met outside of Philippi in northern Greece in early October after nearly a month of buildup. The battle was massive, with each side commanding nearly a hundred thousand troops, and the outcome was indecisive. Antony routed the forces of Cassius so soundly that

Cassius committed suicide. On the other side of the immense battlefield, however, Brutus inflicted such a serious defeat on Octavian
that he captured the triumvir's camp, though a serious illness meant
that Octavian was not there at the time. On October 23, Brutus was
forced into a second bloody battle, which the triumvirs again won.
He and a number of others who had joined his cause committed
suicide. Most of the surviving troops then joined the triumvirs.[37]

Nearly forty thousand Romans had died in the two battles between the triumvirs and the liberators in Greece, but the triumviral
victory did not end the civil war. It merely inaugurated a new phase
of the conflict. All of the men who fought at Philippi fought ultimately for the commanders who recruited and paid them, and, after
the battle, their loyalty remained with their paymasters rather than
with the Republic. Now many of Brutus's and Cassius's soldiers simply replenished Antony's and Octavian's ranks. There was no system
in Rome that could control what the victorious triumvirs would do
with the armies still personally loyal to each of them. This was particularly dangerous because a clear hierarchy developed among the
triumvirs after Philippi. Antony took authority over both Gaul and
the East, the two regions from which successful generals had previously seized power in Rome. Octavian got control of much of the rest
of the West while being forced to run Italy amid the social and economic chaos unleashed by the discharge and settlement of waves of
veterans whose terms of service in the triumviral armies had ended.
Lepidus, now clearly in third place, was given control of Africa. This
was not a sustainable arrangement—and everyone knew it.[38]

Nevertheless, the uneasy balance among the triumvirs held
for most of the next half decade. The specific developments of
those years matter less to the story of the Republic's fall than the
broad pattern through which a society accustomed to a Republic
struggled to adapt to autocracy. In 41 BC, for example, Octavian's
inability to find enough land for veterans in the eighteen cities
whose land the triumvirate had initially confiscated forced him to
expand the land seizures into neighboring areas. Italians naturally

felt tremendous anger at these land seizures, but no political process existed through which to express their concerns or change the hated policy. Armed rebellion was all that remained and, in the zero-sum game of triumviral autocracy, Octavian's failure could become Antony's gain. This was why Antony's wife Fulvia and his brother Lucius both urged the disgruntled Italians to resist Octavian's colonists. Octavian eventually blockaded the rebels in the city of Perusia. When the city fell in the spring of 40 BC, the carnage was horrifying. Octavian's forces plundered the city and then burned it to the ground, after allowing Fulvia to flee to Athens and Lucius Antony to leave for Spain.[39]

Following the Perusine siege, Octavian and Antony both seem to have understood that an all-out war between them was coming. In preparation, both reached out to Sextus Pompey to form an alliance. He ultimately chose to work with Antony and took to raiding the Italian coastline in a reasonably successful effort to block grain supplies from reaching Rome. In the late summer of 40, Antony besieged the city of Brundisium, which was protected by five of Octavian's legions. Octavian and, perhaps more importantly, his best general Agrippa arrived to reinforce those legions, but, before large-scale combat began, troops from both sides began agitating for a compromise so aggressively that their commanders were unsure that they would fight at all. In the end, Antony and Octavian came to another agreement. The two triumvirs redivided the empire, this time in a way that marked them effectively as equals. Antony recognized Octavian's authority over Gaul, Illyricum, and the rest of the West. Lepidus, who was not present or apparently even consulted, retained Africa. Antony got the eastern provinces as well as the right to recruit forces in Italy. Octavian was charged with taking Sicily back from Sextus Pompey, and Antony was to go to Parthia to conduct the campaign that had been delayed by Caesar's murder. The reconciliation between them was to be sealed by Antony's marriage to Octavian's sister Octavia. Then, in 39 BC, Antony and Octavian negotiated an additional treaty with Sextus

Pompey following a famine in Rome caused by Sextus's blockade of the port of Ostia. This, Appian writes, prompted public rejoicing in Rome at the arrival of "peace" and of "liberation from divisive war, conscription of sons,... the plundering of fields, the ruin of agriculture, and above all of famine."[40]

Some of these things were indeed finished for Italians, but Octavian, Sextus, Antony, and even Lepidus were not done fighting. And, as the 30s progressed, the balance of power began to shift increasingly toward Octavian. In the initial division of triumviral territories, Octavian's control over Italy brought with it a host of serious problems—not the least of which was the supervision of a land confiscation program that disrupted Italian agriculture at a time when Sextus Pompey threatened Rome's ability to import food from abroad. But Octavian had successfully weathered that storm—and had gained control of Gaul as well. In 42, Antony's assignment of the East had seemed to offer him the opportunity to tap the region's great wealth and make alliances with its independent kingdoms. But, after the depredations of Cassius and Antony, the East was inflamed against Roman rule. With the support of Parthian forces, a dissident Roman commander named Labienus seized control of Syria and much of Asia Minor in 40. By early 39, the territory under Labienus's control reached as far as the Aegean coast.

The situation had begun to stabilize as Antony sailed back to the East following a winter spent in Athens in 39–38. Antony's deputy had recovered Asia Minor and defeated Labienus. The Parthians had largely pulled back from Syria, and many of the kings and princelings of the East were again willing to take Antony's direction. But, while Antony busily worked to remake a framework of direct and indirect Roman control of the region, he had not won the military victories that had made such a thing possible in previous generations. And, in the meantime, Octavian provoked a resumption of his conflict with Sextus Pompey.

Antony and Octavian met again in Tarentum in 37, a location chosen because the city of Brundisium had barred entry to Antony and his ships as a show of support to Octavian. The peace between them still held well enough that Antony agreed to immediately provide Octavian with 130 ships to help his campaign against Sextus Pompey, and Octavian promised Antony twenty thousand troops at a future point (though Octavian never followed through on his half of the bargain). The two men also addressed the messy question of renewing the triumvirate, which had expired in 38, by securing a popular vote that belatedly authorized their own decision to extend the triumvirate until 33 BC.[41]

By the end of the year 36, however, the comity and military parity between Antony and Octavian had begun to disappear. Much of this had to do with Antony's burgeoning romance with Cleopatra, the queen of Egypt. The two had first met near the Anatolian city of Tarsus in 41 BC when the queen had hosted Antony in spectacular style on her royal party barge. Antony had then proceeded to Alexandria, reviewing affairs in Syria along the way, and spent the winter of 41–40 with the queen in the Egyptian capital. She bore him twin sons during 40, the same year in which Antony married Octavian's sister Octavia. Even then, after his stay in Alexandria had facilitated the Parthian advance into Syria, it was becoming clear that Antony's attachment to Cleopatra caused him to make poor strategic choices. By the mid-30s, however, Antony had come to recklessly disregard the consequences of appearing overly devoted to the Egyptian queen. Upon returning from Italy, Antony took territory from Roman client kingdoms such as Judaea, gave it to Cleopatra, and then compelled the Roman allies to lease the land back from her. She also bore Antony a son in 36, and Antony acknowledged the legitimacy of twins that he had fathered with her in 40 BC, two things that humiliated Octavia. In 36, Antony also mounted an invasion of Parthia that went disastrously wrong, with his army having to make a harried retreat back through Armenia. Rumors subsequently circulated that the calamitous invasion had begun late because Antony had waited too long to leave Cleopatra in Alexandria and was too eager to return to her. And, worst of all, Antony seems to have been oblivious to the damage his affair with Cleopatra was doing to his reputation in Italy.[42]

At the same time, Octavian inflicted a significant defeat on Sextus Pompey, seized Sicily, and destroyed or captured much of Sextus's fleet. Sextus fled to the East, initially seeking some sort of support from Antony. When Sextus heard of Antony's Parthian defeat, however, he tried to seize on the weakness he now perceived in Antony's position. This proved a mistake. Antony's lieutenants and allies hunted him down and, in 35 BC, one of them executed Sextus in Miletus.

Lepidus had also taken part in Octavian's campaign against Sextus from his base in North Africa. Outside of the Sicilian city of Messana, his forces, those led by Agrippa, and eight legions that had once served under Sextus all met. The legions of Lepidus and those formerly belonging to Sextus combined to sack Messana together. This cooperation excited Lepidus's ambition, and he tried to compel Octavian to renegotiate Lepidus's place in the triumvirate. When Octavian arrived for the negotiations, however, the legions all abandoned Lepidus. Lepidus now mattered so little that Octavian did not even have him killed; he was returned forcibly to private life and retained only the title of *pontifex maximus*. Octavian had unilaterally taken Lepidus out of the triumvirate, and he had done this in Sicily without consulting anyone in Rome, a step that indicated his lack of concern for maintaining even the patina of Republican procedure. Octavian now controlled all of Rome's western territories, from Africa around the Mediterranean through Spain and Gaul to Italy, he had forty-five legions at his disposal, and he no longer felt constrained even by the very heavily revised rules of the political game that the triumvirs themselves had set.[43]

After these victories, it seems that Octavian saw war with Antony as inevitable, and he began to prepare his soldiers and the Italian public accordingly. Some of his soldiers had demanded to be demobilized after the victory over Sextus Pompey, and Octavian settled twenty thousand of the longest-serving men on Italian and Gallic lands. But he kept most of his troops at arms by beginning a campaign against Dalmatian barbarians, near the border separating his territory from that administered by Antony. By 33 BC, this resulted in another military success, and Octavian ostentatiously displayed the legionary standards he had recovered during his Dalmatian campaign and even allowed a report to spread about a combat injury he had suffered. Octavian was slowly creating an impression of himself as a successful commander and, implicitly at least, opening up a contrast between his good Roman vigor and Antony's Egyptian-induced sloth.[44]

Octavian and his associates worked in other ways to contrast his energetic stewardship of Italy with Antony's apparent devotion to Cleopatra in Egypt. In the period between 36 and 33 BC, supporters of Octavian built Rome's first stone amphitheater for gladiatorial games, and they restored the Temple of Hercules, the Temple of Bellona, and the Basilica Paula. Octavian's general Agrippa took things even further. He restored and expanded Rome's aging and outdated early-second-century water infrastructure, adding a new aqueduct line along the path of the Aqua Marcia and dedicating new public fountains in the city at the places where the aqueducts ended. Agrippa also secured the city's food supply, emphasizing that the days of shortages and famines had now passed. He sponsored fifty-nine days of games in 33 BC and, on festival days, even paid for barbers that Romans could use for free. All of these things implicitly highlighted not just Antony's deficiencies but also the failure of the Republic in recent decades to adequately address the structural and personal needs of Roman citizens. Octavian was showing Italians that he and his allies were better and more responsive leaders than both his current triumviral rival and his immediate Republican predecessors. Octavian continued to maintain publicly that he was defending and preserving the traditions and structures of the Republic, but he was laying the groundwork to transform the autocracy of the triumvirs into the autocracy of Octavian.[45]

The sense of revival and prosperity that Octavian and his supporters cultivated in Rome worked alongside even more powerful efforts to discredit Antony. These took many forms, but they
largely centered on a portrayal of Antony as a besotted slave to the
foreign queen Cleopatra. Perhaps no weapon was more potent in
making this case than Octavian's sister Octavia, Antony's wife. In
35 BC, Octavian granted both Octavia and Livia, his own wife,
public statues and the official protection against insult usually reserved for tribunes. This elevation of Octavia came at a time when
Antony's relationship with Cleopatra was already well-known in
Italy. Antony's treatment of Octavia, a woman now legally im-
mune to insult, became more brazenly disrespectful as the 30s
wore on. He took to spending the time when he was not campaigning with Cleopatra in Egypt rather than with his wife. In
35 BC, Octavia turned up in the East with troops and military
supplies to help with her husband's eastern campaigns. Antony apparently accepted the soldiers, told Octavia to return straightaway
to Rome, and then spent another winter with Cleopatra in Alexandria. Although, in Plutarch's words, "she was thought to have
been treated with scorn," Octavia returned to Rome, continued
living in the house she and Antony once shared, and looked after
both the children she bore him and those from his earlier marriage. Meanwhile, Octavian made sure that the contrast between
Antony's pious Roman wife and his flamboyant Alexandrian
queen was lost on no one.[46]

Antony made other mistakes as well. Following his capture of
the Armenian king in 34 BC, Antony staged a procession that celebrated the victory—in Alexandria. Octavian and his allies in Italy framed Antony's celebration as a Roman triumph transplanted
to the Egyptian capital and adapted to reflect the stereotypical
decadence of that city. As they told it, Antony entered the city on
a chariot and presented the spoils of the war to Cleopatra. He then
supplied the people of Alexandria with a feast, sat on a gold throne
alongside the queen and their children, and made gifts of Roman

territory to these members of his family. These stories, combined with Antony's treatment of Octavia, permitted Octavian to build a public case that Antony had lost himself and betrayed Rome amid the charms of Cleopatra and the luxuries of her capital.[47]

Octavian would soon exploit Antony's crucial weaknesses. The triumvirate expired at the end of the year 33, and, when it did, the Roman state should theoretically have returned to normal Republican order. The massive military power Octavian and Antony each enjoyed made this impossible in reality. Ensconced in the East, Antony could continue to enjoy a politically liminal status without any real challenge. But Octavian was in Italy and, as the year 32 began, he faced two consuls allied to Antony who had been pre-selected years earlier when Antony and Octavian were on better terms. These Antonians wanted to exploit the fact that the legal authority of the triumvirate had expired in order to attack Octavian as one who held power illegally. On January 1 of 32, one of them delivered a speech attacking Octavian and introducing a motion in the Senate to sanction him. Although the motion was vetoed by a tribune, Octavian, who had stayed away from Rome during the meeting, soon returned to the city with troops. Staying just outside of the city walls, he had a loyal tribune summon the Senate to him. He seated himself on an ivory throne set between the two consuls, mounted a defense against the charges, and promised to provide evidence of Antony's treason at a future senate meeting.[48]

The alarmed consuls and scores of senators also loyal to Antony fled Rome, heading toward Antony and the forces he was gathering in Asia Minor. Later that spring Octavian produced the evidence he had promised. He forced his way past the Vestal Virgins (who were the custodians of Antony's will), read the document, and then repeated what he claimed were its main provisions to the Senate and people of Rome. The will, he said, proclaimed the legitimacy of Caesarion, the son Cleopatra claimed to have conceived with Julius Caesar. It also named Antony's children with Cleopatra as heirs even though Antony remained legally married to Octavia, and it said that Antony wished to be buried in Alexandria alongside Cleopatra even if he died in Rome. These bequests to non-Romans were technically illegal, and the fact that Antony made them anyway was, Suetonius would later write, evidence that Antony had ceased to behave like a Roman. More rumors to this effect soon spread across Italy. Some said that Antony had given the great library in Pergamum, a treasure that belonged to the Roman people, to Cleopatra. Others claimed that Antony intended to defeat Octavian, move the capital to Alexandria, and rule Rome's empire alongside Cleopatra. Few of these things were true. But all were useful for what Octavian did next.[49]

Octavian could now wage war against Antony under the pretext that he alone could protect Roman liberty and control of Rome's empire from the cunning Cleopatra. But, since the triumvirate had lapsed, Octavian held no office and lacked the legal authority to lead a campaign against the Egyptian queen. He decided that this authority could best be obtained through the universal consent of all Italians. Octavian thus arranged it so that "of its own accord, all of Italy swore allegiance to me and demanded me as leader (*dux*)…. The provinces of Gaul and Spain, as well as Africa, Sicily, and Sardinia swore the same oath."[50] Although officially a voluntary oath, there seems to have been very little that actually was voluntary about it. In each town across Italy and the Western Mediterranean, one man stood before the assembled citizens and read the text of the oath out loud. Each citizen then stepped forward and said, "The same for me." One Italian community with strong ties to Antony was exempted, but everyone else swore allegiance to Octavian and charged him with fighting on their behalf.[51] They would be loyal to Octavian and would hold his enemies to be their enemies as well.

Some elements of what came to be called the Oath of All Italy drew on older Republican precedents through which citizens swore allegiance to a military commander when rebellion threatened in Italy. In 32 BC, this communal expression of loyalty had a new and more sinister significance.[52] Its terms bound all of the

Western Mediterranean, soldier and civilian alike, to Octavian in the same way that troops owed allegiance to their commanders. Octavian alone determined Rome's enemies, and the millions of people who swore this oath vowed to fight with him and on his behalf. They were now personally loyal to Octavian, even if he asked them to fight against other Romans.

It would have been lost on few Italians that a functional Roman Republic would never have demanded the oath they had just taken. In the Roman Republic of old, the Senate collectively determined Rome's enemies—and these enemies were shared by all because they threatened all. Now the rest of Italy had no choice but to follow Octavian. But Octavian's propaganda against Antony and Cleopatra had worked well enough that this departure from past Republican practice did not matter for many Italians. Maybe they were willing to allow Octavian to assume unparalleled power because it just seemed like another small step away from political normalcy. Or, perhaps, political norms no longer seemed relevant. After a half century in which Roman generals had often put prices on the heads of their opponents and sacked towns they deemed disloyal, Italians might have judged that they could not really prevent Octavian's empowerment and that the cost of failure would be too high to justify even trying to do so.

Italians proved less willing to pay for the war they were compelled to support. When Octavian finally declared war against Egypt in the late summer or fall of 32, Italians openly expressed their anger at the huge new taxes that he assessed to fund his campaigns. Riots broke out in Rome, but Octavian's military autocracy had become extremely efficient at violently suppressing dissent like this.[53] Perhaps not coincidentally, his associates had become equally effective at rounding up funds from hesitant taxpayers. Octavian's soldiers too could not have relished yet another campaign, though many certainly would have been reassured to know that with just two rivals left, one way or another, the civil wars would soon be coming to an end.

The forces of Octavian and Antony met in Greece in the late summer of 31 BC. Both commanders had massive numbers of troops and ships, but the decisive moment came during a fight at sea on September 2. Antony's land forces had been blockaded by Octavian's ships and afflicted with a brutal outbreak of dysentery. Antony elected to try to break the blockade using his fleet, but, in the midst of the battle, Cleopatra sailed away and Antony, abandoning his flagship, followed her in a smaller, faster vessel. The rest of Antony's fleet surrendered, and his beleaguered army, now left without supplies, did the same a week later. Antony reached Egypt without a fleet and soon saw the defection of the last of his troops, legionaries he had stationed in Cyrene. He was now truly alone, the unarmed Roman consort of a militarily overmatched Egyptian queen.

Octavian took his time to finish the war. He did not land in Egypt until the summer of 30 BC, but, when he arrived, the kingdom quickly capitulated to him. Antony committed suicide on August 1. Cleopatra did the same on August 10. Egypt was now Roman, but in a distinctly different way from the rest of Rome's territories. Egypt effectively belonged to Octavian, not the people of Rome, and its governance would be different from that of any other part of the Roman world. Octavian not only took control of the Egyptian kingdom but also took personal possession of all of the royal lands that had belonged to the old Ptolemaic kings and queens. Effectively the king of Egypt, Octavian received considerable revenues from these Egyptian properties that he controlled as part of his own private fortune. He could use these new funds to personally reward his soldiers, provide for Roman citizens, and build a more stable Roman political order around himself. After nearly fifteen years of political battles, Octavian seems to have understood that the Republic was finished. The empire was ready to begin.[54]

CHAPTER 12

CHOOSING AUGUSTAN LIBERTY

O CTAVIAN'S ROMAN EMPIRE GREW OUT of more than a century of Republican dysfunction. Indeed, Octavian carefully designed the imperial system that replaced the Republic to meet many of the needs of Roman citizens that the late Republic could not. Romans accepted an implicit bargain when they recognized Octavian as their autocrat. They would follow his lead and, in return, he would provide reliable salaries and demobilization benefits for the armies, political stability, protection from enemies, regular food and water supplies, beautiful cities, and relative prosperity. In the years preceding his defeat of Antony, Octavian had come to realize that Romans were ready to make this trade. Octavian's major building projects in Rome, Agrippa's work on the city's water supply, and Octavian's victory over the Dalmatians showed Romans the benefits of this sort of autocracy—and the Oath of All Italy showed their willingness to swear personal loyalty to Octavian during a time of conflict. But, after Antony was defeated and Egypt was annexed, Octavian faced the question of how to restructure the Roman state to make this bargain permanent.

He had no model to follow. He could not imitate Sulla. Sulla had stepped down from the dictatorship before the system he had put in place came under serious stress, and he died long before there was any danger that he might be prosecuted for his crimes. Caesar offered an even less attractive path. Caesar saw the folly in Sulla's decision to relinquish control of Rome and resolved to hold power as a perpetual dictator while allowing the other magistracies to be filled by both allies and former opponents.[1] Perpetual dictatorship meant that Caesar could not be prosecuted, but it also meant that the survival of Caesar's system depended entirely on his ability to stay alive even as he empowered his former enemies by allowing them to hold office. That also would not work for Octavian.

Octavian's crimes had exceeded even those of Sulla, and his young age—he was not quite thirty-three when he conquered Egypt—meant that he needed a much more enduring system than that of Caesar. His experience in the later 30s had shown him what an imperial system needed to deliver for its leader to remain alive. The question he faced, however, was how to craft such a system to survive a time when fears of civil war had receded. He understood that every year he ruled, more Romans would come of age who did not remember the shortages, dangers, and horrors of civil war. Octavian knew that he had to find a way to prevent Rome from longing for *libertas* once the rewards of autocracy that were so attractive to Romans of the late 30s came to seem mundane. Octavian's life quite literally depended on it.

Octavian did not immediately arrive at an enduring solution, but outlines of one began to appear when he returned to Rome to celebrate his conquest of Egypt in 29 BC. Following news of his capture of Alexandria, the Senate and people had voted on new powers and privileges for Octavian, including a requirement that "priests and priestesses in their prayers on behalf of the people and the Senate were to pray for him too and at all banquets, both public and private, everyone was to pour a libation to him." There was also a decree that the doors of the Temple of Janus were to be closed, an act that symbolized that the Roman world was at peace.

12.1. A bronze coin from the Roman imperial period showing the closed doors of the Temple of Janus (*Roman Imperial Coinage*, Vol. 1 [London: Spink and Son, 1984], catalog # Nero 347). Private collection. Photo by Zoe Watts.

Octavian would later note: "Although before my birth it had been closed twice in all recorded memory from the founding of the city, the senate voted three times in my principate that it be closed." The idea of an enduring peace preserved by a divinely inspired ruler was such a fundamental part of the Roman understanding of the benefits of Octavian's regime that, in 13 BC, the Senate dedicated the Altar of Augustan Peace (the *Ara Pacis Augustae*) to commemorate it. This freedom from war that Octavian ensured was not the Republican liberty that Romans had long cherished, but, after the civil wars of the first century, it was seen by many as more valuable.[2]

When the conqueror arrived in Rome, he celebrated his victory in truly unique style. "Not only did all of the citizens offer sacrifice...but even the consul [did this too]...a thing that had never been done in the case of any other person."[3] Octavian then honored his closest ally Agrippa, praised his officers and soldiers, distributed gifts worth 100 denarii to each of the Roman people, and refused to accept gold crowns that had been sent to him by the cities of Italy. Fortified by the wealth of Egypt, he then "paid all of the debts that he himself owed to others...and did not insist on payment of others' debts to him." Romans then "forgot all of their unpleasant experiences and viewed his triumph with pleasure, quite as if the vanquished had all been foreigners."[4] This kicked off a magnificent triple triumph on August 13, 14, and 15. The first day commemorated the victories over the Dalmatians alongside Gaius Carrinas (a general whose father had been killed by Sulla). The second day marked the triumph at Actium, which was framed as a victory over Cleopatra rather than Antony. The third day celebrated the subjugation of Egypt. Following this were dedications of temples and the Curia Julia, a new senate house that Octavian had built to honor Caesar. Then, on August 18, Octavian sponsored magnificent games that displayed the first rhinoceros and hippopotamus ever seen in Rome.

These elements came together to form a rough image of what Octavian's regime would claim to do. Octavian promised a new sort of liberty under his autocracy in which Romans enjoyed security, peace, prosperity, and entertainment. The rule of law even returned. Octavian spared all citizens who asked for pardon, rehabilitated those like Carrinas who had been unjustly wronged by past regimes, and supported those of lower social status like Agrippa whose talents merited recognition. All the while, Octavian stood at the center of this new arrangement. It was Octavian who guaranteed all of these benefits, and he expected his centrality to this new order to be recognized ritually in the sacrifices, prayers, and libations Romans had long given on behalf of the Senate and people, not any one man. Provincial cities like Pergamum went even further, dedicating new sacred precincts to the worship of Octavian as a divine figure.[5]

Over time, the formal powers Octavian possessed ultimately proved less important than the majesty that lay behind their exercise. Indeed, these powers evolved as Octavian experimented with different models for ruling. Throughout his reign, though, he was informed by Caesar's experience, which had taught Octavian the perils of being seen to take too much from the elites who had long tied their family honor to officeholding. Octavian realized early on that it was less important to these men that they accomplish anything in office than that they hold office at all. And so the basic principle on which he would base his formal powers was that he had, in his own words, "transferred the Republic from my own power to the dominion of the senate and people of Rome" and he would now "excel all in influence (*auctoritas*) although I possessed no more official power than others who were my colleagues in several magistracies."[6]

This process, which a modern historian has described as working toward a model for political "business as usual after alterations," began to unfold in the years 28 and 27 BC.[7] Never at any point in this process did Octavian surrender the absolute power he held over the actual running of those Roman affairs that mattered to him, but the process was nonetheless important. Not only did it begin to reopen the paths to the consulships, praetorships, and other senatorial offices that elites craved but it also allowed Octavian to offload onto these elites responsibility for the mundane tasks of governing what was now the world's largest city and empire. This meant that, if things worked as they should, Octavian and the magistrates whose selection by the Senate or the people he approved would share credit. If something went wrong, however, the problem could be blamed on an ineffectual senatorial administration, and Octavian could then step in and use his personal authority and his private wealth to correct it. In this way, Octavian remained indispensable, even when he had stepped back from direct control over such responsibilities as the food supply and the supervision of elections.

This evolution began in 28 BC when Octavian and Agrippa were both consuls and were granted the power of censors, through which they revised the senate lists. As the year progressed, Octavian abolished the special powers that he had claimed as triumvir. In January of 27, he made the dramatic gesture of handing the Republic back to the Senate. The Senate, in turn, gave him control of the provinces along with most of the armies in them. Octavian

would govern these provinces through men he appointed personally, and the troops in these and all other provinces would take
loyalty oaths to him. He would eventually also be sure that these
troops knew that the benefits they would receive upon retirement
came not from the public purse but from his own private funds.[8]
The Senate, meanwhile, resumed its own authority to appoint
magistrates for the more secure provinces that did not have armies
garrisoning them. This arrangement gave senators responsibility
for their administration but prevented governors appointed by
the Senate from gathering military forces that might potentially
be used to challenge Octavian's power. Octavian would also continue as consul, because the people had voted that office to him,
and he would be given control over decisions about peace and
war.[9] For the next several years, Octavian would base his political
powers on continually holding the consulship, even celebrating his
tenth consulship in 24 BC by granting gifts worth 100 denarii to
each citizen of Rome.

But, by 23, it was clear that Octavian's monopolization of one
of the two consulships was becoming a problem, and further ad-
justments occurred. Perhaps in response to either an assassination
plot or a serious illness, Octavian resigned the consulship in July
and communicated that he did not wish to be considered for it
again.[10] In return, his powers were redefined. He gained the right
to make the first procedural motion in the Senate and the ability to propose any law. He also received an enhanced imperium,
imperium maius, that gave him authority over all governors in all
provinces in the event of a conflict. And, most crucially, he gained
tribunicia potestas, a grant of the political powers and personal sacrosanctity traditionally attached to the tribunes of the plebs. The
granting of tribunicia potestas symbolized Octavian's trade of the
actual aristocratic office of the consulship for the symbolic status
of an unelected tribune of the plebs.

The senatorial grant of tribunicia potestas would mark the formal assumption of power for all subsequent Roman emperors for

the next three hundred years, but, for Octavian, nothing encapsulated his political and spiritual preeminence more than the title that the Senate awarded him on January 16 of 27. On that day, he would later write, "I was called Augustus by decree of the Senate, the doorposts of my house were covered with laurels by public act and a civic crown was fixed above my door, and a golden shield was placed in the Curia Julia whose inscription testified that the Senate and people of Rome had given this to me on account of my virtue, justice, and piety."[11] Octavian had become something entirely new. He had become Augustus, Rome's first emperor.

The title Augustus had particular resonance. Dio writes, "He took the title of Augustus, signifying that he was more than human. For all the most precious and sacred objects are termed *augusta*. Because of this, those speaking in Greek addressed him as Sebastos, meaning an august personage, from the verb which means to be revered."[12] The name, Dio continues, "confers no particular power," but it instead "clearly shows the splendor of [his] position."[13]

It is now, at long last, that we can return to the events of 22 BC with which this book began. The winter of 23–22 saw Rome struck by a series of crises as frightening as anything that afflicted it during the civil wars. Plague descended on the city in both years and the Tiber flooded its banks on multiple occasions. At one point, the flooding was so severe that, for three full days, the streets of Rome could only be navigated by boats. Famine followed the flooding. But even more ominous was a series of lightning storms, one of which struck the Pantheon temple, which Agrippa had recently completed. During that storm, a spear fell from the hand of the statue of Augustus that stood amid all of the other gods in the temple. Romans believed that divine entities inhabited cult statues and, when the representation of Augustus dropped its spear, this was seen as a sign of divine displeasure at the state of things in Rome. The year 22 BC was the first year since Actium that Augustus had not held the consulship, and, for the people of

Rome, the lightning strike on the Pantheon served as a sign that showed them the cause of their troubles. "The Romans," Dio would write, "believed that these woes had come upon them for no other reason than that they did not have Augustus as consul at that time."[14]

The mobs that then set upon the senators, locked them in the senate house, and threatened to burn them alive if Augustus were not made dictator were panicked but, in the moment, not irrational. They had been told that Augustus had a higher status than any other Roman. They had come to appreciate that he alone served to control Rome and its empire. They had given offerings of thanksgiving for his victories and prayed for his recovery when he was ill. They believed what he and the Senate had been saying for years, and now, in a moment of crisis, they could not imagine any other source of deliverance. They were convinced that he must be given even more power. And, although Augustus refused the consulship and the dictatorship, he did agree to take control of the grain supply. "In a few days," he would later write, "I freed all people from the fear and danger they experienced using my own funds."[15] Only Augustus, using his private resources, could save Rome and its citizens from danger. It is impossible to say when the last embers of the Republic flickered out, but Augustus's chilling words meant that they would never reignite. Freedom from fear, freedom from famine, and freedom from danger now all came from Augustus and Augustus alone.

Augustus would remain atop the new political structure he had built until his death in AD 14. His stepson Tiberius succeeded him and continued to rule until the year 37. Sixty-eight years passed between the Battle of Actium and the death of Tiberius— probably a decade longer than the average life span of a Roman who lived into adulthood. The average senator at Tiberius's death was probably in his thirties and, because Augustus had instituted a mandatory retirement age of sixty-five for senators, the oldest would have been in his sixties.[16] There was hardly anyone active in

Roman political life in AD 37 who remembered anything but Augustus's empire. In fact, the empire was so entrenched that it continued even though the next emperor, Caligula, proved completely incapable of running its affairs. And the Roman state remained an empire until cannons breached the walls of its last capital of Constantinople in May of the year 1453. It was as close to permanent as any political system in the history of the world.

And yet, Augustus was anything but inevitable. Some historians assume that, had Augustus not ended up at the head of the Roman Empire, perhaps there would instead have been a Roman Empire of Antony or a Roman Empire of Julius Caesar.[17] It is, of course, quite possible that an empire of some sort would have emerged from the wreckage of Rome's republic. But there also might not have been a Roman Empire at all. It is surely just as likely that, if the first Roman to try to create a permanent Roman autocracy had been less skilled or less long-lived than Augustus, Rome's Mediterranean primacy might have ended with the Republic itself. As the dictatorships of Caesar and Sulla both showed, an empire involving all of Rome's territory was by no means inevitable. Spain had split off from Sulla's regime. It had almost succeeded in doing the same under Caesar. Syria, too, remained incredibly difficult to control for both Caesar and the triumvirate, with figures such as Labienus easily peeling it off from central Roman control. Augustus managed to create a stable Roman autocracy that dominated the entire Mediterranean world. If he had not come along, Rome's empire may well have fallen apart.

But there was a real long-term cost Romans paid for the stability of Augustus's empire. The Roman Empire of Augustus ensured peace and stability under good emperors—and Rome would have many such emperors. But it lacked the capacity to prevent cruel or mentally unstable autocrats such as Caligula, Nero, and Commodus from taking the lives and property of Romans simply because they wanted to do so. In moments like those, Romans such as Plutarch and Cassius Dio looked back on the Republic with a sort of nostalgia that celebrated a type of liberty that they had collectively lost—and which Augustus had ensured could never return.

These later Romans recognized that, just as Augustus's empire was an unlikely achievement, the Republic did not need to die. A republic is not an organism. It has no natural life span. It lives or dies solely on the basis of choices made by those in charge of its custody. Rome's republic could have been saved if Tiberius Gracchus had found a compromise with his opponents in 133 BC, or if Livius Drusus had managed to get Romans to accept his citizenship extension to all Italy, or even if Sulla's commanders had refused to follow him when he chose to march on Rome in 88 BC. Even at the time of Augustus's birth in 63 BC, there was a chance that the Republic could still survive. Augustus was born near the end of Cicero's consulship, right around the time of the suppression of Catiline's conspiracy. For much of the 60s, Cicero had proposed an idea of Roman society governed by a basic cooperation among senators, Roman *equites,* and the Roman people.[18] Each would govern with a mind toward the interests of the others. This notion, called the *concordia ordinum,* even found an echo in coins from 62 BC that celebrated the preservation of peace and concord within the Republic.

12.2. The goddess Concordia on a coin minted in 62 BC, the year following Cicero's consulship (Crawford 415/1). Private collection. Photo by Zoe Watts.

Unfortunately, both the time and the messenger were wrong. Cicero's arrogance, Cato's senatorial obstruction, and the intimidating specters of Pompey's military power, Crassus's wealth, and Caesar's immense political talent ensured that the *concordia ordinum* was effectively stillborn—as even Cicero himself acknowledged.[19] Each of these men's selfish, individualized pursuits of glory ensured that Romans quickly returned to a form of elite political competition in which no limits were placed on the tools one would use to vanquish his opponents. And the fact that ordinary Romans did not immediately oppose all of these selfish acts and punish all of these actors by withholding their votes simply encouraged more and more extreme misbehavior. The Republic could have been saved. These men, and many others less famous than they, chose not to save it.

Rome's republic, then, died because it was allowed to. Its death was not inevitable. It could have been avoided. Over the course of a century, thousands of average men, talented men, and middling men all willingly undercut the power of the Republic to restrict and channel the ambitions of the individual, doing so in the interest of their own shortsighted gains. Every time Cato misused a political procedure, or Clodius intimidated a political opponent, or a Roman citizen took a bribe in exchange for his vote, they wounded the Republic. And the wounds festered whenever ordinary Romans either supported or refused to condemn men who took such actions. Sulla, Marius, Caesar, and Augustus all inflicted mighty blows on the Republic, but its death was caused as much by the thousands of small injuries inflicted by Romans who did not think it could really die. When citizens take the health and durability of their republic for granted, that republic is at risk. This was as true in 133 BC or 82 BC or 44 BC as it is in AD 2018. In ancient Rome and in the modern world, a republic is a thing to be cherished, protected, and respected. If it falls, an uncertain, dangerous, and destructive future lies on the other side.

NOTES

Note to the reader: Many of the ancient sources cited below appear as part of the Loeb Classical Library series published by Harvard University Press. The abbreviation LCL in the first reference to such a source indicates that the source is found in the Loeb series. The translations of LCL sources generally follow those presented in the Loeb, with some adaptations for clarity. The exception to this is the translations of Polybius, which use the Loeb Greek text but also draw upon the more accessible English of Ian Scott-Kilvert's translation (*Polybius: The Rise of the Roman Empire* [New York: Penguin, 1979]). Fuller references to ancient sources not found in the Loeb are given following their first mention. References to modern scholarship are not intended to be exhaustive but should instead serve as a point of departure from which further investigation of a topic can commence.

CHAPTER 1

1. Augustus's illness: Cassius Dio (hereafter Dio) 53.30–31 (LCL). Floods: Dio 53.33.5, 54.1. Augustus's use of his own funds: Dio 54.1. 3–4; Augustus, *Res Gestae,* 34. A translation of Augustus's *Res Gestae,* the emperor's own account of his reign, was published as part of the Loeb Classical Library edition of the Roman History of Velleius Paterculus (*Velleius Paterculus/Res Gestae Divi Augusti,* trans. F. Shipley [Cambridge, MA: Harvard University Press, 2002]).

2. Dio 54.3.2–8.

3. Rioting and violence between 21 and 19 BC: Dio 54.6.1–4, 54.10. 1–5. On the conception of a state in antiquity, see now the important

arguments of James Tan, *Power and Public Finance at Rome, 264–49 BCE* (New York: Oxford University Press, 2017), xx–xxv.

4. *Rem publicam a dominatione factionis oppressam in libertatem vindicavi* (*Res Gestae* 1.1). For the most thorough recent discussion of conceptions of *libertas* in the late Republic, see V. Arena, *Libertas and the Practice of Politics in the Late Roman Republic* (Cambridge: Cambridge University Press, 2012).

5. This concept is developed in Vergil, *Eclogue,* 1.26–45 (LCL). For discussion, see K. Galinsky, "Vergil's Use of '*Libertas*': Texts and Contexts," *Vergilius* 52 (2006): 3–19.

6. For US patterning on Rome, see, among many examples, the explicit statements made by John Adams in his *A Defense of the Constitutions of Government of the United States of America,* letter 30. Note, too, the comment of the historian of the ancient world Arnaldo Momigliano that Polybius had such influence on the American Constitution that he should be considered an honorary Founding Father (*Essays in Ancient and Modern Historiography* [Middletown, CT: Wesleyan University Press, 1977], 77). For these examples as well as a concise analysis of Polybius's influence, see C. Champion, "Polybius on Government, Interstate Relations, and Imperial Expansion," in *A Companion to Ancient Greek Government,* ed. H. Beck, 119–130 (Oxford: Wiley-Blackwell, 2013).

7. For a brief summary of these tools and their use, see A. Lintott, *The Constitution of the Roman Republic* (Oxford: Oxford University Press, 1999), 61–63.

8. For this perspective, see the insightful and provocative work of H. Flower, *Roman Republics* (Princeton, NJ: Princeton University Press, 2010).

CHAPTER 2

1. For Pyrrhus's summons to Italy, see Plutarch, *Pyrrhus,* 13 (LCL). For Tarentum's previous appeals to Greek commanders (e.g., its collaboration with Alexander of Epirus in the 330s), see M. Fronda, *Between Rome and Carthage: Southern Italy during the Second Punic War* (Cambridge: Cambridge University Press, 2010), 79–80.

2. Plutarch, *Pyrrhus,* 14.2–7.

3. Pyrrhus's letter: Dionysius of Halicarnassus, *Roman Antiquities* (hereafter *Ant. Rom.*), 19.9.1 (LCL); Plutarch, *Pyrrhus,* 16.4. Lavinius's response: Dionysius of Halicarnassus, *Ant. Rom.,* 19.10.4. Captured spy: Dionysius of Halicarnassus, *Ant. Rom.,* 19.11.1.

4. Romans not barbarous: Plutarch, *Pyrrhus,* 16.5. First battle: Plutarch, *Pyrrhus,* 16.6–17.5; Dionysius of Halicarnassus, *Ant. Rom.,*

19.12; Livy, Book 13 (LCL). Pyrrhus's losses: Plutarch, *Pyrrhus,* 17.4, gives the range of figures, citing two different ancient sources. Roman forces replenished: Plutarch, *Pyrrhus,* 18.1. Pyrrhus's embassy: Appian, *Samnitica,* 10. For Lucanian and Samnite forces that joined Pyrrhus after the battle, see Plutarch, *Pyrrhus,* 17.5, and the discussion of Fronda, *Between Rome and Carthage,* 15n33. Although Plutarch (*Pyrrhus,* 16.2) and Appian (*Samnitica,* 8) both say that the Tarentines were unserious and unable to mount a real army, the quality of the Tarentine contribution was recognized in an inscription erected by Pyrrhus in Dodona and the Tarentine inscription in Delphi, both commemorating their joint victories over the Romans. These are discussed by P. Willeumier, *Tarente: Des origines à la conquête romaine* (Paris: De Boccard, 1939), 116–117; and A. Eckstein, *Mediterranean Anarchy, Interstate War, and the Rise of Rome* (Berkeley: University of California Press, 2006), 156.

5. Cineas is introduced most extensively in Plutarch, *Pyrrhus,* 14. 1–2. For this system of diplomacy in the ancient world, see Eckstein, *Mediterranean Anarchy,* 56–72.

6. Pyrrhus's terms: Plutarch, *Pyrrhus,* 18.3–5. The speech is alluded to in a partial inscription commemorating the career of Appius Claudius (*Corpus Inscriptionum Latinarum* [Berlin, 1863, hereafter *CIL*], 6.40943) and another, evidently with the same text fully preserved, found at Arretium (*CIL,* 11.1827). Both indicate that "he prevented the agreement of a truce with king Pyrrhus." The text of his speech continued to circulate at least until the time of Cicero (see de *Senectute* 6 [LCL—hereafter *Sen.*], "the speech of Appius himself is extant," and *Brutus,* 61). The quotations here come from Plutarch, *Pyrrhus,* 19.4.

7. This view of the third-century Roman alliance structure owes much to the impressive work of Fronda, *Between Rome and Carthage,* 13–34. For the Celtic army, see Eckstein, *Mediterranean Anarchy,* 156.

8. Dionysius of Halicarnassus, *Ant. Rom.,* 14.1–2. Plutarch (*Pyrrhus,* 20.1–5) has a slightly different account involving a sequence of conversations with Fabricius over a number of days. Fabricius's encounter with Pyrrhus would later become proverbial and would be alluded to many times by subsequent authors (e.g., Ennius, Book 4:186–193 [LCL]; Vergil, *Aeneid,* 6.843–844 [LCL]; Cicero, *De oratore,* 2.268 [LCL]).

9. Dionysius of Halicarnassus, *Ant. Rom.,* 14.2.

10. Dionysius of Halicarnassus (*Ant. Rom.,* 15.1–18.7) offers a fictionalized reconstruction of Fabricius's response. For similar ideas, see, for example, Cicero, *de Re Publica,* 5.4 (LCL).

11. Plutarch, *Pyrrhus,* 21.14–15.

12. The notion of the Republic as a mechanism to channel the energies of individual Romans toward a collective good is developed at great

length in Book 2 of Cicero's *de Re Publica*. For a concise description of the Republic of the *nobiles*, see Flower, *Roman Republics*, 25–27.

13. For an excellent and concise summary of the display of tokens of bravery, see N. Rosenstein, "Aristocratic Values," in *A Companion to the Roman Republic*, ed. N. Rosenstein and R. Morstein-Marx, 365–382 (Oxford: Wiley-Blackwell, 2010). Note, too, the more detailed discussions of H. Flower, *Ancestor Masks and Aristocratic Power in Roman Culture* (Oxford: Oxford University Press, 1996). For the crowns and war spoils: Aulus Gellius, *Attic Nights*, 5.6.13 (*corona civica*), 2.11.3 (spoils) (LCL). For the epitaphs of Lucius Cornelius Scipio Barbatus and his son, see *CIL* 1.2.7 (father) and *CIL* 1.2.9 (son). For a discussion of the father's epitaph and the odd erasure that precedes the surviving text, see Flower, *Ancestor Masks*, 176–177.

14. Eulogy of Metellus: Pliny, *Historia Naturalis*, 7.139–140 (LCL— hereafter *HN*). Display of war spoils: E. Malcovati, *Oratorum Romanorum fragmenta*[4] (hereafter *ORF*[4]) (Turin: Paravia, 1976), Cato no. 8.97; Pliny, *HN*, 35.7. Note here Rosenstein, "Aristocratic Values," 374.

15. This notion of liberty at the heart of the Republic is best articulated by Cicero more than two hundred years later, but he likely describes sentiments at the core of Roman notions of liberty. For discussion, see V. Arena, "Invocation to Liberty and Invective of Dominatus at the End of the Roman Republic," *Bulletin of the Institute of Classical Studies* (hereafter *BICS*) 50 (2007): 49–73, at 58.

16. For a discussion of the workings of this system, see the important study of A. Lintott, *Constitution of the Roman Republic*, as well as the concise introduction of J. A. North, "The Constitution of the Roman Republic," in Rosenstein and Morstein-Marx, *A Companion to the Roman Republic*, 256–277. Flower (*Roman Republics*) offers a compelling and accessible reconstruction of the Republic's structural evolution. On the consulship in the Republic, see the essays contained in H. Beck, A. Duplá, M. Jehne, and F. Pina Polo, eds., *Consuls and Res Publica: Holding High Office in the Roman Republic* (Cambridge: Cambridge University Press, 2011).

17. For a thorough discussion of the praetorship, see the magisterial work of T. C. Brennan, *The Praetorship in the Roman Republic*, 2 vols. (Oxford: Oxford University Press, 2000).

18. No magistrates except for a tribune had a genuine veto power. More senior magistrates could effectively veto the actions of juniors by prohibiting them from taking a certain action. A magistrate could also cancel the actions of a colleague through an *intercessio*, though there are not many attested examples of this actually happening. For discussion, see Lintott, *Constitution of the Roman Republic*, 100–101.

19. Cicero, *de Re Publica*, 2.22, describes the political principles behind this assembly. At some point in the Republic, the actual voting within the centuries was apparently reorganized so that it was done according to a division of the thirty-five Roman tribes. For further discussion, see Lintott, *Constitution of the Roman Republic*, 55–61.

20. The question of whether there were one or two assemblies remains a subject of some controversy among scholars. Here I follow the discussion of Lintott, *Constitution of the Roman Republic*, 49–55. Although some have questioned the existence of a *comitia tributa* distinct from the *comitia plebis*, note the discussion of Lintott, *Constitution of the Roman Republic*, 53–55. It is well-known that tribunes proposed legislation in the *concilium plebis*. For praetors and consuls proposing legislation, see, for example, M. H. Crawford, *Roman Statutes* (London: Institute of Classical Studies, University of London, 1996), 1:12. Livy 45.35 gives an instance of a patrician speaking to an assembly convened by tribunes of the plebs to discuss the triumph of Aemilius Paullus in 167 BC. I am not aware of any account of patricians voting in a plebeian assembly, however.

21. The number of rural tribes grew as Roman territory and citizenship expanded until the thirty-first and final rural tribe was established in 241 BC. For a concise discussion of the Roman tribes, their origins, and their expansion, see Lintott, *Constitution of the Roman Republic*, 50–51.

22. On the *contio*, see R. Morstein-Marx, *Mass Oratory and Political Power in the Late Roman Republic* (Cambridge: Cambridge University Press, 2004), 34–42. For Roman voting procedures before their reform in the 130s, see Lintott, *Constitution of the Roman Republic*, 46–61.

23. So says the text of a *Lex Ovinia* from the fourth century BC (Festus 290 L); for discussion, see T. Cornell, "The *Lex Ovinia* and the Emancipation of the Senate," in *The Roman Middle Republic: Politics, Religion, and Historiography c. 400–133 BC*, ed. C. Bruun, 69–89 (Rome: Institutum Romanum Finlandiae, 2000).

24. Appian, *Civil Wars*, Pro. 1 (LCL). All of the surviving works of Appian belong to one historical project. The initial phase of this project consisted of a series of books narrating Rome's conquests of the regions that made up its empire. The next phase, a series of books narrating the civil wars, offered a unified narrative of these conflicts across the entire Mediterranean. The final phase (now lost) provided an imperial history that ran from the time of Augustus until the second century AD. I refer to the books from the first part of the project by the abbreviated names of the regions on which they focus. The *Civil Wars* hereafter is referred to as *BC*.

25. Polybius 6.18 (LCL). The conceptual puzzle of how to fit Rome into this Greek and barbarian dichotomy animated the work of Polybius and other contemporary Greeks. For a compelling discussion of this

issue within and beyond Polybius, see C. Champion, *Cultural Politics in Polybius's Histories* (Berkeley: University of California Press, 2004). For a different take on Polybius's goals, see A. Eckstein, *Moral Vision in the Histories of Polybius* (Berkeley: University of California Press, 1995). On the concept of the Republic of the nobles, see Flower, *Roman Republics,* 35–57.

26. Polybius 6.2.

27. Polybius 1.20.13–16. For First Punic War and the idea of Rome stumbling into it, see the careful discussions of B. D. Hoyos, *Unplanned Wars: The Origins of the First and Second Punic Wars* (Berlin: De Gruyter, 1998), 33–131; and N. Rosenstein, *Rome and the Mediterranean 290–146 BC: The Imperial Republic* (Edinburgh: Edinburgh University Press, 2012), 53–70.

28. Polybius 1.38.6.

29. The Roman reluctance to build a fleet goes back to 253 BC. For discussion of that incident, see Tan, *Power and Public Finance,* chap. 4. Individual financial support for new fleet: Polybius 1.59.6–7. Success in 241: Polybius 1.61.1.

30. For discussion of the agrarian law and the process that led to it, see Polybius 2.21.8–9; Cicero, *de Inventione* (hereafter *Invent.*), 2.52; *Brutus,* 57; *de Academica* (hereafter *Acad.*), 2.13 (all in LCL); Valerius Maximus, *Facta et Dicta Memorabilia* (hereafter Valerius Maximus), 5.5.4 (LCL). For the abrogation of his military command resulting from the bad omens and the triumph, see Plutarch, *Marc.,* 1–3 (LCL); Zonaras, *Epitomē Historiōn* (hereafter Zonaras), 8.20. On the career of Flaminius and the reasons for the uniformly negative portrayal he receives in literary sources, see R. Feig Vishnia, "A Case of 'Bad Press'? Gaius Flaminius in Ancient Historiography," *Zeitschrift für Papyrologie und Epigraphik* (hereafter *ZPE*) 181 (2012): 27–45.

31. For details of the war's outbreak and the military campaigns within it, see the excellent, accessible studies of J. F. Lazenby, *Hannibal's War: A Military History of the Second Punic War* (Warminster: University of Oklahoma Press, 1978); A. Goldsworthy, *The Punic Wars* (London: Cassell, 2000); and Rosenstein, *Rome and the Mediterranean,* 119–175.

32. Although only later sources indicate that Hannibal was familiar with Pyrrhus's strategy (e.g., Livy 35.14.5–12; Appian, *Syr.,* 9–10; Plutarch, *Flam.,* 21), Hannibal's strategy when in Italy seems to have been informed by Pyrrhus's campaigns. On this, see Fronda, *Between Rome and Carthage,* 45–48.

33. Livy 21.63.5–15, 22.1.5–20, 3.11–13.

34. Livy 21.63.

35. For Fabius's strategy, see P. Erdkamp, "Polybius, Livy, and the 'Fabian Strategy,'" *Ancient Society* 23 (1992): 127–147.

36. For some recent studies on the Battle of Cannae, see A. Goldsworthy, *Cannae: Hannibal's Greatest Victory* (London: Cassell, 2001); G. Daly, *Cannae: The Experience of Battle in the Second Punic War* (London: Routledge, 2002).

37. Casualty reports vary. They include 70,000 dead (Polybius 3.117), 60,000 (Quintilian, *Institutio Oratoria,* 8.6.26), 50,000 (Plutarch, *Fabius,* 16.8, and Appian, *Hannibalic War,* 4.25), and 48,200 (Livy 22.49). For modern discussion, see P. A. Brunt, *Italian Manpower 225 BC–AD 14* (Oxford: Clarendon Press, 1971), 419n4.

38. On the scene when news of Cannae reached Rome: Livy 22.53, though this anecdote functions primarily to foreshadow the eventual success of Scipio Africanus. For human sacrifices: Livy 22.57. The only subsequent occurrence was in 113 BC, on which see the report of Plutarch, *Roman Questions,* 83, and *Marcellus,* 3 (both in LCL), as well as the discussion of M. Beard, J. North, and S. R. F. Price, *Religions of Rome: A History* (Cambridge: Cambridge University Press, 1998), 1:81. The act was banned in 97 BC (Pliny, *HN,* 30.3.12).

39. Livy 22.57.

40. The revolts and the local background to them are masterfully reconstructed by Fronda, *Between Rome and Carthage.* On the revolt of Capua and the hegemonic aspirations that may have laid behind it, see Livy 23.6.1–2; Fronda, *Between Rome and Carthage,* 103–125.

41. War with Macedon seems to have actually not been officially declared until 214 BC. For Philip's objectives, see Polybius 7.9.1–17; Livy 23.33.1–12. On the general scrambling in the Mediterranean as a result of Rome's troubles, see A. Eckstein, *Rome Enters the Greek East: From Anarchy to Hierarchy in the Hellenistic Mediterranean, 230–170 BC* (Oxford: Wiley-Blackwell, 2012), 78–91.

42. For estimates of Roman manpower during the war, see N. Rosenstein, *Rome at War: Farms, Families, and Death in the Middle Republic* (Chapel Hill: University of North Carolina Press, 2004), 90; Brunt, *Italian Manpower,* 417–422.

43. N. Rosenstein, "Competition and Crisis in Mid-Republican Rome," *Phoenix* 47 (1993): 313–338.

44. For the economic impact, see P. Kay, *Rome's Economic Revolution* (Oxford: Oxford University Press, 2014), 16; Tan, *Power and Public Finance,* chap. 5.

45. The *prorogatio* of commands was not new to the period of the Second Punic War, though this practice became much more widespread

during and following the war. For discussion, see Lintott, *Constitution of the Roman Republic,* 113–115.

46. Sale of confiscated land: Livy 26.35–36, 28.45–46. On the logistics of this currency reform, see M. Crawford, *Roman Republican Coinage* (hereafter *RRC*) (Cambridge: Cambridge University Press, 1983), 3–46; M. Crawford, *Coinage and Money under the Roman Republic: Italy and the Mediterranean Economy* (London: Methuen, 1985), 52–62; K. Harl, *Coinage in the Roman Economy, 300 B.C. to A.D. 700* (Baltimore: Johns Hopkins University Press, 1996), 21–37.

47. This threat was particularly meaningful given the financial power that the taxpayers in the assembly had at this moment (Tan, *Power and Public Finance,* chap. 5).

48. For the denial of Scipio's triumph and his election: Livy 28.38; Dio 17.57.5–6; Valerius Maximus 2.8.5. Fabius's speech: Livy 28.40–42. Although Livy created the speech he puts in the mouth of Fabius, he is probably correct to imagine that Fabius attributed Scipio's proposal to invade Africa to a desire for personal glory rather than a wise military tactic. Commissioners' impression of the troops: Livy 29.16–22.

49. Literally, *"mater Idaea a Pessinunte Romam advecta foret"* (Livy 29.10). The best analysis of this situation and its connection to the political tension caused by Scipio's rise remains E. Gruen, "The Advent of the Magna Mater," *Studies in Greek Culture and Roman Policy* (Berkeley: University of California Press, 1996), 5–33.

CHAPTER 3

1. Roman embassy to Egypt in 213: Polybius 9.11a. The gold coins are Crawford, *RRC* 44/2-4 and 72/2. For discussion see Kay, *Rome's Economic Revolution,* 16, and A. Meadows, "The Mars/Eagle and Thunderbolt Gold and Ptolemaic Involvement in the Second Punic War," in *Coins of Macedonia and Rome: Essays in Honor of Charles Hersh,* ed. A. M. Burnett, U. Wartenberg, and R. Witschonke, 125–134 (London: Spink and Son, 1998). Egyptian embassy in 208: Appian, *Mace.,* 9.3.1. On Roman relations with Pergamum in this period, see A. Eckstein, *Rome Enters the Greek East,* 122.

2. Roman vigilance after the first Macedonian war: Livy 30.26.2–4, though note the comments of Eckstein, *Rome Enters the Greek East,* 123. For the Egyptian rebellion in 207 or 206 and the climate shocks precipitating it, see F. Ludlow and J. Manning, "Revolts under the Ptolemies: A Paleoclimatological Perspective," in *Revolt and Resistance in the Ancient Classical World and the Near East: In the Crucible of Empire,* ed. J. Collins and J. Manning, 154–174 (Leiden: Brill Academic Publishers,

2016), 160–163 (for the revolt) and 164*ff.* (for the climatological conditions). For the pact of Philip V and Antiochus III, see Eckstein, *Rome Enters the Greek East,* 3–28. For Philip's interest in western expansion, see Polybius 5.105.4–8.

3. Reports from allies: Appian, *Mace.,* 4; Livy 31.2–6. For the idea that Galba had an incentive to prosecute this war with Philip, see W. Harris, *War and Imperialism in Republican Rome* (Oxford: Oxford University Press, 1979), 217–218.

4. Livy 31.6.3. The tribune blamed for this was Quintus Baebus. On the events leading to the second Macedonian war, see Eckstein, *Mediterranean Anarchy,* 280–288.

5. Galba's speech: Livy 31.6; cf. Zonaras 9.15. For Roman concerns about their credibility and prestige in Greece, see E. Gruen, *The Hellenistic World and the Coming of Rome* (Berkeley: University of California Press, 1986), 391–398. Exemptions of previous soldiers from repeat service: Livy 31.8.6.

6. Philip's defenses against Galba: Zonaras 9.15. Flamininus's breakthrough: Zonaras 9.16. Sabotage of negotiations: Appian, *Mace.,* 8; Polybius 18.1.1–12.5; Zonaras 9.16. See as well A. Eckstein, "T. Quinctius Flamininus and the Campaign against Philip in 198 BC," *Phoenix* 30 (1976): 119–142.

7. The superiority of the Roman formation over the phalanx at Cynoscephalae: Polybius 18.28–32. For the "Freedom of Greece," see Polybius 18.46. The announcement at the games apparently freed only those cities in Greece, though it was communicated separately to representatives of Antiochus III that the cities of Asia Minor once controlled by either Philip or the Ptolemies were to be free as well. For liberation of Asia Minor: Polybius 18.47. Livy 33.30 and Zonaras 9.16 both affirm that the freedom of Greek cities in Asia was part of the set of terms dictated to Philip by the Senate.

8. For an analysis of the situation after Antiochus's defeat, see Eckstein, *Mediterranean Anarchy,* 342–381. Roman disinterest subsequently is described at, for example, Polybius 24.8–10.

9. Perseus filling the leadership void left by Rome: Livy 42.12.2. Offenses detailed by Pergamum: Livy 42.11–13.

10. The most thorough assessment of the Republic's second-century involvement in Spain is J. S. Richardson, *Hispaniae: Spain and the Development of Roman Imperialism, 218–82 BC* (Cambridge: Cambridge University Press, 1986), 62–155. A change in the intensity of the warfare after 178 is illustrated by the relative lack of triumphs or ovations awarded for service in Spain between 177 and 166, after averaging almost one a year between 195 and 178 (noted by Richardson, *Hispaniae,* 105).

11. For example, Polybius 36.9. On this point, see the excellent study of C. Champion, *Cultural Politics in Polybius's Histories* (Berkeley: University of California Press, 2004).

12. The numbers for 234–233 appear in Livy, *Periochae,* 20. Those for 209–208 are found in Livy, *History,* 27.36.7. The question of how to trace Roman population trends during and after the Second Punic War has received a great deal of recent attention. Among the most important studies, see S. Hin, *The Demography of Roman Italy: Population Dynamics in an Ancient Conquest Society, 201 BCE–14 CE* (Cambridge: Cambridge University Press, 2013); L. De Ligt, *Peasants, Citizens, and Soldiers: Studies in the Demographic History of Roman Italy 225 BC–AD 100* (Cambridge: Cambridge University Press, 2012); and N. Rosenstein, *Rome at War.* These revise the more pessimistic assessment of Brunt, *Italian Manpower.*

13. For casualty numbers in the second century, see Rosenstein, *Rome at War,* 143, though note the cautions of Hin, *Demography,* 157–160.

14. Livy, *Periochae,* 54. This was a census of 142–141. For a table with all known Republican and early imperial census figures, see Hin, *Demography,* 351–353.

15. Rosenstein (*Rome at War,* 162–169) argues persuasively that colonies were of only limited use as a release valve for building population pressures.

16. Rosenstein, *Rome at War,* 165. On the Aelii, see Valerius Maximus 4.4.8. As Rosenstein notes, poverty was not the only reason that multiple generations of the same family might live together. It must have been the cause of the situation with the Aelii because Valerius Maximus places his discussion of the Aelii with other anecdotes illustrating poverty (the section heading is *De paupertate*). For a similar case in another context, note, for example, Plutarch, *Crassus,* 1.1 (LCL).

17. Rosenstein, *Rome at War,* 144–145. This figure is derived from N. Morley, *Metropolis and Hinterland* (Cambridge: Cambridge University Press, 1996), 39, 46. For a survey of various other figures put forward for the population of the city, see Hin, *Demography,* 220n31.

18. Livy's comment: 39.3. Tooth enamel patterns: Hin, *Demography,* 218–220.

19. Livy 30.45.3 (Scipio); 31.20 (Lentulus).

20. Scipio brought 1,720 talents of silver; the combined tributes from Carthage, Antiochus, and Greek states totaled between 1,200 and 1,300 talents between 187 and 177 BC. For a chart tracing this, see Kay, *Rome's Economic Revolution,* 39, table 2.2.

21. On Roman mining income, see Kay, *Rome's Economic Revolution,* 43–58. New supply crashing the gold market: Polybius 34.10.10–15.

22. Tax refund: Livy 39.7.1–5. As Tan (*Power and Public Finance,* 141–142) has shown, the abolition of the *tributum* eliminated a fiscal burden, but it also diminished the influence that Roman citizens could have over the conduct of wars that they no longer funded. Denarii minting: Crawford, *Roman Republican Coinage, 640ff.* sees 157 BC as a date when a regular and steady increase in the amount of denarii minted began. See, too, the discussion of K. Hopkins, "Taxes and Trade in the Roman Empire (200 BC–AD 400)," *Journal of Roman Studies* 70 (1980): 101–125, at 106–112.

23. Cloaca Maxima: Dionysius of Halicarnassus, *Ant. Rom.,* 3.67.5. Aqua Marcia: Frontinus, *de aquis.,* 1.7 (LCL). For discussion of this and other construction in the period, see Kay, *Rome's Economic Revolution,* 217–220.

24. Polybius 6.17.

25. Cato's Spanish plunder: Livy 34.46.2–3. Cato's interest in commercial farming in Italy is best indicated by his treatise *de Agricultura* (hereafter *Agr.*).

26. Cato recommended that thirteen slaves work on a 180-acre olive farm (Cato, *Agr.,* 10—LCL) and sixteen work on a 66-acre vineyard (*Agr.,* 11).

27. Plutarch, *Cato Maior,* 21.5 (LCL). For discussion, see Kay, *Rome's Economic Revolution,* 230–231.

28. The restriction on seaborne trade using a vessel that carried more than 300 amphorae came with the *plebiscitum Claudianum* of 218 (Livy 21.63.3). For Cato's partnerships, see Plutarch, *Cato Maior,* 21. 5–6, as well as the excellent explanation of Kay, *Rome's Economic Revolution,* 145–146.

29. For the use of credit in the Roman economy, see the important work of W. Harris, "A Revisionist View of Roman Money," *Journal of Roman Studies* 96 (2006): 1–24. For the implications of this development on Roman economic growth and wealth creation, see Kay, *Rome's Economic Revolution,* 107–268.

30. Land grant and property for self: Livy 31.49.4–5. Lavish games: Livy 37.3.7.

31. Fulvius Flaccus gave his foot soldiers the equivalent of 30 denarii, his centurions 60 denarii, and his cavalry 90 denarii (Livy 40.59.3).

32. Twenty-five pairs of gladiators: Livy 31.49.9; 120 gladiators: Livy 39.46. For temples, see the cases of M. Acilius Glabrio (Livy 40.34.5; Valerius Maximus 2.5.1) and L. Aemilius Regillus (Livy 40.52.4–6). Public feasts in 180s: Livy 39.46. Limits on silver: Aulus Gellius, *Noctes Atticus* (hereafter *NA*), 2.24.2 (LCL).

33. For Antiochus: Livy 39.6.7–9; Pliny, *HN,* 33.138; for Perseus: Polybius 31.25. For Crassus: Pliny, *HN,* 33.134. See discussion of Kay, *Rome's Economic Revolution,* 194.

34. Cato, *Agr.,* 144–150, details his recommendations for the use of seasonal laborers based in nearby towns.

CHAPTER 4

1. Tan, *Power and Public Finance,* 61–64, on contracting and tax farming.

2. On hesitancy to serve in Spain, see Rosenstein, *Rome at War,* 276–277n76, with references to earlier scholarship.

3. For discussion of this, see W. Kunkel, *Untersuchungen zur Entwicklung des römischen Kriminalverfahrens in vorsullanischer Zeit* (Munich: Bayerische Akademie der Wissenschaften, 1962).

4. First corruption court: Flower, *Roman Republics,* 69–70. Brennan, *Praetorship in the Roman Republic,* 1:235–256, speaks about earlier steps to prevent misconduct by governors abroad.

5. For a figure "observing" the votes, see Livy 4.49, 45.39.20; Plutarch, *Aemilius Paullus,* 31.10: "But come, take these people off to their voting; and I will come down and follow along with them all, and will learn who are base and thankless and prefer to be wheedled and flattered in war rather than commanded." On these processes more generally, see Flower, *Roman Republics,* 73; Lintott, *Constitution of the Roman Republic,* 46–61; U. Hall, "Greeks and Romans and the Secret Ballot," in *Owls to Athens: Essays on Classical Subjects Presented to Sir Kenneth Dover,* ed. K. Dover and E. Craik (Oxford: Clarendon Press, 1990), 190–194.

6. Gabinian reform: Cicero, *Laws,* 3.35; Livy, *Per.,* 54.193. For discussion, see A. Yakobson, "Secret Ballot and Its Effects in the Late Roman Republic," *Hermes* 123 (1995): 426–442; and Yakobson, "Popular Power in the Roman Republic," in *A Companion to the Roman Republic,* 383–400, at 388–390. Cassian reform: Cicero, *Laws,* 3.35; *Brutus,* 97. Reform of 131: Cicero, *Laws,* 3.36.

7. Gabinius: Cicero, *Laws,* 3.35 (a sordid nobody); *De Amicitia,* 42 (estranging Senate and people). Cassius: Cicero, *Laws,* 3.36. Carbo: Cicero, *Laws,* 3.35.

8. The fact that observation remained a possibility after the reforms of the 130s is suggested by the fact that, in 119, Marius attracted a great deal of resistance when he pushed for narrowing the platform on which a voter walked when presenting his ballot. On Marius's reform, see Plutarch, *Marius,* 4.2–4; Cicero, *Laws,* 3.38; Yakobson, "Secret Ballot," 438–439.

9. Yakobson, "Popular Power," 390.

10. The Dioscuri were most often depicted on the reverse through the 180s BC, though they continued to appear regularly through the 150s (e.g., *RRC* 198/1, a coin of 157–156 BC). They again became the most common reverse from c. 150 BC through the end of the 140s BC (e.g., *RRC* 209/1, a coin of 149 BC, and *RRC* 224/1) and occasionally after that as well. The divine figures in chariots began appearing in the 180s. Luna was most popular in the 180s, though she continued to appear intermittently after that (e.g., from the 180s, *RRC* 140/1, 141/1, 163/1, 187/1; from the 140s, *RRC* 207/1). Diana appeared most frequently in the 170s and 160s (e.g., *RRC* 158/1, 159/2). Victory was common in the 150s and 140s (e.g., *RRC* 197/1a–b, 199/1a–b, 202/1a–b, 203/1a–b, 204/1, 205/1, 206/1, 208/1). The gods and goddesses depicted in the chariot begin to vary more widely at the end of the 140s, with Victory, Diana, Juno, and Jupiter all appearing in issues from 142 and 141 BC.

11. Four moneyers signed off on denarius issues that year. Two of them used standard designs (P. Aelius Paetus had the Dioscuri on the reverse [*RRC* 233/1] and M. Baebius Q. f. Tampilus depicted Apollo in a chariot [*RRC* 236/1a–e]). The other two were radically different.

12. The coin is *RRC* 234/1, issued by Ti. Veturius. For discussion of this coin and its significance, see Crawford, *RRC*, p. 266 (with bibliography). The connection of this coin with the *foedus Numantinum* of 137 has been debated by, among others, C. Stannard ("Numismatic Evidence for the Relations between Spain and Central Italy at the Turn of the Second and First Centuries," *Schweizerische Numismatische Rundschau* 84 [2005]: 47–79, at 58–60) and Flower, *Ancestor Masks*, 79–86. Stannard's argument that this coin should be dated later seems implausible because the coin was tariffed at 10 asses and the retariffing of the denarius to 16 asses is clearly evident on later issues.

13. These moneyers were C. Minucius Augurinus (moneyer in 135 BC, responsible for *RRC* 242/1) and T. Minucius C. f. Augurinus (moneyer in 134 BC, responsible for *RRC* 243/1). For discussion of these coins, see Crawford, *RRC*, 273–276; T. P. Wiseman, "The Minucii and their Monument," in *Imperium Sine Fine*, ed. J. Lindersk (Stuttgart, 1996), 57–74. On the grain distribution of 439 BC, see A. Momigliano, "Due Punti di Storia Romana Arcaica," in *Quarto Contributo alla Storia degli Studi Classici e del Mondo Antico* (Rome: Ed. di Storia e Letteratura, 1969), 329–361, at 331–349.

14. For a survey of the family background of Tiberius Gracchus, see D. Stockton, *The Gracchi* (Oxford: Oxford University Press, 1979), 23*ff*.

15. For Tiberius's intervention in the trial, see Valerius Maximus 4.1.8; Livy 38.57, among others. On the fanciful nature of elements of this account, see Stockton, *The Gracchi*, 23–24.

16. His teachers were said to have been the rhetorician Diophanes of Mytilene and the Stoic philosopher Blossius of Cumae. For this, see Plutarch, *Tiberius Gracchus*, 1.3 (LCL); Cicero, *Brutus*, 104; Tacitus, *Dialogus*, 28 (LCL); Quintilian 1.1.6.

17. Bravery in war: Plutarch, *Tiberius Gracchus*, 4. Triumph of Appius Claudius: Cicero, *de Cael.*, 34; Valerius Maximus 5.4.6.

18. For the context of the treaty, see Appian, *Spain*, 80. For Tiberius's role in the negotiations, see Plutarch, *Tiberius Gracchus*, 5–6.

19. On the treaty: Appian, *Spain*, 13.83; Plutarch, *Tiberius Gracchus*, 7. Scipio's army: Appian, *Spain*, 14.84.

20. For Tiberius's sense that Scipio had betrayed him, see Cicero, *Brutus*, 103, *de har. resp.* 43; Velleius Paterculus 2.2 (LCL).

21. Tiberius's concerns are summarized in Plutarch, *Tiberius Gracchus*, 8. Appian, *BC*, 1.1.7 echoes the same point. On the reality of Italian landholding patterns in the second century, see, among many others, Rosenstein, *Rome at War*, 141–169.

22. On the probability that he campaigned on this issue, see C. Steel, *The End of the Roman Republic, 146 to 44 BC* (Edinburgh: Edinburgh University Press, 2013), 16. For slogans painted across the city, see Plutarch, *Tiberius Gracchus*, 9. For the speech, see Appian, *BC*, 1.9.

23. Appian, *BC*, 1.8. Cato (in the *pro Rhodiensibus*, found in *ORF²*, 65–66) suggests that the law was in effect without enforcement mechanisms in 167 BC.

24. The status of non-Roman Italians under this law is unclear. Cicero (*de Re Publica*, 3.41) says that Italians did not benefit, though Appian (*BC*, 1.12.7) seems to suggest otherwise. For discussion, see Stockton, *The Gracchi*, 42–43.

25. Laelius's proposal: Plutarch, *Tiberius Gracchus*, 8. See, too, Stockton, *The Gracchi*, 33. Tiberius's prominent supporters: Plutarch, *Tiberius Gracchus*, 9.

26. Republic balancing wealth distribution: Appian, *BC*, 1.11. Land rented mainly by Italian allies: Appian, *BC*, 1.19–21, though note the critical reading of this passage in H. Mouritsen, *Italian Unification: A Study in Ancient and Modern Historiography* (London: Institute of Classical Studies, University of London, 1998), 16–22.

27. Plutarch, *Tiberius Gracchus*, 10.

28. Plutarch, *Tiberius Gracchus*, 10.4–6.

29. Plutarch (*Tiberius Gracchus*, 11–12) offers a dramatic ancient account of this action. For a more measured assessment, see Appian, *BC*, 1.12.5; Stockton, *The Gracchi*, 65–67.

30. Both Plutarch (*Tiberius Gracchus*, 12) and Appian (*BC*, 1.12) mention that the threat of violence by mobs or armed associates of Tiberius hovered over the proceedings.

31. Plutarch, *Tiberius Gracchus*, 13.

32. Plutarch, *Tiberius Gracchus*, 14–15. Livy, *Per.*, 58, suggests that Tiberius proposed gifting the money to the urban poor who did not receive land allotments. On this, see the comments of Stockton, *The Gracchi*, 67–69. For finance and foreign relations as the unquestioned preserve of the Senate, see Polybius 6.13.

33. On this point, see Arena, *Libertas and the Practice of Politics*, chap. 3.

34. Plutarch, *Tiberius Gracchus*, 14; suggested as well in Cicero, *de Amicitia*, 41.

35. This was Titus Annius. The speech he gave and the particular question he framed would both become so legendary that grammarians later studied them (Festus, in *ORF²* 106 for the speech; Plutarch, *Tiberius Gracchus*, 14.5, preserves the question). Annius's most powerful comment was framed as a *sponsione provocare*, a sort of judicial wager in which Annius invited Tiberius to legally contest with him the validity of the charge that Tiberius had dishonored a fellow tribune in violation of the law. For this, see J. Crook, "*Sponsione Provocare*: Its Place in Roman Litigation," *Journal of Roman Studies* 66 (1976): 132–138, at 133.

36. According to Cicero, the Campanian public land only becomes subject to redistribution in 59 BC, under actions taken by Caesar. On this, see F. De Martino, *Storia della costituzione romana*, 2nd ed. (Naples: Eugenio Jovene, 1973), 3:169n3; Stockton, *The Gracchi*, 55. There exists, however, a boundary stone with the names of land commissioners found near Capua (H. Dessau, *Inscriptiones Latinae Selectae*, vol. 1 [Berlin: Weidmann, 1892] [hereafter *ILS*], number 24) that suggests activity in the region.

37. For the estimate of fifteen thousand families: K. Bringmann, *A History of the Roman Republic* (Cambridge: Polity Press, 2015), 151. On the limitations on the power of the Roman poor, see, for example, the discussion of H. Mouritsen, *Politics in the Roman Republic* (Cambridge: Cambridge University Press, 2017), 61–64.

38. Plutarch, *Tiberius Gracchus*, 13 (poisoning rumor); Appian, *BC*, 1.1.13 (escorted by crowds).

39. Second tribunate: Appian, *BC*, 1.2.14; Plutarch, *Tiberius Gracchus*, 16. Personal canvassing in advance of the vote: Appian, *BC*, 1.2.14.

40. Supporters spending the night on guard: Plutarch, *Tiberius Gracchus*, 16; Appian, *BC*, 1.2.15. For accounts of Tiberius's murder, see Plutarch, *Tiberius Gracchus*, 18–19; Appian, *BC*, 1.2.14–17; Dio, 24.83.8. For a modern summary, see Stockton, *The Gracchi*, 75–77.

41. Plutarch, *Tiberius Gracchus*, 20.1.

42. Cicero, *de Re Publica,* 1.31.

43. Appian, *BC,* 1.1.2 (first to die in civil strife), 1.2.17 (polarization).

44. Appian, *BC,* 1.2.17.

45. οἱ μὲν οἰκτείροντες αὑτούς τε κἀκεῖνον καὶ τὰ παρόντα ὡς οὐκέτι πολιτείαν, ἀλλὰ χειροκρατίαν καὶ βίαν (Appian, *BC,* 1.2.17, lines 9–11).

46. Functioning and funding of land commission after Tiberius's death: Plutarch, *Tiberius Gracchus,* 21; Appian, *BC,* 1.3.18. For the idea that work continued until 118 (based on a reading of Appian, *BC,* 1.27), see D. Gargola, "Appian and the Aftermath of the Gracchan Reform," *American Journal of Philology* 118 (1997): 555–581. For later land laws, see, for example, Cicero, *Brutus,* 136 (on the *lex Thoria*) and an agrarian law of 111 BC. For discussion of the latter, see A. Lintott, *Judicial Reform and Land Reform in the Roman Republic: A New Edition, with Translation and Commentary, of the Laws from Urbino* (Cambridge: Cambridge University Press, 1992), 49–55.

47. Cicero (*de Re Publica,* 1.6) and Valerius Maximus (3.2.17) both suggest that the appointment to Asia was made out of concern for his safety or to prevent a trial.

48. Plutarch, *Tiberius Gracchus,* 21.

49. Appian, *BC,* 1.3.19–20.

50. Flaccus's citizenship proposal: Appian, *BC,* 1.3.21; Valerius Maximus 9.5.1. Note, too, the discussion of Mouritsen, *Italian Unification,* 112–113. Revolt of Fregellae: P. Conole, "Allied Disaffection and the Revolt of Fregellae," *Antichthon* 15 (1981): 129–141.

51. Appian, *BC,* 1.3.21.

52. Appian, *BC,* 1.3.21; Cicero, *Sest.,* 103, Livy, *Per.,* 60. For a summary of Gaius's reforms in 123, see Stockton, *The Gracchi,* 114–176.

53. Tan, *Power and Public Finance,* 61–64.

54. The sources for the violence include Cicero, *De oratore,* 2.132–134; Plutarch, *G. Gracchus,* 13–18; Appian, *BC,* 1.3.25–26. For a narrative reconstruction, see Stockton, *The Gracchi,* 176–205. For the unsanctioned public policy discussion as the cause of the disturbance that led to Gaius's death, see R. Morstein-Marx, *Mass Oratory,* 39, on the basis of *de vir. ill.* 65.5; Orosius 5.12.5; Plutarch, *C. Gracchus,* 13–14. On the broader moment, see J. Lea Beness and T. W. Hillard, "The Theatricality of the Deaths of C. Gracchus and Friends," *Classical Quarterly* 51.1 (2001): 135–140.

55. Plutarch, *C. Gracchus,* 1. This dream is also mentioned by Cicero, *Div.,* 1.56, citing as his source Gaius's contemporary Lucius Coelius Antipater.

CHAPTER 5

1. For Opimius's construction of the temple, see Appian, *BC,* 1.26; Plutarch, *G. Gracchus,* 17; Cicero, *pro. Sest.,* 140.

2. Caecilii Metelli were consuls in 123, 119, 117, 115 (the year of the consulships of M. Caecilius Metellus and M. Aemilius Scaurus), 113, and 109. Other consuls belonging to the same family in this period included Q. Fabius Maximus Allobrogicus (consul in 121) and Q. Fabius Maximus Eburnus (consul in 116); C. Papirius Carbo (consul in 120) and Cn. Papirius Carbo (consul in 113); and M. Porcius Cato (consul in 118) and C. Porcius Cato (consul in 114).

3. Sallust, *Jugurtha*, 41.9 (LCL).

4. On this incident, see Plutarch, *Quaest. Rom.*, 83 (LCL) and the discussion of Steel, *End of the Roman Republic*, 27.

5. On the live burial of the two Greeks and two Gauls, see Z. Vár-helyi, "The Specters of Roman Imperialism: The Live Burials of Gauls and Greeks at Rome," *Classical Antiquity* 26 (2007): 277–304. For the conviction of the priest C. Sulpicius Galba as part of the corruption investigations related to the activities of Jugurtha, see Cicero, *Brutus*, 128, as well as the discussion below. For politicians seizing on this moment: E. Rawson, "Religion and Politics in the Late Second Century BC at Rome," *Phoenix* 28 (1974): 193–212.

6. On Jugurtha's background, see Sallust, *Jugurtha*, 5–16. For his friendships with Scipio and other Romans: Sallust, *Jugurtha*, 7.7.

7. Sallust, *Jugurtha*, 8.1.

8. Bribery of senatorial commission: Sallust, *Jugurtha*, 13.8. Attack on Cirta: Sallust, *Jugurtha*, 26. On the likelihood that these merchants had been active participants in the defense of Cirta and, thus, were not civilians killed indiscriminately, see R. Morstein-Marx, "The Alleged 'Massacre' at Cirta and Its Consequences (Sallust *Bellum Iugurthinum* 26–27)," *Classical Philology* 95 (2000): 468–476.

9. Sallust, *Jugurtha*, 30.1–2.

10. "Not to forsake Republic": Sallust, *Jugurtha*, 30.3. "Arrogant cabal": Sallust, *Jugurtha*, 31.2. For the context, see Morstein-Marx, *Mass Oratory*, 267–269. For a parallel idea in a speech of Gaius Gracchus (quoted in Gellius, *NA*, 11.10), see F. Millar, "Politics, Persuasion and the People before the Social War (150–90 BC)," *Journal of Roman Studies* 76 (1986): 9. This Gracchan speech suggests the basic plausibility that Sallust may indeed reproduce the sentiments Memmius expressed.

11. Sallust, *Jugurtha*, 31.6 (no violence), 31.18 (courts). Jugurtha's bribery of tribune: Sallust, *Jugurtha*, 34.

12. Workings of tribunal: Sallust, *Jugurtha*, 30. See the concise summary of Steel, *End of the Roman Republic*, 28–29. "Bitterness and violence": Sallust, *Jugurtha*, 40.5. For the corruption tribunal generally, see Sallust, *Jugurtha*, 30. See the concise summary of Steel, *End of the Roman Republic*, 28–29.

13. Sallust, *Jugurtha*, 63; Plutarch, *Marius*, 8 (LCL).

14. Depending on the context, the term *novus homo* (new man) could mean either the first member of a family to qualify for the Senate or the first to hold the consulship. See the discussion of D. R. Shackleton Bailey, "*Nobiles* and *Novi* Reconsidered," *American Journal of Philology* 107 (1986): 255–260.

15. On Marius's connection to the Caecilii Metelli: Plutarch, *Marius*, 4, and E. Badian, *Foreign Clientelae (264–70 BC)* (Oxford: Clarendon Press, 1958), 194–195. Voting law: Cicero, *Laws*, 3.39; Plutarch, *Marius*, 4; Lintott, *Constitution of the Roman Republic*, 46. For an assessment of Marius's subsequent electoral failures (and Sallust's attempts to skate over them), see R. Syme, *Sallust*, 2nd ed. (Berkeley: University of California Press, 2002), 161. On the bribery charges, see Plutarch, *Marius*, 5.2–5; Valerius Maximus 6.9.14.

16. Sallust, *Jugurtha*, 63.7.

17. Sallust, *Jugurtha*, 64.2; cf. Plutarch, *Marius*, 8.

18. Plutarch, *Marius*, 8; Dio 26.3; and Sallust, *Jugurtha*, 64.4, all preserve the same comment.

19. Sallust, *Jugurtha*, 64.

20. Plutarch, *Marius*, 8; Sallust, *Jugurtha*, 65.5, 73.3–7.

21. Sallust, *Jugurtha*, 73.4.

22. Command given to Marius: Sallust, *Jugurtha*, 73.7. Consulships as spoils: Sallust, *Jugurtha*, 84.1.

23. Cicero (*de Re Publica*, 2.40) indicates that the lowest property class eligible for military service possessed at least 1,500 bronze asses, a modest amount equaling less than 150 denarii. On the poor seeing Marius's command as a plunder opportunity, see Sallust, *Jugurtha*, 84.4. For Marius enrolling the poor, see Plutarch, *Marius*, 9; Sallust, *Jugurtha*, 86; Valerius Maximus 2.3.1; Gellius 16.10.10.

24. For the casualty numbers at Aurasio, see Livy, *Per.*, 67 (80,000); Granius Licinianus (70,000). For the defeat, see as well Sallust, *Jugurtha*, 114; Plutarch, *Life of Camillus*, 19.7; *Life of Lucullus*, 27.7 (both LCL); and Granius Licinianus, Book 33 in *Grani Liciniani Reliquae*, ed. N. Criniti (Leipzig: Teubner, 1981); Dio 27 (91.1–3) on the incompetence of the Roman commanders.

25. Gnaeus Domitius Ahenobarbus prosecuted Scaurus (Dio 27 [92.1]). Norbanus prosecuted Caepio (see Cicero, *Brutus*, 163, for the defense of Caepio). Ahenobarbus was consul in 96, and Norbanus became consul in 83, albeit in a very different political climate.

26. Saturninus's quaestorship: Cicero, *Sest.*, 17.39. Pushing Marius to run for consulship: Plutarch, *Marius*, 14.

27. The coin is *RRC* 326/1. For Marius as the third founder of Rome, see Plutarch, *Marius,* 27.

28. Plutarch, *Marius,* 28.

29. This is the comment of Plutarch, *Marius,* 28.1, though admittedly Plutarch was extremely hostile to Marius.

30. For Metellus getting credit for victory against Jugurtha, note Plutarch, *Marius,* 10. This is, of course, as untrue as the idea that Marius had won the war despite Metellus. For Marius's cooperation with allies against Metellus: H. Evans, "Metellus Numidicus and the Elections for 100 BC," *Acta Classica* 30 (1987): 65–70, and E. Gruen, "The Exile of Metellus Numidicus," *Latomus* 24 (1965): 576–580. On the bribery charges, see Livy, *Per.,* 69; Velleius Paterculus 2.12.6; Plutarch, *Marius,* 28.5.

31. Plutarch, *Marius,* 29; Appian, *BC,* 1.29.

32. For previous laws with oaths attached and the senatorial discomfort with the violent circumstances of this law's passage, see Appian, *BC,* 1.30; Gruen, "Exile of Metellus," 576nn2–3.

33. Plutarch, *Marius,* 29; Appian, *BC,* 1.30.

34. Livy, *Per.,* 69, and Orosius 5.17.4 both indicate that the trial of Metellus was to be conducted before the people, not before an equestrian jury. So, apparently, do Cicero (*Laws,* 3.26) and Appian (*BC,* 1.31). Given that Saturninus was a tribune, this must refer to some sort of trial before the *concilium plebis,* the only assembly he could lawfully summon.

35. Such is the interpretation of Gruen, "Exile of Metellus," 579–580.

36. The dating of the *maiestas* law is unclear. Brennan (*Praetorship in the Roman Republic,* 2:366–367) dates it to 103 and connects it to the prosecutions of the commanders in the war against the Cimbri. For consideration of its place in 100, see Steel, *End of the Roman Republic,* 32; Millar, "Politics, Persuasion and the People," 3.

37. Appian (*BC,* 1.32) comments, "Memmius was the more illustrious man by far, and Glaucia and Apuleius [Saturninus] were anxious about the result."

38. Crowd chanting: for example, Appian, *BC,* 1.32. Plutarch (*Marius,* 30) speaks about Saturninus being killed in the forum. For these events, see J. Lea Beness and T. W. Hillard, "The Death of Lucius Equitius on 10 December 100 BC," *Classical Quarterly* 40 (1990): 269–272, as well as the longer reconstruction of E. Badian, "The Death of Saturninus," *Chiron* 14 (1984): 101–147.

39. Appian, *BC,* 1.33.

40. Plutarch, *Marius,* 30.

CHAPTER 6

1. Appian, *BC,* 5.1.

2. Furius's actions and murder: Appian, *BC,* 1.33; A. Russell, "Speech, Competition, and Collaboration: Tribunician Politics and the Development of Popular Ideology," in *Community and Communication: Oratory and Politics in Republican Rome,* ed. C. Steel and H. van der Blom (Oxford: Oxford University Press, 2013), 101–115. Metellus's return: Appian (*BC,* 1.33) comments that "a whole day was not sufficient for those who wanted to greet Metellus at the city gates."

3. Tooth enamel from skeletons offers an interesting portrait of the sorts of Italian immigrants in Rome in the late second and early first centuries. For discussion, see Hin, *Demography,* 218–221.

4. The introduction of Gaius Gracchus's grain dole, for example, required the Republic to create an organized system of tax collection in Asia Minor to fund the program. On this, see Kay, *Rome's Economic Revolution,* 59–86.

5. This law is the *lex Licinia Mucia,* described by Cicero, *de Off.,* 3.47. For this as a response to Italian elite requests for help, see C. Steel, *End of the Roman Republic,* 35–36.

6. Steel (*End of the Roman Republic,* 37–38) plausibly suggests that Drusus's measure proposed mixed juries of *equites* and senators, which would be a dilution, but not an elimination, of the effects of the earlier reform.

7. Appian, *BC,* 1.35–36.

8. A situation made clear by Marius's decision to violate the law by granting Roman citizenship to some of his allied soldiers from Camerium so that they might be eligible for land in his veteran colonies. For discussion, see H. Mouritsen, *Italian Unification,* 90. On the Drusus reform, see Mouritsen, 142–151.

9. As Appian (*BC,* 1.36) indicates.

10. Velleius Paterculus 2.14.

11. Velleius Paterculus 2.14; Appian, *BC,* 1.36.

12. For the events in Asculum, see Appian, *BC,* 1.38; Velleius Paterculus 2.15. For the background to the revolt as an action motivated by a desire to push back against Roman power rather than a drive for Roman citizenship, see Mouritsen, *Italian Unification,* 130–142.

13. Asconius 22C. For discussion, see E. Badian, "*Quaestiones Variae,*" *Historia* 18 (1969): 447–491; Mouritsen, *Italian Unification,* 133–137. For a list of prosecutions or possible prosecutions undertaken because of this law, see Steel, *End of the Roman Republic,* 82.

14. Arming slaves: Appian, *BC,* 1.49. Law of Caesar: Appian, *BC,* 1.49; Cicero, *Pro Balbo,* 21 (LCL). Note, however, the arguments against

Appian's version of events made by Mouritsen, *Italian Unification,* 153–156. Although Mouritsen is certainly correct that increases in Roman manpower led to the Roman successes of 89 BC, I am not persuaded that the Umbrians and Etruscans revolted after the law was issued. Lex Calpurnia: Cicero, *Pro Archia,* 4.7 (LCL). Extension of Latin rights: Asconius 3C.

15. Plutarch, *Sulla,* 1 (LCL). Sulla's ancestor P. Cornelius Rufinus held the consulship in 290 and 277 BC as well as a dictatorship during the conflict with Pyrrhus. He was subsequently expelled from the Senate because he held more than ten pounds of silver plate, a violation of a sumptuary law in effect at that time.

16. Sulla styled himself "Lucky" (*Felix* in Latin). Sulla's *Memoirs,* which were cited extensively by Plutarch, offer a detailed account of Sulla's own recollections of incidents where such divine communications occurred. It is unclear when Sulla came to this realization. It was perhaps as early as 106 BC, when he was serving alongside Marius in the war with Jugurtha, though Plutarch (*Sulla,* 5) indicates that this may have grown out of a conversation with some Chaldeans during Sulla's meeting with a Parthian envoy. For discussion of the origins of this conviction, see J. P. V. D. Balsdon, "Sulla Felix," *Journal of Roman Studies* 41 (1951): 1–10, at 9 (for the year 106 BC); A. Keaveney, *Sulla: The Last Republican,* 2nd ed. (New York: Routledge, 2005), 33–34 (for 93 BC).

17. Plutarch, *Sulla,* 2 (inheritance); *Sulla,* 3 (signet ring); *Sulla,* 5 (use of Bocchus connection in campaign for aedile). Bocchus himself reinforced this when, in the 90s BC, he paid for the erection in the Roman Forum of a gold statue of Sulla accepting the surrender of Jugurtha (Plutarch, *Sulla,* 6).

18. Plutarch, *Sulla,* 5, describes this period in Sulla's career. For discussion, see Keaveney, *Sulla,* 27–35; D. Magie, *Roman Rule in Asia Minor,* Vol. 1 (Princeton, NJ: Princeton University Press, 2015), 206–207.

19. Plutarch, *Sulla,* 5 (extortion case), 6 (Bocchus statue).

20. Plutarch (*Sulla,* 6) describes Sulla's conviction that fortune ensured that his intuition would lead to good outcomes.

21. Plutarch, *Sulla,* 6.

22. On Nicomedes: Appian, *Mithridates,* 11–12 (on Nicomedes's debts) and 13–17 (on the embassies). On Mithridates's career and life, see A. Mayor, *The Poison King: The Life and Legend of Mithridates, Rome's Deadliest Enemy* (Princeton, NJ: Princeton University Press, 2009).

23. For a concise summary of the initial phases of the campaign, see J. Hind, "Mithridates," in *The Cambridge Ancient History,* Vol. 9, *The Last Age of the Roman Republic, 146–43 BC,* 2nd ed., ed. J. Crook, A. Lintott, and E. Rawson (Cambridge: Cambridge University Press, 1994), 129–164, at 144–148. For the massacre, see Appian, *Mith.,* 22; Valerius Maximus 9.2.3; Dio fr. 109.8; Plutarch, *Sulla,* 24.4.

24. Cicero described how "very many people lost large fortunes in Asia...there was a collapse in credit at Rome, because repayments were interrupted. Indeed, it is not possible for many people in one state to lose their property and fortunes without the result that many others are dragged into the same calamity with them" (*De imp. Cn. Pomp.*, 19—LCL). For the resultant reforms as well as the murder of Asellio, see, for example, Appian, *BC*, 1.54. For discussion of the financial crisis of 88 BC, see Kay, *Rome's Economic Revolution*, 243–252.

25. For Asian taxes funding the grain distribution program, see Kay, *Rome's Economic Revolution*, 59–83; Tan, *Power and Public Finance*, 158–160.

26. For Sulpicius's private army, see Plutarch, *Sulla*, 8.

27. On this shift, see the comments of Cicero, *Har. resp.*, 43 (LCL); Velleius Paterculus 2.18.5–6; T. Mitchell, "The Volte-Face of P. Sulpicius Rufus in 88 BC," *Classical Philology* 70, no. 3 (1975): 197–203; and the cautions of Steel, *End of the Roman Republic*, 87–93. Steel's suggestion that Sulpicius's tribal reforms are separate from the Marian command proposal (92n49) is sensible, even though Appian, *BC*, 1.55–56, conflates the two.

28. Though, as Steel (*End of the Roman Republic*, 93) notes, there was no precedent for ending a command before it even began.

29. Appian, *BC*, 1.57.

30. For Sulla's advance and capture of the city, see Appian, *BC*, 1.58; Plutarch, *Sulla*, 9; Velleius Paterculus 2.19.

31. Punishment of soldiers: Appian, *BC*, 1.59, probably following Sulla's memoirs in its account of these events. Condemnation of Marius and others: Appian, *BC*, 1.60, makes this clear.

32. A point made most powerfully by Flower, *Roman Republics*, 117–134.

33. Appian, *BC*, 1.62.

34. Marius's Etruscan army: Appian, *BC*, 1.67. Samnites: Dio, fr. 102.7.

35. Steel, *End of the Roman Republic*, 97, gives a list of the dead. Appian (*BC*, 1.72–74) gives a litany of the ways the condemned lost their lives. For heads on the speaker's platform, see Appian, *BC*, 1.73; Cicero, *De or.*, 3.8–10.

36. Plutarch, *Sulla*, 12.

37. Death of Cinna: Appian, *BC*, 1.78. Defection of Italian armies: Velleius Paterculus 2.25.2.

38. Appian, *BC*, 1.82, speaking of the forces of the consuls arranged to meet Sulla on his approach.

39. On the Battle at the Colline Gate, see, for example, Velleius Paterculus 2.27.1–3; Appian, *BC*, 1.93; Plutarch, *Sulla*, 29. Paterculus

is notable for describing this battle as one against a foreign adversary, describing the Samnite leader as presenting a threat to Rome as severe as anything since Hannibal. Steel (*End of the Roman Republic*, 106n105) is likely correct in seeing this view of the battle as ultimately deriving from Sulla's own memoirs.

40. Executions of Samnites: Plutarch, *Sulla*, 30; Dio 109.6–7. On the proscriptions and confiscations, see Velleius Paterculus 2.28.1–4; Appian, *BC*, 1.95–96; Plutarch, *Sulla*, 31; F. Hinard, *Les proscriptions de la Rome républicaine* (Rome: École Française de Rome, 1985). For convictions simply because of wealth, see the anecdotes in Plutarch, *Sulla*, 31.

41. On these figures, see, for example, Sallust, *Catiline*, 28. On their loyalty, see Appian, *BC*, 1.96.

42. Appian, *BC*, 1.101.

43. Appian, *BC*, 1.79.

CHAPTER 7

1. Sallust, *Histories*, 1.49.1 (LCL).

2. Sallust, *Histories*, 1.49.2.

3. Sulla's use of the property of the proscribed as a way to spread guilt: Plutarch, *Crassus*, 2 (LCL); Sallust, *Hist.*, 1.49.18–19. Sulla fronting the money for purchases: Sallust (*Hist.*, 4.1) and Cicero (2 *Verr.*, 3.81), both of whom speak about proposals in the later 70s to get some of the beneficiaries of these policies to pay the money back to the state. Livy values the land confiscated by Sulla at 350 million sesterces (*Per.*, 89). Appian counts 120,000 Sullan veterans settled on seized land (Appian, *BC*, 1.104).

4. Crassus, who was one of these men, was even said to have remarked that no one could be thought rich unless he had the resources to buy an army (Plutarch, *Crassus*, 2).

5. On the integration of new citizens in 86 BC, see Livy, *Per.*, 84; Steel, *End of the Roman Republic*, 125; M. Crawford, "How to Create a *municipium*: Rome and Italy After the Social War," in *Modus Operandi: Essays in Honour of Geoffrey Rickman*, ed. M. Austin, J. Harries, and C. Smith (London: Institute of Classical Studies, University of London, 1998), 31–46.

6. Sulla stripping citizenship: Sallust, *Hist.*, 1.49; Cicero, *Dom.*, 79 (LCL). The case of Roscius: Cicero, *Rosc. Am.*, 20 (LCL); Steel, *End of the Roman Republic*, 133–135. Oppianicus: Cicero, *Pro Cluentio*, 21–25 (LCL). Pompey in Picenum: Plutarch, *Pompey*, 6 (LCL). Punishment of later generations: Sallust, *Hist.*, 1.49.6.

7. Cicero, *Pro Cluentio*, 21, 162. For discussion, see Steel, *End of the Roman Republic*, 135.

8. For the Sullan elimination of the grain dole in 84 BC and its consequences, see Kay, *Rome's Economic Revolution*, 300–301.

9. On the dispute and the funeral, see the description of Appian, *BC*, 1.105–107.

10. For the grain measure, see Sallust, *Hist.*, 1.55, 67; Granius Licinianus Bk. 36, p. 34F; Exsuper. 6 (37Z), and R. Seager, "The Rise of Pompey," in *Cambridge Ancient History*, 9:208–209. For the land restorations, see Appian, *BC*, 1.107; Sallust, *Hist.*, 1.67. On Lepidus's position regarding the tribunate, Granius Licinianus Bk. 36, pp. 33–34, indicates that Lepidus was first to oppose an attempt by tribunes to get Sulla's restrictions removed. Sallust (*Hist.*, 1.49) indicates that he quickly reversed this position, likely after Sulla's funeral.

11. Sallust, *Hist.*, 1.60.

12. The sources describing these events make the chronology difficult to reconstruct. Appian mentions the provincial assignment and conflict with Catulus (*BC*, 107), but not the revolt in Eturia. Sallust (*Hist.*, 1.57–72) describes the revolt in Etruria, but not the assignment in Gaul. Granius Licinianus (Bk. 36, pp. 34–35) suggests the chronology laid out above, though Lepidus's provincial governorship can only be inferred based upon one of the text's final fragments. For this reconstruction, see, too, Seager, "Rise of Pompey," 208. On the coup more generally, see E. Badian, *Foreign Clientelae (264–70 BC)*, 275*ff*; E. Gruen, *The Last Generation of the Roman Republic* (Berkeley: University of California Press, 1974), 12–16.

13. For the second consulship demand, see Sallust, *Hist.*, 1.67.15. Death of Lepidus and survivors fleeing to Spain: Appian, *BC*, 1.107. For discussion, see Seager, "Rise of Pompey," 209.

14. For these points, see, for example, Plutarch, *Pompey*, 16 (on Sulla's example inspiring Lepidus), Sallust, *Hist.*, 1.67.7–8 (which places Lepidus amid the litany of other challenges facing Rome at that time).

15. Plutarch, *Pompey*, 20; Sallust, *Hist.*, 2.86. This situation will be discussed below. Sallust, however, makes it clear that Pompey's request for supplies covers both his army and that of Metellus, who, he indicated, was supplied from Gaul in the previous year but could not get supplies in 74 because of a food shortage in that province.

16. Sallust, *Hist.*, 2.41.

17. This was the campaign of M. Antonius, launched in 74 BC. Given that the grain shortage hit Italy, Gaul, and the armies in Spain, a climate event seems a more likely cause of the grain shortage than pirate activity.

18. *lex Aurelia:* Sallust, *Hist.*, 2.44. For context, see B. Marshall and J. Lea Beness, "Tribunician Agitation and Aristocratic Reaction 80–71 BC," *Athenaeum* 65 (1987): 361–378. Grain allowance passed in 73: Sallust, *Hist.*, 3.15.19; Cicero, *2 Verr.*, 3.163 (LCL).

19. Sallust, *Hist.*, 3.15.1, 3.15.13.

20. For an excellent survey of materials related to the revolt of Spartacus, see B. Shaw, *Spartacus and the Slave Wars* (Boston: Bedford/ St. Martin's, 2001); T. Urbainczyk, *Slave Revolts in Antiquity* (Stocksfeld: Acumen, 2008), 64–73. For free laborers joining the revolt, see Appian, *BC,* 1.116; Steel, *End of the Roman Republic,* 115.

21. On his machinations, see Appian, *BC,* 1.66–68; Plutarch, *Pompey,* 1. For discussion of his career, see R. Seager, *Pompey the Great,* 2nd ed. (Oxford: Blackwell, 2002), 20–23; A. Keaveney, "Pompeius Strabo's Second Consulship," *Classical Quarterly* 28 (1978): 240–241.

22. On this strategy as practiced by Strabo, see Seager, *Pompey,* 23.

23. Described in Plutarch, *Pompey,* 4–5. For Pompey's situation at this time, see the discussion of A. Keaveney, "Young Pompey: 106–79 BC," *L'Antiquité Classique* 51 (1982): 111–139, at 113–117.

24. Pompey leaving camp of Cinna: Plutarch, *Pompey,* 5. Raising revolt in Auximum: Plutarch, *Pompey,* 6–8; Diodorus Siculus 38–39.9. For discussion, see Keaveney, "Young Pompey," 117–118. Soldiers from other districts: Plutarch, *Pompey,* 6; Appian, *BC,* 1.80. This secondary recruitment probably occurred after Pompey had reached Sulla (Keaveney, "Young Pompey," 120).

25. Appian, *BC,* 1.80; Valerius Maximus 5.2.9 (Sulla rising at Pompey's entrance); Plutarch, *Pompey,* 8; *Crassus,* 6 (Sulla greeting Pompey as imperator).

26. Imperium in Sicily: Cicero, *Leg. Man.,* 61 (LCL); Livy, *Per.,* 89.2; Granius Licinianus Bk. 36, p. 31, as well as the discussion of Keaveney, "Young Pompey," 122–123. Execution of Carbo: Plutarch, *Pompey,* 10.3–4. *adulescentulus carnifex:* Valerius Maximus 6.2.8. For discussion of this passage, see B. X. de Wet, "Aspects of Plutarch's Portrayal of Pompey," *Acta Classica* 24 (1981): 119–132. Building relationships in provinces: Seager, *Pompey,* 27; Badian, *Foreign Clientelae,* 304.

27. On Pompey's marital alliances, see the survey of S. Haley, "The Five Wives of Pompey the Great," *Greece and Rome* 32 (1985): 49–59. Haley (on p. 49) dates this marriage to 82. For a date of 81 BC, following Pompey's return from Africa, see Keaveney, "Young Pompey," 132–133.

28. Plutarch, *Pompey,* 13. For discussion of how Strabo's example influenced Pompey, see Seager, *Pompey,* 28–29.

29. Keaveney ("Young Pompey," 128–130) and T. P. Hillman ("Pompeius in Africa and Sulla's Order to Demobilize [Plutarch, *Pompeius,* 13, 1–4]," *Latomus* 56 [1997]: 94–106) both argue against the idea, put forward by Ernst Badian ("The Date of Pompey's First Triumph," *Hermes* 83 [1955]: 107–118, at 115) and others, that Pompey had orchestrated the mutiny. This is almost certainly true, but Pompey

also managed the affair so that the soldiers' will was clearly expressed in a way that insulated Pompey himself from charges of inciting rebellion.

30. Plutarch, *Pompey,* 14.

31. Plutarch, *Pompey,* 14.

32. Plutarch, *Pompey,* 14. On the significance of the elephants and the larger thematic program of the triumph, see G. Mader, "Triumphal Elephants and Political Circus at Plutarch 'Pomp.' 14.6," *Classical World* 99, no. 4 (2006): 397–403.

33. Plutarch, *Pompey,* 15; *Sulla,* 34. For the idea of Pompey anticipating chaos by backing Lepidus, see Seager, *Pompey,* 30. Syme (*Sallust,* 185) is certainly correct that no candidate could stand for the consulship while exhibiting active hostility toward Sulla, but Sulla clearly did not favor Lepidus even if Lepidus's animosity may not have been clear during the campaign. The speech that Sallust puts in his mouth (*Hist.,* 1.49) ostensibly dates to when Sulla was still alive, but, if Sallust accurately reproduces the sentiments of Lepidus's original, the speech likely reflects an evolution of Lepidus's public position after the election. It is certainly possible, however, that Pompey either anticipated this evolution or knew that Lepidus's private hostility toward Sulla would likely manifest itself publicly over time.

34. Plutarch, *Pompey,* 15.

35. Plutarch, *Pompey,* 16; Appian, *BC,* 1.108; Sallust, *Hist.,* 1.67 (on calls for the *Senatus consultum ultimum* [SCU]), 68–72 (on the fight against Lepidus).

36. Post-Lepidus command: Plutarch, *Pompey,* 17. Pompey's self-financing in Spain: Sallust, *Hist.,* 2.84, 2.86. Ratification of Spanish citizenship extensions: Cicero, *Balb.,* 19, 32–33, 38 (LCL). Burning of Perpenna's papers: Plutarch, *Pompey,* 20.

37. If Sallust is to be believed, Pompey may have floated his support for such a restoration as early as 73 BC (Sallust, *Hist.,* 3.15.23). On the background to this, see Gruen, *Last Generation,* 24–25. For other populist ideas floated by Pompey before the election, see Sallust, *Hist.,* 4.32; Plutarch, *Pompey,* 21.

38. Sallust, *Hist.,* 2.17–18.

39. Livy, *Per.,* 80.7; Plutarch, *Crassus,* 4.

40. For his actions under Sulla, see Plutarch, *Crassus,* 6.

41. Plutarch, *Crassus,* 2, 6.

42. Gruen, *Last Generation,* 67, drawing on statements about his ambitions in Cicero, *De Offic.,* 1.25; Dio 37.56.4; and Velleius Paterculus 2.44.2.

43. Plutarch, *Crassus,* 2.

44. For this characterization of Crassus, note Gruen, *Last Generation,* 66–74. For his lending activities, see Sallust, *Catiline,* 48.5;

Plutarch, *Crassus*, 3. For his support of political initiatives of his allies in the 70s, note Plutarch, *Crassus*, 7.

45. Plutarch, *Crassus*, 3 (trans. Warner, slightly adapted).

46. For the nature of his position, see Brennan, *Praetorship in the Roman Republic*, 432–434.

47. The ferocity of Spartacus's forces is made clear from Plutarch's comment (which is certainly exaggerated) that, of the 12,000 followers of Spartacus killed by Crassus in one battle, only 3 had wounds in the back (*Crassus*, 11). The other 11,997 presumably were killed while standing and fighting Crassus's forces. On Crassus's use of decimation, see Plutarch, *Crassus*, 10; Appian, *BC*, 1.118. On the "improvement" in Roman morale because of this, note Appian, *BC*, 1.119.

48. Plutarch, *Crassus*, 11; Appian, *BC*, 1.120.

49. Plutarch, *Crassus*, 11; Appian, *BC*, 1.121.

50. Gellius, *NA*, 5.6.20–23. For discussion, see Steel, *End of the Roman Republic*, 117. For the difference between an *ovatio* and a triumph, see Plutarch, *Crassus*, 11; *Marcellus*, 22. On Crassus's *ovatio* in particular, see B. A. Marshall, "Crassus' Ovation in 71 B.C.," *Historia* 21 (1972): 669–673.

51. Appian (*BC*, 1.121) is the main source.

52. Plutarch, *Crassus*, 12; Sallust, *Hist.*, 4.40 (*collegam minorem et sui cultorem exspectans*).

53. Pompey's push for court reforms: Cicero, *Verr.*, 1.45; F. Millar, *Rome, the Greek World, and the East*, Vol. 3 (Chapel Hill: University of North Carolina Press, 2002), 169–170; Seager, *Pompey*, 36–39. On the land grants to his troops, see Dio 38.5 (which indicates that the law was passed and some land distributions occurred but others were postponed). Plutarch (*Lucullus*, 34) suggests that troops serving under other commanders knew of Pompey's success in getting land for his veterans and felt angry that their commanders could not do the same for them. For discussion of this larger issue, see R. E. Smith, "The *Lex Plotia Agraria* and Pompey's Spanish Veterans," *Classical Quarterly* 7, nos. 1–2 (1957): 82–85.

54. Crassus, *obtrectans potius collegae quam boni aut mali publici gravis exactor* (Sallust, *Hist.*, 4.41); cf. Plutarch, *Crassus*, 12.

55. Calls for reconciliation: Plutarch, *Crassus*, 12; Appian, *BC*, 1.121.

CHAPTER 8

1. Gabinius and mob of supporters: Dio 36.24. Cornelius: Asconius 57C–59C (in A. C. Clark, ed., *Q. Asconii Pediani Orationum Ciceronis Quinque Enarratio* [Oxford: Clarendon, 1907]) details some of the issues Cornelius sought to address. For discussion of the larger situation, see Steel, *End of the Roman Republic*, 144–146. Manlius: Asconius 45C, 65C–66C.

2. On this command, note Velleius Paterculus 2.31.1; Plutarch, *Pompey*, 25; Dio 36.24.3; Appian, *Mith.*, 94.428. On the expectation that Pompey would hold it, see Cicero, *leg. Man.*, 44; Dio 36.23.5.

3. Caesar's advocacy for Pompey command: Plutarch, *Pompey*, 25; Seager, *Pompey*, 44n49. Hortensius's comment: Cicero, *leg. Man.*, 52; Seager, *Pompey*, 44. Roscius's gesture: Dio 36.30.3. On the size of his forces, see Plutarch, *Pompey*, 26.2; Seager, *Pompey*, 45n62 (passage), 63 (increase in forces). Price of bread: Plutarch, *Pompey*, 26.2.

4. Dio 36.23 (attempt to secure patronage), 36.24.5 (disgrace he could not bear), 36.34.4 (Catulus's speech).

5. For a thorough survey of piracy in this period, see P. de Souza, "Rome's Contribution to the Development of Piracy," *Memoirs of the American Academy at Rome, Supplementary Vol. 6, The Maritime World of Ancient Rome* (Ann Arbor: University of Michigan Press for the American Academy in Rome, 2008), 71–96. On Roman maritime domination as a cause, see N. Rauh, *Merchants, Sailors, and Pirates in the Roman World* (Stroud, UK: Tempus, 2003), 33. The connection of poverty and piracy is explained in Dio 36.37.5. Note, too, Seager, *Pompey*, 48. On Pompey's campaign, see P. de Souza, *Piracy in the Graeco-Roman World* (Cambridge: Cambridge University Press, 1999), 167–178.

6. It was, of course, impossible to end piracy. Piracy is not a state of being but an activity that people engage in—and the definition of what constitutes this behavior is similarly fluid. For discussion, see de Souza, "Rome's Contribution," 89–94, and, in a different time period, L. Mylonakis, "Transnational Piracy in the Eastern Mediterranean, 1821–1897" (PhD diss., University of California, San Diego, 2018), 6. On renewed pirate activity in the 50s, see de Souza, *Piracy*, 179–185.

7. Timing after tribal reform: Dio 36.42.1-3; Asconius 45C, 65C–66C. On the ability to wage war without senatorial consultation and the precedent it set, see Seager, *Pompey*, 52.

8. On these various motivations, see Dio 36.42–44.

9. Both Pliny (*Letters*, 10.79–80, 112, 114, 115 [LCL]) in the early second century AD and Dio in the early third century AD (37.20.2) make reference to Pompey's laws and constitutions still being in use in their times.

10. Seager, *Pompey*, 80; E. Badian, *Publicans and Sinners* (Cornell University Press, 1983) (hereafter *PS*), 100*ff.* on the ways that senators could underwrite business undertaken by *equites*.

11. Dio 38.12.7.

12. The examples of this are myriad, but note, for example, the comments of Dio 38.12.6.

13. Plutarch, *Caesar*, 1; Suetonius, *Caesar*, 1 (LCL).

14. Velleius Paterculus 2.22; Florus 2.9 (LCL).

15. For evidence of these views of Sulla, see, for example, Dio 36.34.4; Appian, *BC,* 1.104.

16. Plutarch, *Caesar,* 5.1–2. Suetonius, *Caesar,* 6.1, preserves a small section of the speech on Julia that describes her mother's family as descended from the king Ancus Martius and her father from Venus. For the date of 69, see T. R. S. Broughton, *The Magistrates of the Roman Republic* (hereafter *MRR*), vol. II (New York: American Philological Association, 1952), note 7; *MRR,* vol. III (Atlanta: American Philological Association, 1986), 105–106.

17. Plutarch, *Caesar,* 5.2.

18. So says Plutarch (*Caesar,* 4.5).

19. Plutarch, *Caesar,* 5.9; Dio 37.8.1–2.

20. Plutarch, *Cato,* 1.1 (LCL).

21. Not laughing: Plutarch, *Cato,* 1.2. Dangled from a window: Valerius Maximus 3.1.2b; Plutarch, *Cato,* 2.1–4. Killing Sulla: Plutarch, *Cato,* 3.4.

22. Inheritance: Plutarch, *Cato,* 4.1. Plutarch (*Crassus,* 2.2–3) explains that Crassus inherited 1.8 million denarii and grew the fortune to 42.6 million denarii. In 62 BC, Cicero (*ad Fam.,* 5.6.2; Gellius 12.12) bought a house from Crassus for 3.5 million sesterces (875,000 denarii). Ostentatious modesty: Plutarch, *Cato,* 6.4, though Plutarch interprets Cato's motivation differently.

23. Plutarch, *Cato,* 7.2.

24. Dressing as a common soldier: Plutarch, *Cato,* 9.1–5. Soldiers placing garments on ground: Plutarch, *Cato,* 12.1. Conflict with Catulus: Plutarch, *Cato,* 16. Legal proceedings against Sullans: Plutarch, *Cato,* 17.4-5.

25. Cicero (*de lege agraria* 3) would comment that his election as a new man was "almost the first [such instance] in living memory."

26. Cicero (*Letters to Atticus,* 1.2.1, LCL) actually contemplated defending Catiline in this case.

27. The speech itself is lost, but such is the testimony of Asconius, 84–85. Antonius too was attacked in the speech. For analysis, see D. Berry, *Cicero Pro Sulla oratio* (Cambridge: Cambridge University Press, 1996), 265–272.

28. For Catiline's cynical appeals to the downtrodden, see Sallust, *Catiline,* 35.3–4 (LCL); Cicero, *Mur.,* 50–51 (LCL). On the plausibility of Cicero's report, see Steel, *End of the Roman Republic,* 154. For the Sullan fondness of some of his other supporters, note Sallust, *Catiline,* 5.6, 37.6. Cato's threat (which apparently happened in early July of 63) is recorded by Cicero, *Mur.,* 51. The election was held in mid-July.

29. This is the suggestion of Steel, *End of the Roman Republic,* 157–158.

30. On this sequence of events, see Plutarch, *Cicero,* 15 (LCL); *Crassus* 13.3; Dio 37.31.1–3.

31. Letters read aloud: Sallust, *Catiline,* 47.2–3. Supplicatio: Cicero, *Cat.,* 3.15; speech to people: Sallust, *Catiline,* 48.

32. Sallust, *Catiline,* 48.7.

33. Sallust, *Catiline,* 49.

34. Sallust, *Catiline,* 51.27. Sallust has likely adapted the texts of both Caesar's and Cato's speeches, but, because Cicero had ordered the minutes of the senate proceedings on these days recorded by a stenographer, Sallust and his audience both likely had access to the transcripts of the original speeches. Sallust must then be generally true to the sentiments spoken at the time.

35. Sallust, *Catiline,* 52.

36. Rumored punishment of Caesar: Plutarch, *Caesar,* 8.4–5. Execution of conspirators: Sallust, *Catiline,* 55. Cicero's escort: Plutarch, *Cicero,* 22.2–4; Appian, *BC,* 2.6; Velleius Paterculus 2.35.4.

37. Cicero, *Fam.,* 5.2, *Pis.,* 6–7; Asconius 6C. For discussion and additional bibliography, see Steel, *End of the Roman Republic,* 159n65.

38. Nepos blocked from reciting law: Plutarch, *Cato,* 28.1–2. For the incident in general: Dio 37.43–44; Plutarch, *Cato,* 26–29; Suetonius, *Caesar,* 16.

39. Sallust, *Catiline,* 51.34.

CHAPTER 9

1. The location of Jericho comes in Josephus, *Bellum Judaicum* (hereafter *BJ*), 1.138 (LCL); *Jewish Antiquities* (hereafter JA), 14.53 (LCL). In a complicated section designed perhaps to foreshadow the deaths of both Pompey and Caesar, Dio 37.10–13 groups the deaths of Mithridates and Catiline together and prefaces the discussion with the comment that "changing circumstances often render very weak even those who are exceedingly powerful."

2. Plutarch, *Pompey,* 42.

3. On the implicit expectation from some that Pompey would march: Cicero, *ad Fam.,* 5.7.1 (LCL). On Cicero's arrogant suggestion that Pompey ought to congratulate him more heartily: Cicero, *ad Fam.,* 2–3. On Crassus's flight: Plutarch, *Pompey,* 43.1.

4. Disembarking in Brundisium: Dio 37.20.4. Dismissing army: Plutarch, *Pompey,* 43.2.

5. With some exaggeration, Plutarch writes that the army of soldiers that Pompey had dismissed was soon replaced with a new civilian army

made up of "people streaming forth to show their gratitude" who accompanied the victorious general to the gates of Rome (Plutarch, *Pompey*, 43.3).

6. Dio 37.20.6.

7. Plutarch, *Pompey*, 42.7, offers adultery as an explanation. Cicero, *Att.*, 1.12.3, can be read as supporting this. For the divorce as a repudiation of Nepos, see Steel, *End of the Roman Republic*, 160–161.

8. Cato seeing Pompey's marriage proposal as a plot: Plutarch, *Pompey*, 44.3; compare Plutarch, *Cato*, 30.1–5.

9. Cato had already used this coalition to block Pompey's request to help his former legate Pupius Piso campaign for consul in the summer of 62 (Plutarch, *Pompey*, 44.1–2; *Cato*, 30; Dio 37.44.3).

10. Indeed, by emphasizing the shock that Cato's wife and female family members had at his decision to reject Pompey, Plutarch demonstrates how counterintuitive his resonant decision had seemed.

11. Seager, *Pompey*, 78, on the basis of Cicero, *Att.*, 1.14.2.

12. On Pompey's triumph, note M. Beard, *The Roman Triumph* (Cambridge, MA: Harvard University Press, 2009), 7–41; Seager, *Pompey*, 79–80.

13. For Pompey's list of regions and revenues: Diodorus Siculus 40.1.4 (LCL).

14. On Metellus Celer's animosity toward Pompey because of the divorce, note Dio 37.49.

15. Dio 37.50.6.

16. Cicero, *Att.*, 1.17.8–9, describes this incident.

17. Cicero, *Att.*, 2.1.8.

18. On Caesar's Spanish command and the triumph, see, for example, Plutarch, *Caesar*, 11–12; Dio 37.52.

19. Bibulus feared being overshadowed: Suetonius, *Caesar*, 19. Cato's filibuster: Plutarch, *Cato*, 31.3, *Caesar*, 13.2; Dio 37.54.2. Woods and pastures: Suetonius, *Caesar*, 19.2. Seager (*Pompey*, 84) has suggested that this appointment may have been an effort to hold the consuls in reserve in case their forces were needed elsewhere. Cato's bribery: Suetonius, *Caesar*, 19.1.

20. Plutarch, *Crassus*, 7.6.

21. Dio 37.55.1–3.

22. Plutarch, *Crassus*, 14.2.

23. Ancient sources differ over when the reconciliation actually took place. For the formation of the agreement before the election, see Livy, *Per.*, 103; Plutarch, *Crassus*, 14.1–3, *Caesar*, 13.1–2, *Pompey*, 47, *Cato*, 31.2–5. For formation after the vote, see Suetonius, *Caesar*, 19; Velleius Paterculus 2.44.1. For discussion, see Gruen, *Last Generation*, 88–90.

24. Dio 37.57.1.

25. Dio 38.2.2.

26. Dio 38.3.

27. Steel, *End of the Roman Republic,* 165.

28. Threat of force: Plutarch, *Pompey,* 47, *Caesar,* 14. For discussion, see Seager, *Pompey,* 87. Opponents' fear when recognizing alliance of Caesar, Pompey, and Crassus: Dio 38.4.5.

29. Dio 38.7.3.

30. On the chronology, see L. R. Taylor, "On the Chronology of Caesar's First Consulship," *American Journal of Philology* 72 (1951): 254–268, at 255, on the basis of Cicero, *Att.,* 2.16.2. Cato refusing to mention Caesar's name: Dio 38.7.6.

31. Taylor, "Chronology," 264, on the basis of Cicero, *Att.,* 2.16.

32. Dio 38.7.3.

33. Dio 38.8.2; dating suggested by Cicero, *Att.,* 2.18.3 and 2.19.5. Note the discussion of Taylor, "Chronology," 265–268.

34. On Clodius's career generally, see W. Jeffrey Tatum, *The Patrician Tribune: Publius Clodius Pulcher* (Chapel Hill: University of North Carolina Press, 2010). For Cicero "overwhelming Clodius in the senate to his face," see *Att.,* 1.16, a letter of May 61.

35. Clodius was the son of Appius Pulcher (consul in 79 BC) and the grandson of Appius Claudius Pulcher (consul in 143).

36. The process of approval usually involved the scrutiny of the college of Roman priests and then a formal approval by the *concilium plebis,* following a three-week delay. For discussion of this process and Clodius's divergence from it, see C. Meier, *Caesar* (New York: Basic Books, 1982), 215.

37. On this incident, see Seager, *Pompey,* 91–92. Steel, *End of the Roman Republic,* 167, doubts that this event could have precipitated Caesar's actions.

38. Dio 38.10–12.

39. For this as a legislative package, see Dio 38.13.1–2.

40. Milo occupying Campus Martius: Cicero, *Att.,* 4.3.4–5. Senate disruptions: Cicero, *Q Fr.,* 2.1.1–3.

41. On Caesar's commentaries, see T. P. Wiseman, "The Publication of *De Bello Gallico,*" in *Julius Caesar as Artful Reporter: The War Commentaries as Political Instruments,* ed. A. Powell and K. Welch (Swansea, UK: Duckworth, 1998), 1–9. For his ability to inspire troops, see, for example, Plutarch, *Caesar,* 15–17.

42. On this particular historical moment, see T. P Wiseman, "Caesar, Pompey, and Rome, 59–50 B.C.," in *Cambridge Ancient History,* 9:368–424, at 184n143; Asconius 30C–42C; Dio 40.46.

43. Asconius 35–36.

44. Cicero, *Att.,* 7.1.4. On the law permitting this, which Pompey and all ten tribunes backed, see Steel, *End of the Roman Republic,* 186n152. Caesar was also explicitly exempted from a later law sponsored

by Pompey requiring all candidates to present themselves in person when seeking election (Seager, *Pompey*, 138–139; Cicero, *Att.*, 8.3.3).

45. The comment appears in Cicero, *Fam.*, 8.8.9. For analysis, see Steel, *End of the Roman Republic*, 190.

46. Cicero, *Fam.*, 8.6.5.

47. For Caesar's fear that his election might be blocked or delayed, see R. Morstein-Marx, "Caesar's Alleged Fear of Prosecution and His *ratio absentis*," *Historia* 56 (2007): 159–178. For a survey of other possibilities, see Steel, *End of the Roman Republic*, 193–194.

48. Appian, *BC*, 2.118.

CHAPTER 10

1. These preparations are described in *Gallic Wars* (henceforth *BG*), 8.49–51 (LCL), reports written by a narrator other than Caesar. The report of these spectacles would also have enhanced perceptions of Caesar in Rome, which was certainly part of the purpose of these displays of enthusiastic loyalty.

2. Caesar, *BG*, 8.52.

3. Cicero, *Pro Cluentio*, 146. Note as well Arena, "Invocation to Liberty," 58.

4. On sedition of this sort in the context of Roman Republican political thought, see, for example, Cicero, *de Re Publica*, 6.1.

5. On this incident, see Caesar, *BG*, 8.55; Dio 40.66; Appian, *BC*, 2.30–31; Cicero, *ad Fam.*, 2.17.5.

6. On the SCU, see Caesar, *BC*, 1.4 (LCL). For Pompey's command of the forces, see Appian, *BC*, 2.33.

7. Pompey and Senate conspiring against him: Caesar, *BC*, 1.4–5. Pompey concerned about dignity: Caesar, *BC*, 1.6.

8. Appian, *BC*, 2.30; Plutarch, *Caesar*, 16.1.

9. Caesar, *BC*, 1.11.

10. Pompey's retreat is discussed in Caesar, *BC*, 1.14–27; Appian, *BC*, 2.36–39; Dio 41.5–13.

11. Appian, *BC*, 2.40; Plutarch, *Caesar*, 34.6–9.

12. Cato's retreat: Appian, *BC*, 2.41; Caesar, *BC*, 1.30–31. Curio's defeat and death in North Africa: Appian, *BC*, 2.45.

13. For example, Appian, *BC*, 2.43.

14. Steel (*End of the Roman Republic*, 197) offers a list of the imperium holders. Dio 41.43.2 speaks of two hundred senators. For a survey of Pompey's forces, see Appian, *BC*, 2.49; Caesar, *BC*, 3.3.

15. Appian, *BC*, 2.63; Caesar, *BC*, 3.73–74.

16. Senators force Pompey to move aggressively: Appian, *BC*, 2.67; Caesar, *BC*, 3.82; Plutarch, *Caesar*, 40–41. Caesar's victory at Pharsalus:

Caesar, *BC,* 3.88–89, and Appian, *BC,* 2.70 (following Caesar), give the sizes of the two armies.

17. On Pompey's fate, see Plutarch, *Pompey,* 77–80; Appian, *BC,* 2.83–86; Caesar, *BC,* 3.103–104; Velleius Paterculus 2.53. Excepting Caesar, most of these sources drew on the earlier account of Asinius Pollio. For discussion, see L. Morgan, "The Autopsy of Asinius Pollio," *Journal of Roman Studies* 90 (2000): 51–69, at 52.

18. Appian, *BC,* 2.91, and Plutarch, *Caesar,* 50, both preserve the phrase in Greek translation. Dio (42.48.1) paraphrases it. Appian indicates that the phrase formed the text of a report of the campaign that Caesar sent by letter to Rome. Suetonius (*Caesar,* 37) gives the Latin, indicating that it was displayed on a tablet during Caesar's triumph.

19. The loan situation is described in Caesar, *BC,* 3.20. Appian, *BC,* 2.48, seems to follow Caesar's narrative here. Dio (41.37.3) indicates that the issue involved repayment of the principal of loans in cash. For discussion, see Kay, *Rome's Economic Revolution,* 260–264. For the hoarding of precious metal, see Kay, *Rome's Economic Revolution,* 261, on the basis of Dio 41.38.1.

20. For Caesar's responses, see Caesar, *BC,* 3.1.2; Dio 41.37.3; Kay, *Rome's Economic Revolution,* 260–264.

21. Caelius's loan measures: Dio 42.22; Caesar, *BC,* 3.20–21. Caelius's alliance with Milo and their eventual defeat: Dio 42.24–25; Caesar, *BC,* 3.22.

22. Antony occupying the Forum: Dio 42.29–33 discusses these events in detail. Appian, *BC,* 2.91, alludes briefly to them. Caesar's return: Dio 42.33.2 says explicitly that Caesar's mere presence served to calm the city. On the other measures, see, for example, Dio 42.50.

23. Dio 42.52–55; Appian, *BC,* 2.92–94.

24. Appian, *BC,* 2.94. Dio records the riot at greater length but does not mention the promise to use his own money to fund supplies for the discharged soldiers.

25. Caesar's triumph and forum: Appian, *BC,* 2.102; Dio 43.21–22. Caesar's control of the public revenues: Dio 43.45.1, dated by Dio to 45 BC.

26. Cicero, *Fam.,* 7.30.1, repeated by Dio 43.46.4.

27. Caesar approving election results: Dio 47.1. Octavian as master of the horse: Dio 43.51.6–7.

28. Dio 43.20.3, cf. Horace, *Ep.,* 1.59–60.

29. Caesar greeted as king: Suetonius, *Caesar,* 79, reproduced almost verbatim in Appian, *BC,* 2.108. Lupercalia: Suetonius, *Caesar,* 79; Plutarch, *Caesar,* 61; Dio 44.11; Nicolaus of Damascus, *Aug.,* 21 (in M. Toher, ed., *Nicolaus of Damascus: The Life of Augustus and the Autobiography* [Cambridge: Cambridge University Press, 2017]); among

others. For discussion, see J. North, "Caesar at the Lupercalia," *Journal of Roman Studies* 98 (2008): 144–160.

30. For a summary of these measures, see Dio 43.45.

31. The Roman hatred of kingship is often expressed in Republican authors (e.g., Cicero, *de Re Publica*, 2.30). For the selection process, note, for example, the description of Cicero, *de Re Publica* 2.23–24.

32. Dio alone devotes the first eleven chapters of the forty-fourth book of his history to the decrees passed honoring Caesar in those years. For these lists as a later comment on Caesar's arrogance, see A. Lintott, "The Assassination," in *A Companion to Julius Caesar*, ed. M. Griffin (Oxford: Wiley-Blackwell, 2009), 72–82. For statues in cities and temples: Appian, *BC,* 2.106; Dio 44.4; Suetonius, *Caesar,* 76.

33. This coin is *RRC* 443/1. For the interpretation of its iconography, see D. Backendorf, *Römische Münzschätze des zweiten und ersten Jahrhunderts v. Chr. Vom italienischen Festland* (Berlin: Phillip von Zabern, 1998), 210. For the dating, see Crawford, *RRC,* p. 89.

34. This coin is *RRC* 458/1.

35. These coins are *RRC* 480/2a–c (DICT QUART); 480/3, 480/4, 480/5a–b, 480/17 (variations of IMP); and 480/6-15, 480/18 (variations of DICT IN PERPETUO). The last group must have been first issued before February 15, 44 BC—which suggests that the other two must date to the beginning of the year. On their chronology and iconography, see Crawford, *RRC,* pp. 492–495.

36. For example, Appian, *BC,* 2.112.

37. On the person of Brutus more generally, see K. Tempest, *Brutus the Noble Conspirator* (New Haven, CT: Yale University Press, 2017). The Libertas coin is *RRC* 433/1. The date of 54 BC is suggested by Crawford. For alternative dates, see S. Cerutti, "Brutus, Cyprus and the Coinage of 55 BC," *American Journal of Numismatics* 5–6 (1993–1994): 69–87. The Ahala coin is *RRC* 433/2. On the Ahala incident, see Livy 6.13, 14.

38. On this conception of political liberty in the late Republic, see Arena, *Libertas and the Practice of Politics,* chap. 2.

39. This question prompted a shift in Cicero's definition of liberty from a judicial conception tied to one's rights within a state in *de Re Publica* to one centered on the freedom of the individual from the interference of others in works from the 40s such as *de Officiis* and the *Philippics*. On this evolution, see Arena, "Invocation to Liberty," 49–73.

40. Plutarch (*Brutus,* 8–10) describes how Cassius's persuasion of Brutus to take part in the plot against Caesar centered on the idea that the defense of liberty required the dictator's murder.

41. Suetonius, *Caesar,* 82.

42. Brutus's choice of the Senate: for example, Appian, *BC*, 2.114. On this response within the city: Appian, *BC*, 2.118.

CHAPTER 11

1. Appian, *BC*, 2.119, describes the cap and spear.

2. Appian, *BC*, 2.122; Dio 45.21.

3. For Cicero's actions: Cicero, *Att.*, 14.10.1 (call the Senate), 15.11 (kill Antony). For Lepidus: Appian, *BC*, 2.124; Dio 44.34.5; Nicolaus of Damascus, *Aug.* 27.

4. Cicero, *Att.*, 14.10.1, 15.11.2.

5. The date of his speech is not completely clear, though Plutarch's placing of it on the sixteenth seems most likely (Plutarch, *Caesar*, 67.7; see E. Rawson, "The Aftermath of the Ides," in *Cambridge Ancient History*, online edition [2008], 9:468–490, at 459). Appian (*BC*, 2.137–142) offers a re-creation of the address, though evidently places it after the meeting of the Senate on March 17, timing that would be curious. The actual speech, probably the *contio Capitolina* that was later published, is described by Cicero, *Att.*, 15.1a.

6. Dio (44.34.6) rightly emphasizes that Lepidus would gain the most by using force immediately.

7. The meeting is described at Dio 44.22.3; Appian *BC*, 2.126–129. For a summary, see J. S. Richardson, *Augustan Rome, 44 BC to AD 14* (Edinburgh: Edinburgh University Press, 2012), 13; J. Osgood, *Caesar's Legacy: Civil War and the Emergence of the Roman Empire* (Cambridge: Cambridge University Press, 2006), 13–14; Rawson, "Aftermath," 469. For tentativeness of speakers: Appian, *BC*, 2.127. For Antony's point: Appian, *BC*, 2.128.

8. Appian, *BC*, 2.131–132.

9. For Caesar's will, see Dio, 44.35.1–4; Appian, *BC*, 2.143; Plutarch, *Caesar*, 68. For a concise description of the dating of its public reading, see Richardson, *Augustan Rome*, 15.

10. Appian, *BC*, 2.143. On Appian's use of Pollio here, see Osgood, *Caesar's Legacy*, 12n1.

11. Dio 44.35.4. Appian (*BC*, 2.147), by contrast, says that the body itself could not be seen by the crowd.

12. The most extensive account is that of Appian, *BC*, 2.144–147. See, too, among others, Dio 44.35; Plutarch, *Caesar*, 68; Suetonius, *Caesar*, 84. On the theatricality of the production, see Osgood, *Caesar's Legacy*, 13.

13. Appian, *BC*, 2.147.

14. On this character (also called Hierophilus), see Appian, *BC*, 3.2–3; Livy, *Per.*, 116; Valerius Maximus 9.15.1; Cicero, *Phil.*, 1.5; and the discussion of B. Scardigli, "Il falso Mario," *Studi italiani di filogia classica* n.s. 52 (1980): 207–221.

15. Appian, *BC*, 3.2.

16. Appian, *BC*, 3.4–5.

17. Caesar's intention to take Octavian on campaign: Appian, *BC*, 3.9. Octavian counseled to reject will: Appian, *BC*, 3.10–11; Nicolaus of Damascus, *Aug.*, 18; Suetonius, *Augustus*, 3.

18. Appian, *BC*, 3.11.

19. For this date, see M. Toher, "Octavian's Arrival in Rome, 44 B.C.," *Classical Quarterly* 54, no. 1 (2004): 174–184, on the basis of Appian, *BC*, 3.105–106; Nicolaus, *Aug.*, 28; Cicero, *Att.*, 14.5.3 and 14.6.1.

20. This is suggested strongly by Nicolaus, *Aug.*, 28, and Appian (*BC*, 3.28). For discussion, see Toher, "Octavian's Arrival," 175.

21. Dio, 45.5.3–4; Florus 2.15.2–3.

22. Legacies to Romans: Appian, *BC*, 3.21. Lawsuits: Appian, *BC*, 3.22. Prohibition on standing for tribune: Appian, *BC*, 3.31; Dio 45.6.3. Meetings of reconciliation: Appian, *BC*, 3.30.

23. On the comet appearance: Osgood, *Caesar's Legacy*, 40–41; J. T. Ramsey and A. L. Licht, *The Comet of 44 BC and Caesar's Funeral Games* (Oxford: Oxford University Press, 1997). On the departures of Brutus and Cassius: Plutarch, *Brutus*, 24; Nicolaus, *Aug.*, 30; Cicero, *Phil.*, 10.8. For the dating, see Rawson, "Aftermath," 476n50.

24. On this incident, see Cicero, *Fam.*, 12.23.2, Nicolaus of Damascus, *Vit. Aug.*, 30; Appian, *BC*, 3.39.

25. Octavian's problems with his soldiers: Appian, *BC*, 3.44. Defection of Antony's soldiers: Appian, *BC*, 3.45; Dio 45.13.

26. Octavian pledging forces against Antony: Appian, *BC*, 3.47; Dio 45.14 frames Octavian's action as making himself a friend of Decimus Brutus rather than the Senate. Octavian dissuading his soldiers from demanding title in Rome: Appian, *BC*, 3.48.

27. Cicero's praise: Cicero, *Phil.*, 3.37–39, narrated by Dio 45.15; discussion at Richardson, *Augustan Rome*, 26–27. Authority to Octavian: Dio 46.29; Appian, *BC*, 3.48. Vote that Republic should not come to any harm: Cicero, *Phil.*, 8.6; Augustus, *Res Gestae*, 1.3; Dio 46.29.5; Appian, *BC*, 3.63.

28. On the battles more generally: Dio 46.36–38. On the *legio Martia* in particular: Cicero, *Phil.*, 14.29–35; Osgood, *Caesar's Legacy*, 52.

29. Dio 46.40.3–4; Cicero, *Ep. ad Brutum*, 24.9, speaks about the honors voted in this meeting.

30. For larger narration: Dio 46.39, Appian, *BC*, 3.80–81.

31. On these events: Appian, *BC*, 3.86–88; Richardson, *Augustan Rome*, 31–32; Osgood, *Caesar's Legacy*, 58–59.

32. Velleius Paterculus 2.69.5 indicates that Pedius introduced the law imposing banishment on all of Caesar's murderers.

33. For this moment, see the concise description of Richardson, *Augustan Rome*, 34, and, for the many unknowns of the world it created, C. Pelling, "The Triumviral Period," in *Cambridge Ancient History* 10:1–5. The ancient sources for the triumvirate include Appian, *BC*, 4.2–3; Dio 46.54–55; Suetonius, *Augustus*, 96; Plutarch, *Cicero*, 46; *Antony*, 18–19.

34. Osgood (*Caesar's Legacy*, 63–150) offers the most compelling reconstruction of the consequences of the land confiscations and proscriptions. Ancient authors such as Appian, Dio, and Valerius Maximus provide catalogs of stories about the victims of the proscriptions and those who avoided their effects. Though these have been dismissed as fantasies by some scholars, Osgood (*Caesar's Legacy*, 81) shows that there is good reason to believe that they capture something of the reality of the moment.

35. Triumvirs' entry: Appian, *BC*, 4.7; Dio 47.2. Cicero's capture: Appian, *BC*, 4.19–20; Dio 47.8, 11; Plutarch, *Cicero*, 47–48, *Antony*, 20. Initial killings: Appian, *BC*, 4.5, gives these numbers. Livy, *Per.*, 120, notes 130 senators and many *equites*. Plutarch, *Antony*, 20, counts 300 senators but does not mention *equites*. Dio 47.3–14 gives no numbers. The tax on women and the response of Hortensia: Appian, *BC*, 4.32, and the analysis of Osgood, *Caesar's Legacy*, 84–87.

36. Judaea: Osgood, *Caesar's Legacy*, 88–89, following Josephus, *JA*, 14.272, and *BJ*, 1.220. Dio 47.28.3 alludes to this. Tarsus: Dio 47.31 (generally); Appian, *BC*, 4.64 (on the 1,500-talent fine). Rhodes: Appian, *BC*, 4.65–73 (the Rhodian proscriptions are found at 4.73) and Dio 47.33. Brutus's sack of Xanthus and Patara: Appian, *BC*, 4.76–81; Dio 47.34. Brutus portrait on coins: *RRC* 507.1a and b.

37. On Philippi: Augustus, *Res Gestae*, 2; Dio 47.37–49; Appian, *BC*, 4.107–138; Suetonius, *Augustus*, 13; Plutarch, *Brutus*, 43–53. Note, too, the discussion of Osgood, *Caesar's Legacy*, 95–104.

38. Casualty figures for Philippi: Plutarch, *Brutus*, 45; Appian, *BC*, 4.112. Former "liberator" soldiers joining triumviral armies: Appian, *BC*, 4.138; Velleius Paterculus 2.71.1; Osgood, *Caesar's Legacy*, 103–104; Brunt, *Italian Manpower*, 485–488.

39. For a detailed discussion of the horrors of the Perusine war, see Osgood, *Caesar's Legacy*, 152–166.

40. Brundisium: Appian, *BC*, 5.59, goes so far as to say that Octavian's forces claimed they had come to defend Brundisium "with the intention of bringing them to an agreement or, if Antony refused and continued the war, of defending Octavian against him." On Brundisium and its context, see Osgood, *Caesar's Legacy*, 188–207; Pelling, "Triumviral Period," 17–21. Agreement with Sextus Pompey: Appian, *BC*, 5.74.

41. On this question, see Appian, *BC*, 5.95, and Pelling, "Triumviral Period," 27.

42. Territorial grants to Cleopatra: Plutarch, *Antony,* 36; Dio 49.32; Josephus, *JA,* 15.94–95. For discussion, see Pelling, "Triumviral Period," 29; Osgood, *Caesar's Legacy,* 244. Cleopatra as cause of Parthian calamity: Livy, *Per.,* 130; Plutarch, *Antony,* 37–38; Pelling, "Triumviral Period," 32.

43. For the Messana events and Lepidus's reduction, see Appian, *BC,* 5.122*ff.*; Dio 49.12.4; Paterculus 2.80.4.

44. Combat injury: Appian, *Illyricum,* 28.82; Augustus, *Res Gestae,* 29.1. Contrast of vigor of Octavian with Antony: Appian, *Illyricum,* 16.46; Plutarch, *Antony,* 55. For these developments, see the discussions of Osgood, *Caesar's Legacy,* 325–326; Pelling, "Triumviral Period," 46.

45. Construction projects: Osgood, *Caesar's Legacy,* 329–330. There were some projects undertaken by supporters of Antony, but, as Osgood shows, these were fewer in number and completed less efficiently. Agrippa activities: Osgood, *Caesar's Legacy,* 330–336; Pelling, "Triumviral Period," 47–48.

46. On this incident and its aftermath, see Plutarch, *Antony,* 53–54; Dio 49.33; and the discussion of Osgood, *Caesar's Legacy,* 336. About Octavia returning to the marital home, Plutarch (*Antony,* 54.2) comments, "Without meaning it, she was damaging Antony by this conduct of hers; for he was hated for wronging such a woman."

47. Dio 49.40; Plutarch, *Antony,* 50.4 (pseudo-triumph), 54.3 (territory distribution); cf. Horace, *Ep.,* 9. On these events and the dubious nature of the ancient evidence, see Osgood, *Caesar's Legacy,* 338–339.

48. For the senate meeting: Dio 50.2.3 (January 1 meeting), 50.2.4–6 (Octavian's meeting).

49. Flight of senators to Antony: Dio 50.2.7. Antony's will: Dio 50.3.4–5, 50.20; Plutarch, *Antony,* 58.3–4. On the validity of the will, see J. R. Johnson, "The Authenticity and Validity of Antony's Will," *L'Antiquité Classique* 47 (1978): 494–503. Antony ceased to act like a Roman: Suetonius, *Augustus,* 17.2. Library of Pergamum to Cleopatra: Plutarch, *Antony,* 58.5. Moving capital to Alexandria: Dio 50.4.1. For discussion of these rumors and their context, see Osgood, *Caesar's Legacy,* 354–355.

50. Augustus, *Res Gestae,* 25.2.

51. This was Bononia, described in Suetonius, *Augustus,* 17.2, and analyzed in Osgood, *Caesar's Legacy,* 359.

52. Osgood (*Caesar's Legacy,* 357–364) offers a thoroughly compelling reconstruction and contextualization of the oath, its Republican antecedents, and the precedent it set for loyalty oaths in the imperial period.

53. Dio 50.10 describes these riots.

54. For discussion of Egyptian property as a component of the patrimonium of the emperor, see D. Rathbone, "Egypt, Augustus, and Roman Taxation," *Cahiers du Centre Gustave Glotz* 4 (1993): 81–112, at

99–110, and D. Rathbone, "The Imperial Finances," in *The Cambridge Ancient History*, Vol. 10, *The Augustan Empire, 43 BC–AD 69*, 2nd ed., ed. A. Bowman, E. Champlin, and A. Lintott (Cambridge: Cambridge University Press, 1996), 315–316.

CHAPTER 12

1. Suetonius, *Caesar*, 77.1.

2. Libations poured: Dio 51.19.6. Temple of Janus: Augustus, *Res Gestae*, 13.

3. Dio. 51.21.1–2.

4. Dio, 51.21.4.

5. Dio 51.20.6.

6. Augustus, *Res Gestae*, 34.

7. For this concept, see J. A. Crook, "Political History, 30 BC to 14 AD," in *Cambridge Ancient History* 10:76*ff*.

8. Augustus, *Res Gestae*, 17.

9. For this moment, see Dio 53.11; Strabo 17.3.25.

10. On his illness, see Dio 53.31.1. Dio places the assassination attempt in 22 BC (54.3.4–8), though many scholars have redated it to 23 on the basis of a lacunose entry in the *Fasti Capitolini* related to the consulship of a Murena who may have been involved. These threats would then be seen a precipitating event for the constitutional redefinition. Against this see the concise summary of Richardson, *Augustan Rome*, 103–104. The dating question is, however, not important for our purposes.

11. *Res Gestae*, 34.

12. Dio 53.16.8. Compare Suetonius, *Augustus*, 7.2; Velleius Paterculus 2.91.1.

13. Dio 53.18.2.

14. Dio 54.1.1–2.

15. *Intra paucos dies metu et periclo praesenti populum universum meis impensis liberarem* (*Res Gestae*, 5).

16. Age range of senators: T. Parkin, *Old Age in the Roman World* (Baltimore: Johns Hopkins University Press, 2003), 104.

17. J. A. Crook, "Augustus: Power, Authority, Achievement," in *Cambridge Ancient History* 10:146.

18. Cicero expresses this idea frequently in the mid-60s, from at least 66 BC when it appears in *Pro Cluentio*, 151–153. For other references or allusions, see, for example, *Catil.*, 4.14–17; *Rab. Perd.*, 27; *ad Fam.*, 5.2.8. The most recent substantial discussion of the concept in Cicero is J. Zarecki, *Cicero's Ideal Statesman in Theory and Practice* (New York: Bloomsbury Academic, 2014), 49–59.

19. For example, Cicero, *Att.*, 1.18.3.

INDEX

Credit: Katharine Calandra

EDWARD J. WATTS holds the Alkiviadis Vassiliadis Endowed Chair and is Professor of History at the University of California, San Diego. The author and editor of several prize-winning books, including *The Final Pagan Generation*, he lives in Carlsbad, California.